THE
WITCHES'
COVEN
TOOLS AND ACTIVITIES

TAMARA VON FORSLUN

BALBOA.
PRESS

A DIVISION OF HAY HOUSE

Balboa Press books may be ordered through booksellers or by contacting:

Balboa Press
A Division of Hay House
1663 Liberty Drive
Bloomington, IN 47403
www.balboapress.com.au
1 (877) 407-4847

Print information available on the last page.

ISBN: 978-1-5043-1496-1 (sc)
ISBN: 978-1-5043-1497-8 (e)

Balboa Press rev. date: 10/04/2018

Table of Contents

Introduction

The Craft of the Wise is far more than Ritual and Celebration. A Temple of Wicca is not only called a coven, but also a circle, a church or a fellowship. It is far more than just a group of acquaintances doing ritual and celebrating the Sabbats and Celebrations together as solitary's. It is about a growing family dedicated to learning all the ancient ways of Wiccecraft and honouring the Goddess and Her Consort, The Horned God, with a program that is rich, diverse and educational which will help your Coven grow towards Perfect Love and Perfect Trust and allow you to be Wicces together in many free and diverse ways, not only honouring the 'Religion of Old' but the honouring of each other.

Are all these tools and activities necessary? Altars, robes, athames, candles, social gatherings, recreational outings, service projects? Yes, they are indeed. Esbats, Sabbats and Training Courses are the mainstay of most covens programs. But if our faith is a Holistic one, which permeates every part of our lives, then it is good to share many aspects of life as a Wiccan Temple; to work together, serve the Craft and the community together and seek social changes together, but to honour the diversity in our many paths.

If you want acceptance, then fight for acceptance! This not only helps to erase the negative way of thinking but also lets those of interest seek us out and know where and how to find us. It also helps to erase the line between Religion and Living, and also helps fellow Wiccans, Wicces and Pagans bond together, to become friends and family rather than just mere affiliates or acquaintances as solitary Wicces who occasionally come together.

This book, which is Book Four of the series is a resource towards that goal. It contains all the Working Tools of a Wicce and a Coven, with ideas for more than a hundred varied activities and ideas for workshops for the Wiccan Coven and its Fellowship.

Many have been part of a program of small covens that I have used for decades, but to truly grow we must all experience the fruits of the tree and not just learn by one branch. I would also add this thought; the planning of an activity is an exercise in bonding as much as the event itself.

I encourage different covens to share and rotate responsibilities for design and preparation of Wicca. So that different pairs and combinations of members work together on each succeeding activity. This will not only strengthen ties among all the Fellowship but will foster leadership and organisational skills throughout the Wicca.

And if you have children affiliated with your Coven, let them also have a voice in some of the planning, and let them help to prepare activities, and participate as fully as possible in many Wiccan events. If we let them be Pagan now, then perhaps they will choose to be Wiccan when they have grown into young adults. Besides, they deserve to share the fun and beauty as much as the rest of us. Keeping a Circle vital and healthy requires a great deal of time, energy, skill and imagination from ALL the members. It requires a big commitment from EVERYONE.

It is easy to always blame the teacher, and many rebel at any rule and blame the training for their own inability to learn and progress. But the truth is that not everyone fits into your circle energy, and we all need to find just the right fit to become a part of the circle jigsaw. Many people are swimming in fresh water crying – I THIRST when what they seek is actually all around them. Teach them not to fight with the ways of the Coven, for the BATTLE is always within and never without. We must all accept responsibility for our own life. If you are asked to leave a specific circle, then go with grace knowing that, that circle is not for you, as you will eventually, if true to your Craft find the Coven and Spiritual Family that is the perfect balanced home for you.

Remember always that a life without COMMITMENT is no life at all! If you can't handle it and think of failure-then you have already failed. We have always heard the saying "Live for the moment-as the future will take care of itself". No, it won't, if you do not work for a good present, then the future is destined to be the same routine of failure. If you want a great future then plan for it, work for it, and dream constantly of it and infuse your Magickal thoughts into building on what you already have. Laziness infused with a bit of Magick here and there will give you nothing but grief and a feeling of emptiness and loneliness.

If you go through your days of training within the Wicca, squeezing every bit of life out of every minute-then you need not be a failure. The Traditional Covens of the Wicca and Wiccecraft have taken decades to train their Priesthood and learn their Craft, and have the abilities to offer you what you CANNOT get as a Solitary. It is always up to you. Look for the things that you disagree with and you will surely find them. Look for the true Magick of the Goddess in everything and She will welcome you home to your true Spiritual Family and all will be revealed. Remember always that you do not only let yourself down, but you let down all your fellow sisters and brothers of the Wicca and bring disrepute upon all its followers. There are many Elders of this world who have over the past 60 years worked hard to bring the Craft out into the open and away from persecution. Many of you are not aware of how hard it actually was and how hard the Elders of Wicca worked to give you the luxury and freedom that you have these days. So respect the Elders and the teachers that gave you this light to find your Truth. May this book help you, as you enjoy and fulfil the commitment you have made to Wicca and to your entire fellow Wiccans, and to the Goddess? If you need to find a genuine working Coven, then let me know and I will try if possible to get you into contact with a genuine Traditional Coven.

Blessed Be
Tamara Von Forslun
The Witch of Oz

Tools of the
Seeker

Anointing Oil

Anointing oil is a special consecrated oil blend that we make in the Magick Circle. When seekers ask for wiccaning, I get them to make their own anointing oil so they can start their Magickal journey and consecrate and bless their tools. It is a simple blend (if not sure, see an aromatherapist) of your favourite fragrances combined with just one drop of your blood. Do not put more than a drop as blood goes off and can turn quite rank. It has a base oil, and then you add several of your own personal Magickal essential oils to the mix to get the perfect blend and aroma for all your anointing and Magickal purposes.

This is a very important item in Wiccecraft to have as it is used to anoint every item or Wiccetool that you will be using in the Magick Circle. Every tool must be consecrated and anointed. And I mean every tool, especially yourself. Whenever you enter a Magick Circle, you must anoint yourself with your anointing oil.

Start by facing the altar. Put a pentagram with the oil on your forehead to open your mind and bless yourself. Then draw an inverted triangle on your left palm with the oil and an upward triangle on your right hand. Finish with an equal-armed cross (the tau) over your heart.

Cakes—Lunar or Sabbat

Whenever we have a gathering, we always make an offering of cakes or bread. These are differently made to suit the ceremony or festival you are having. It is not an offering so much to the Goddess and God but to yourself and those attending your gathering.

If it is a New or Full Moon, we make what are called Luna cakes, which are made in the shape of crescent moons. We make enough for all in attendance, one each for the Goddess and God, and one for the centre of the Magick Circle.

Recipe

I find the best recipe is the following.

1 cup oats

1 tablespoon raisins

1 tablespoon sultanas

1 to 2 tablespoons honey

½ cup red wine or Port

½ cup mixed chopped nuts

self-rising flour (enough to make a good blend)

These are all evenly mixed together and then formed into crescent moons. Glaze with egg wash and sugar, and then baked in the oven until ready. For Sabbat cakes, which are traditionally used at festivals, we can use any shape we desire. I prefer to make a large loaf with above ingredients, so it can be used and broken into pieces for all to partake. This is also used at the Harvest Festival by adding a mixture of grains and seeds.

If you are making a harvest loaf as an offering, bake a normal loaf of grain and seed bread but inside, place an emptied eggshell filled with red food colouring and then bake.

The loaf of bread is placed on the altar and for a sacrificial offering. Consecrate the loaf under the God name Cernunnos, and as at all harvests, the old God is slain so that the God can be reborn. When you are ready for the sacrificial act, bring down your dagger and plunge it into the loaf of bread. As you do, the loaf of bread will bleed, with the red dye coming out of the concealed egg filled dye in the loaf. The bread is then broken into pieces and shared by all participants who take the God into themselves as an act of devotion.

Candles

Candles are very much a necessity in the craft as they are used for so many things. We all know how easy it is to buy candles, but is what the candle is made from important? So many inexpensive candles come out of Asia that are not real wax. They are forms of plastic called paraffin, a petroleum product, and include many hardening agents. They can be toxic, and some should never be burned in confined spaces, let alone anywhere near your family, especially your children.

There are also many candles out there made by people who are pure and beautiful. These candles contain essential oils. But with Wiccecraft and Magick, you are required to have certain colours, aromas, and so on, for specific rituals and ceremonies.

Magick of Colour

Colour has an intense energy that radiates powerful influences on humans, especially psyche and emotions. Our emotions are sometimes triggered by certain colours, and they become integral parts of our innate creativity and self-expression. Colours give life to our homes and our hearts. And when we wear certain colours, our feelings and emotions are elevated so that we feel more attractive, sexy, businesslike, or strong. In Magick, colour takes on a very important role as it triggers not only our inner emotions and psyche but also raises and elevates the psychic energies on an astral level in Magick. So in connecting deeper to these Magickal colours, we must understand their deeper meanings and the vibrations they relay to our psyches.

The sun, an emitted source of solar light, is the source of all colour. White light has within its spectrum all the colours but is not actually a colour itself; it is a carrier of colour. By the power of the Source and its certain energy, it also activates the energy frequency of all colours that vibrate at certain frequencies to omit the Magickal vibration we use in our rituals and spells.

- **Red**—The most powerful colour is of energy, power, strength, and expansion. It resonates a high sexual vibration as well and is a creative force that gives life to its colour. But on the flip side, in its negative mode, it represents anger, destruction, pain, war, and hate. It is the colour of survival, self-pleasure, and lust. It associated with the fire element and the ancient primordial earth, Pachamama—the first Earth Mother—followed by Gaia.
- **Pink**—When you mix the power of red with the softness of white, it reflects the gentler side of red. It softens sexual and survival instincts to a more sensitive and sensuous nature to protect and care. It resonates love more than sex or lust; it is about sensuality and the desire to give to others emotionally. It is the heart chakra. All relationships built on the foundation of pink are far superior and last longer than those built of red.

- **Orange**—Again we use red, combining its power with yellow to create this colour of fertility and change. Yellow is mental, while red is physical. This colour radiates rationale and assertiveness, and self-worth when in a positive mode. When in its negative mode, it is about survival and logic. But foremost about fertility is the creation of something new.

- **Gold**—This colour resonates with yellow but has a higher vibration. It resonates joy, happiness, laughter, and good cheer. Gold is a gentle masculine force that is about the communication of truth and love to others. It is the higher essence of creativity, sharing its beauty, colour, and artistry with warmth and unconditional love to the world. It is the colour of perfection combined with the vibration of wisdom. This colour is attuned to the yellow of the chakra the solar plexus.

- **Yellow**—Yellow is of the high intellect of the mind, very analytical, full of knowledge and a lust to learn, and quite logical. It must always have a sense of learning or boredom will set in. Yellow is of the outer sun and the internal sun, the solar plexus. The colour yellow encourages rational thinking and logic. Yellow is magnetic and attracts and sends out vibrations of desire. It is associated with the magnetic ability to receive and send telepathic responses. This is the colour of the true teacher, the mentor, as it is always the student first and then the teacher.

- **Green**—The beautiful colour of life and nature, green is the power of being restful and regenerative. It is also about calmness and the ability to take your time and replenish your energy reserves. It is a soft, cool colour associated with the feminine aspects of life. It teaches trust and love, knowing that as you give, so shall you also be given. This means not only with others but more important, with self-love. Too much green creates vanity, conceit, and lack of consideration towards others. But green is the radiance of life and love combined and is the bridge between the two. It, like red, is associated with the heart chakra but on a higher frequency and represents spiritual and Divine love.

- **Brown**—Representing the surface and energy of the life of the earth, brown is the deeper vibration of the earth, the very soul; it is the primordial nature and the need for continued life. All life starts in green and ends in brown. The cycle is complete with its reabsorption. Brown is about stability of home life and material wealth. Too much brown, and you are filled with greed; too little, and you lose the zest for life. It is at the base of your chakras and is the root, or base, chakra.

The Personality of Colour

Colour, as we have seen, is an integral part of our lives. But we also need colour to show individuality, and we must know what its vibrations portray. In Wiccecraft, colour enhances our rituals and spells and makes it less hard and simpler. If everything is in sync with each other, they act on their own with just with a little Magickal intervention from us. Let your ritual or spell speak for itself. Each will act upon another, making the vibration clearer and more powerful.

Each colour vibration also has a numerical vibration, which is in balance with each other. Numerology is a science of Magick and like Colour can determine your life and actions and events. By adding and using your alphabet, in sync with the numbers sets off a colour rainbow vibration that we can use in everyday life and in Magick. Here is a Personality Chart that will give you your Magickal Personality number and colour, which is your *"Soul Number"* or *"Wicce Number"*.

LETTERS	NUMBERS	COLOURS
AJS	1	RED
BKT	2	ORANGE
CLU	3	YELLOW
DMV	4	GREEN
ENW	5	BLUE
FOX	6	INDIGO
GPY	7	VIOLET
HQZ	8	PINK
IR	9	GOLD

EXAMPLE: TAMARA

NAME:	T	A	M	A	R	A
NUMBER:	2	1	4	1	9	1
COLOUR:	Orange	Red	Green	Red	Gold	Red

Total Number 18 – when broken down to a single digit is 1. 1 + 8 = 9

The Colour of Personal Expression

- **Red**: The Leader. With power, creative, leader, sexual and master of they're destiny. Stand securely and firmly on the ground full of ambition and creativity. Red people hate to follow; they need to be leaders, as they get frustrated and confused easily. Red people live their lives to the fullest with aggression, sometimes to the detriment of their own lives.
- **Orange:** The Listener, gentle natured, peacemaker, with plenty of energy and interest to be challenging, they love to organize and always persuasive. They love the quiet and calm and seek peace and harmony. Balance is their key tendency of searching their Truth. But can be demanding.
- **Yellow:** The Dreamer, who is thoughtful, creative, and intelligent and loves to move forward, Yellows truth is in the future; they live little in the past or present and usually miss opportunities. They constantly are building castles in the sky and need to be grounded often. Although they are Intellectual and love to be the centre of attention with a large array of friends, they at many times prefer to be alone.
- **Green:** The Nature Lover. A Lover of Life, Earthy, understanding, tolerant, peaceful, and accepting, seeking truth for their own well-being. They love to create and achieve in a positive way, through honesty. But sometimes get caught up in their personal ideas and views. They need to nurture, reflect, connect and nourish.
- **Blue:** The Psychic. A spiritual person, reliable and dependable, but has a free spirit. They seek Truth on all levels and build their lives based on devotion, trust, loyalty and a deep connection with the Environment. Blue can be an activist for the preservation of species, planet, and seeks knowledge and skills to help the Natural Earth.
- **Indigo:** The Philosopher, The Priest or Priestess who is a Spiritual leader, and lover. Indigo sees beauty in all things, always strong in their positivity to understand and accept others. Indigo believes in unconditional love, for without this emotion there is no purpose in their life. Good at solving problems but sometimes loses concentration

and gets off track. Needs to be away from turbulence and negative people. As they absorb this negative energy and can lose sight.

- **Violet:** The Spiritual Teacher. Has deep perception and understand of Spirit. Violet needs to know WHY in everything, and in everything do they question. They are the true Occultist to searches the closed off areas restricted from lay people. They yearn for tranquillity in their Environment. They are the Lucifuge, The Light Bearer who brings the gift of Spirit and the Goddess to man. Violet does need to be grounded so they do not become too Heavenly and ignore their own physicality. If this happens they have flights of fantasy and will not find their Truth.

- **Pink:** The Lover. Pink is the true friend and is usually friends to everyone; they connect with reality especially in Nature and have few illusions, as they always understand material life. Pink can judge fairly and be arbitrator between people, as they can always see both sides truthfully. Pink loves to succeed and achieve their dreams especially for their family, as they are the Provider.

- **Gold:** The Hope of the World. This masculine colour denotes intellect, gentle energy, god force, especially Universal hope and love to the world. They love to be the centre of positive attention, always spreading laughter and joy and are a ray of sunshine. Gold find it hard to live up to other ideals, and sometime needs to aware of depression, as they become disappointed within themselves if they fail their families.

Working With Candles

The first step in Candle Magick is to choose a candle by selecting a colour and shape, which represents your Magickal purpose and desire. Next you will have to anoint the candle this is done by wiping the entire candle with specific Magickal Consecration Oil. The oil is usually made of some plant or flower, which also represents your desire. Place some oil on your fingertips. As you concentrate on your desire, rub the oil into your candle, starting from the centre and rubbing upward. Then rub the oil from the centre downward. Be sure to cover the entire candle with the oil, even the wick, as doing this infuses it with your desire, or rhyming spell.

When you are planning a Magick Candle Spell, try to keep all your symbolism or vibrations the same. For example: if you were doing a love Spell, you would want to use a green candle and love drawing oil, like rose, lavender or Venus Oil. For a peaceful home, use blue candle and Tranquillity oil, I would even burn matching incense. The whole idea is to keep your colours, objects, and thoughts similar in meaning and symbology. By doing this, your energy is focused for a maximum positive result.

REMEMBER CANDLE MAGICK IS SIMPLE, IT IS ONE OF THE EASIEST AND SIMPLEST MAGICKAL RITUALS YOU CAN DO. ALWAYS REMEMBER MAGICK IS LIKE A DOUBLE-EDGED SWORD; AS IN ALL MAGICK USED, IF IT IS USED FOR THE WRONG REASON, IT COULD AND WILL REBOUND THREEFOLD! SO ALWAYS DO YOUR SPELL WITH A FULL HONEST HEART AND NOT FOR WRONG REASONS.

COLOUR DAY	DAY	ZODIAC	ANGEL	PLANET	TIME	MEANING
Red	Tuesday	Aries	Samael	Mars	1 hour	Power, strength, lust, courage, action, protects from Fire.
Pink	Friday	Libra	Anael	Venus	1 hour	Love, calming, friendship, heart opener, beauty, peace, the Arts.
Orange	Sunday	Leo	Michael	Sun	2 hours	Career, action, sales, finance, healing, attraction, results.
Yellow	Wednesday	Gemini	Raphael	Mercury	3 hours	Intellect, healing, communication, selling oneself, writing, persuasion.
Green	Friday	Taurus	Anael	Venus	4 hours	Love, fertility, luck, health, money, Art and music, creativity, goals.
Blue	Friday	Libra	Anael	Venus	3 hours	Creativity, perception, beauty, peace, tranquillity, harmony, the Arts.
Indigo	Thursday	Sagittarius	Sachiel	Jupiter	2 hours	Psychic powers, self-awareness, Wisdom, prestige, awareness, truth.
Violet	Tuesday	Pisces	Asariel	Neptune	1 hour	Ambition, spiritual development, Ocean connection, power, secret life.
Silver	Monday	Cancer	Gabriel	Moon	3 hours	One with the Moon Goddess, love, Magick, female empowerment, Insight, clairvoyance.
Gold	Sunday	Scorpio	Azrael	Pluto	1 hour	One with the Horned God, nature, Wealth, prosperity, mining, death.

White	All Days	Aquarius	Gabriel	Uranus	N/A	All Magick, universal colour, male energies, spiritual knowledge, all healing.
Black	Saturday	Capricorn	Gabriel	Saturn	1 hour	Protection, secrets, karma, occult knowledge, dissolve negativity, property.
Brown	Monday	Virgo	Raphael	Mercury	4 hours	Stability, Earth energy, indecision, Grounding, healing the Earth.

Candle Magick Hints

- If you can make your own candles. While the wax is in a liquid form add a corresponding oil, herb or flower, even colour. For example, if you are doing a money spell you could add Heliotrope Oil and mint leaves, green dye.
- When anointing a candle, close your eyes and concentrate, visualize, see in your mind's eye, what the candle represents. Anoint with your fingers from the centre of the candle upwards and downwards, removing all negative energies, and then from the outside of the candle to the centre, bringing in positivity.
- Always allow the burning time of the candle to complete its time as shown in the graph.
- Read and know your Spell or Ritual, rehearsal makes perfect. Know your Spell.
- Don't forget to make your ritual check list "PROPERLY PREPARED YOU SHOULD ALWAYS BE."
- But remember the law of threefold return! Only do the ritual or Spell if you are 100% sure!

DEVELOPING:

1. Make sure to always keep records in your book, write down the preparation, the tools, the time and date, your emotions, phase of the Moon, even the successes or failures, as this is how you learn.
2. You must always be comfortable, with loose clothing or robe and a relaxed meditative body. Know your Spell, this will make you more sure and comfortable.
3. Have a total fast at least 3 hours prior to your ritual or Spell.
4. Meditation first prior to your ritual and Spell.
5. You are now ready to enter your Magick Circle, so acknowledge the Goddess always, and call to the Elements and the Elements to guide you and assist when necessary.

Altar Candles

Altar Candles represent the Divine Feminine – the Goddess and the Divine Masculine – The Horned God. They are traditionally place either side of the Altar. Goddess Candle to the West, usually is a Black Candle representing Women's Mysteries and the Moon (Night). God Candle to the East, usually a White Candle representing Men's Mysteries and the Sun (Day).

Spirit Candle

The Spirit Candle in Traditional Wiccecraft is the first Light brought into the Magick Circle and represents the Light of the Universe, it is from this White Spirit Candle that all other flames are lit, even the Charcoal and Incense as well as the Heart Fire in the centre.

Festival Candles

Are traditionally the colour to represent the Seasonal changes such as:

Samhain – Black and Jack O Lanterns

Winter – white and green

Lughnasadh – blues and greens

Spring – Rainbow Colours

Beltane - Red

Summer – reds, yellows and oranges

Imbolg - blues

Autumn – brown.

The Yule Log is a special piece that is designed each and every year and decorates the Yule House to bring in light and life for the following year and then at the next Yule Ceremony it is traditionally offered to the fire as an offering of thanks for the past year.

Akashic Quarter Candles

- East – Blue to bring in the energy and light of the Rising Sun of the East and new beginnings, to open the mind and allow our Creativity to flow to bring more light and Magick into our world.
- South – Red to bring the power and Passion of the Noon-day Sun and the Masculine power of the God Force. It is the realm of Emotion and all balanced emotion comes in through this direction.
- West – Green to bring the strength of Magick and the Invisible within the Visible. It is about the ebb and flow of the cosmic tides of life and the very ocean that moves within us. It is about tapping into the Magick Power of everything in life.
- North – Amber to bring Foundation and Grounding and all Physical Power of life and growth. About Law of Nature and Commitment. Learning to honour the brotherhood of all life as one essence.
- Centre – White to bring spirit and Divine Light of the Goddess and God as one universal energy to illumine our Soul and awaken us to Truth.

Fif-faths

Fif-faths are what is called "Dolly Magick", similar to Voodoo dolls, but for good. You can use any item to make them from clay, wax, plasticine, fabric etc. It is used to draw two lovers together then they should either look like the couple or at least be the colour of passion which is red. You need to make the two poppets as close to the resemblance as the couple, if you have nails, hair, photos, etc they should all be used in the dolls. Also it is great to have some material from an old shirt etc from the person you are making the Fif-fath of.

Cape

I love the look of Capes and find them very welcoming when it is a cold evening, as it can be spread wide enough to keep others warm as well. But when it comes to ritual I dislike them as they have too much fabric that flows and gets in the way of the ritual, and I have seen many a Wicce go up in flames. They also flap and cause the candles to be extinguished. I feel that unless it is really cold, then avoid having capes during any ritual. We use them at Festivals and when it is cold only, so they do not hinder the ritual.

The Chakra's

Chakras are your psychic centres, or energy centres. The word Chakra is Sanskrit, meaning "**WHEEL**". The Chakra's are power centres, which gather and attract energy and information within the body. This is associated with the Endocrine Glands, and the nerve plexus. By the Indian Mystics it is often referred to as "Organs of Psychic Perception" or even "Etheric Organs". The Chakra's serve as Channels for our Spiritual and psychic information. So, wherever we find a major gland in our body, there is a nerve plexus, and one of the Seven Major Sacred Chakra's. I wish to also advise you that although the Chakra's are associated with the Endocrine System, they are not to be confused with the actual physical organs of the body.

- **The First Chakra (Root or Base Chakra):** This is at the base of the spine, at the tailbone or anus, and has a direct relationship to the ovaries and testicles, which is called Kundalini. The first Chakra also has to do with SURVIVAL. All survival data and genetic information necessary to keep the body alive is found at this psychic centre. It also tells you what you need for survival in an individual, the proper foods, shelter, rest, exercise, sexuality, etc.! The question here is do you allow yourself to have physical and material pleasures such as joy, happiness, sexual fulfillment; and do not deny ourselves these things. The problems in this Chakra are usually apparent when we have grounded or earthed ourselves properly at all. This sometimes occurs when you focus on *another's survival and needs and neglect your own*. This Chakra also gets overloaded if you are trying to keep two bodies alive, in this case you will tend to get very ill. As maintaining another life is only good with children, or in an immediate life or death situation. It is wise to question yourself. *"Am I trying to prove myself, by keeping another alive?"*
- **The Second Chakra or Sacral Chakra:** This is located just below the naval and has a direct relationship to the Pancreas. This Chakra is related also to CLAIRSENTIENCE, which is the feelings and emotions of other people, it picks up all the vibrations, sometimes it can even duplicate their emotions. Reflected here

is the degree of your own personal reality. This Chakra also governs the erotic world, it rules sexuality, sensuality and desire and even lust. Problems usually occur in this Chakra when you are too open to the feelings of others, when this happens there is a tendency to duplicate their emotions and enter into a sympathetic state of anger with them, rather than just being and having empathy for their feelings. If you allow yourself to be invaded by another's feelings, then your body is alive via the stimuli of another - which is an unhealthy state.

- **The Third Chakra - The Solar Plexus:** This Chakra is located at the Solar Plexus and has a direct relationship to the Adrenal Gland. It governs energy distribution and distributes vital energy throughout the body; it is your CONTROL AND POWER CENTRE. Through this Chakra you can regulate and balance your own energy, by learning when to give and when to take energy. The problem associated with this Chakra occurs when you allow your energy to be given away, giving in the demands of people. *"Give me your energy, I want your energy and support. I control you."* You must know why you choose this, and why you agree to give up or take too much energy, control or be controlled. It is this contrast between you as a spiritual being and you as a physical body, and consequently this is how you operate. When you allow others to hook into your energy or even when you try to control the energies of others, you do not own your own power, and therefore cannot trust it. Being hyperactive and sending energy all over the place indicates that the Solar Chakra is too open causing depletion of your own energies; the draining feeling. When tension in the Solar Chakra occurs, ask if your energies have been where you want them, or if you have given too much away. To rid yourself from outside energies from others that drain your own, it is important to always ask yourself; ***"Why you agree to these situations and what are you getting from it."***

- **The Fourth Chakra - The Heart Chakra:** This is located under the ribs at the Sternum and has a direct relationship to the Thymus Gland. The Heart Chakra has to do with affinity, your ability to love and to enter a state of oneness with yourself (self-love) with another person, or a group. It is the centre of your Path and your goals. Everything is usually found around this Chakra, as it is the meeting between your being and your 'body'. It is the inner you that does know.

  The problems in the Heart Chakra occur when we are out of affinity with ourselves or when we are operating with others on a pure affinity level. If we cannot look at ourselves, or when we are operating with others on a pure affinity level. If we cannot look at ourselves with love, we cannot accomplish very much. To manifest your body in the most capable positive, joyful, and loving way, you must have love and affinity for it. When you are out of the present time occurrences re-stimulate past pictures or incidents, which say; "Nobody likes me!" This relationship doesn't work, so I am no good! Then you are kept from affinity with yourself. It is difficult to have to ask you, but you must always ask yourself where and why you stopped being close to yourself. Realise your Goddessness and who and what took your right away, who played one-upmanship with you, and who placed judgments on you.

If people around you cannot be themselves, and you cannot be yourself, then get rid of them, so be it, I did, and I have. You do not have to play games with other people; you do not need other people laying their trips on you. Push out the dark pictures and the negative energy of others. Return it to neutral or send it back without malice. Energy that is not yours in your Heart Chakra should be pushed out to enable you to have affinity with your SELF.

- **The Fifth Chakra - The Throat Chakra:** This is located at the cleft of the throat and is connected to the Thyroid Gland. This Chakra is COMMUNICATION - which is the vehicle with which we communicate as beings. It helps to give us the ability to express what we feel, verbalize clearly, communicate clearly with other people. It is your inner voice. It gives you communication between your personality and your soul. It is your most vital and rapid form of growth. You learn through words, "Heal the Words, and receive the words." Problems occur in the Heart Chakra when your communication with others is not very clear and direct an honest. We always grow through words and we learn from each other with words. But it is important to find out whose words you are using and you're expressing what needs to be said.

We must let go of unfinished conversations whether an hour ago or ten years ago for these keep us out of the present time. The programming of others can also cause frozen energy in the Throat Chakra that you should say things in a certain way you cannot say what you feel, and you cannot express your emotions in a certain way. You cannot get good grades in English etc. Such programming keeps away spontaneity, which prevents you from being in the present time and thinking about yourself in new terms. Ask yourself: "Who won't let me say my feelings are hurt; who won't let me be angry; tell someone I love them, verbalize affection and healing? Who blocks or blocked me from using communication in the best way possible? Who told me I didn't have anything to say, wasn't important enough to speak and express my thoughts and feelings?"

Eliminate all the inner voices from those people who prevented you from speaking up. Do you have pictures that say; if you don't have something profound to say, don't speak! If you can't say something nice, don't say it at all. KNOW you have the right to express what you want to express. It might not be good insight but get it out. If others can't effectively incorporate what you have said, then that is their problem. If you choose not to say it, write it, get it out of your system in order to keep the Throat Chakra clear. You cannot deal with any problem until you have made it real by either writing it or verbalizing it.

Be aware of heat in the back of the neck and let go of all unspoken thoughts and unexpressed emotions and send them back. Those conversations are over - finished. Rid yourself of self-judgments that say; "I don't know how to say it right, others express themselves better. I don't have creative dialogues. Nobody listens to me anyway." Also, be aware of people who 'demand' that you hear them. They are trying to plug your fifth Chakra without equal communication.

- **The Sixth Chakra - The Third Eye Chakra:** This is located between the eyebrows and is connected to the Pituitary Gland and is the Sixth Chakra which is the Third Eye, the centre of the individual CONSCIOUSNESS, consciousness defined as SOUL quality. It has to do with CLAIRVOYANCE, which is the ability to see the invisible within the visible: such as Auras, levels of energy and pictures, also the Spirit World. It is also the ability to arrive at a concept without going through rational processes, i.e. abstract intuition. Through the Third Eye, individual consciousness is expanded into Universal Consciousness. By this, you reach up into the Manifested Universal Mind. The problems associated with the Sixth Chakra occur in two ways. The first is that people want you to see the world in their way (Conditioning). This clogs your own intuitive sense of things, and if you are not aware, cautious, you will respond to the data and see the world their way. When their more permissive data prevents you from acting on your own data, we begin to operate off their people's pictures. It becomes difficult to distinguish what is the real us, from their pictures of us. The result can be a feeling of craziness, headaches and confusion. The second way the Brow Chakra becomes jammed from people plugging into it is trying to see where you are at or wanting your validation. (I want to see you; I want you to see me). This creates enormous tension.

Get rid of people with whom you have tried to share your reality, but who were incapable of recognizing it. Another thing to be aware of in this Chakra is pressure behind the eyes. When this happens, you may be trying to visualize what you are seeing or perceiving with your Third Eye through your physical eyes. Be aware of this and redirect your energy.

- **The Seventh Chakra - The Crown Chakra:** This is located at the top read of the head. It is the soft spot on a baby's head. This concerns KNOWINGNESS, the ability to sit still and know. It is the controller of all the other Chakra's, the centre of Cosmic Consciousness or Spirituality. It is supreme consciousness, eternal peace, eternal knowledge, etc.! It connects humans with the infinite. The problems of the Seventh Chakra come from people trying to own you or run you, trying to manipulate you. Such situations block communications between the being and the body.

Someone is trying to communicate with your body.

This ownership message is: *"You don't have a thought or desire of your own"*. Because this Chakra is the ultimate control of the other Chakra's, people who desire to own you, plug in there. When this happens you must ask yourself why are you willing to play the victim game? Ask what the agreement is, the key picture of what is holding them there. It's not trusting your knowingness, not taking time to be still enough to touch with your spirituality and feel the Oneness with all creation? Try to get rid of energy that is not your own. Tell yourself that you want Cosmic Consciousness to meet your body and be responsible for what happens to your body. Situations, where someone speaks of someone as my woman, my man, are not ownership qualities if the agreement is to work together. However, having a pattern of having men in control or vice versa in a relationship is one of ownership.

Self-Blessing Ritual

The Self-Blessing Ritual is an activity, using the Chakras and your Anointing Oil, which many Wiccans do less and less as time goes by. In the times of our ancestors, everyone did some form of Self-Blessing To be in touch with your true Inner and Higher Self. You should do this ritual every morning and evening. With SELF-EMPOWERMENT central to ritual and to your own spirituality, the Self-Blessing Ritual is very simple, beautiful and a powerful cleansing process. The High Priestess usually leads but you can do this on your own. This one I wrote in 1976 and use it every day.

Touch the Crown Chakra:
"BLESS ME MOTHER, FOR I AM YOUR CHILD, AND I AM PART OF YOU!"

Touching the Third Eye:
"BLESS ME MOTHER, THAT I MAY SEE MY WAY CLEAR, AND SEE YOU IN ALL THINGS!"

Touching the Throat Chakra:
"BLESS ME MOTHER, AND BLESS MY WORDS, THAT I MAY SPEAK CLEARLY AND TRUTHFULLY, WITH LOVE AND POWER!"

Touching the Heart Chakra:
"BLESS ME MOTHER AND BLESS MY HEART THAT IT BE OPEN TO ALL LIFE AND FILLED WITH COMPASSION AND STRENGTH!"

Touching the Solar Plexus Chakra:
BLESS ME MOTHER WITH DIVINE LIGHT AND ENERGY AND ALLOW MY DIVINE LIGHT TO TOUCH OTHERS IN YOUR NAME!

Touching the Sacred Chakra:
"BLESS ME MOTHER AND BLESS MY BEING WITH THE POWER TO HEAL ALL WOUNDS AND THE EARTH!"

Touching the Base Chakra:
"BLESS ME MOTHER, AND BLESS MY SEXUALITY, THE GATEWAY OF LIFE AND DEATH, AND TEACH ME TO FEAR NEITHER!"

Touching the Souls of your Feet:
"BLESS ME MOTHER AND BLESS MY FEET THAT HAVE BROUGHT ME ALONG THE PATH THAT LEADS TO YOU AND JOY DIVINE!"

Touching the Palms of your Hands: (with fingers of opposite hand touching palm)
"BLESS ME MOTHER AND BLESS MY HANDS THAT THEY MAY DO YOUR GREAT WORK, TO HELP ALL OTHER LIFE!"

Stand in Pentagram Position with head tilted back:
"BLESS ME MOTHER IN THE RADIANCE OF YOUR MAJIKAL SIGN, FOR I AM YOUR CHILD NOW AND FOREVER BLESSED!

Being in Balance

THE HEAD: The forepart is electric; the back of the head is magnetic and so is the right side; the left side is electric and so is the inner of your being.

THE EYES: The forepart is neutral and so is the background. The right side is electric and so it is with the left side. The inside is magnetic.

THE EARS: Forepart neutral, back-part also. Ride side magnetic, left side electrical, inside neutral.

MOUTH AND TONGUE: Forepart neutral, back-part as well as right side and left side both neutral, inside magnetic.

THE NECK: Forepart, back part, and right side magnetic, left side and inside electrical.

THE CHEST: Forepart electro-magnetic, back part electrical, right side and inside neutral, left side electrical.

THE ABDOMEN: Forepart electrical, back-part and right side magnetic, left side electrical, the inside neutral.

THE HANDS: Forepart neutral, back part also, right side magnetic, left side electrical, the inside neutral.

THE FINGERS OF THE RIGHT HAND: Fore and back part neutral, right side electrical, left side also the inside neutral.

THE FINGERS OF THE LEFT HAND: Fore and back part neutral, right side electrical, left side as well, the inside neutral.

THE FEET: Fore and back part neutral, right side magnetic, left side electrical, inside neutral.

THE MALE GENITALS: Forepart electrical, back part neutral, right and left side also, the inside magnetic.

THE FEMALE GENITALS: Fore part magnetic, back part, right and left side neutral, the inside electrical.

THE LAST VERTEBRA TOGETHER WITH THE ANUS: Fore and back part neutral, right and left side as well, the inside magnetic.

Exercise: 4 x 4 breathing

(This is where you breathe in to the count of 4, then hold to the count of 4, then exhale to the count of 4. Keep this up for at 5-10 minutes)

Charcoal Blocks

If you have the luxury of having a Temple or Magick Circle set up outdoors, then you are one of the lucky ones, as having our Spiritual Temple built encompassing Mother Nature with the stars as our roof, the trees as our walls, and the living grass beneath our feet as the floor, that the Goddess created for us, this is the real Temple of the Goddess. If this is the case, then there is nothing more beautiful and Magickal than using Charcoal Blocks to burn your Incense in your Thurible (Incense Burner).

You can buy them at most new Age stores in rolls of about 10, but it works out much cheaper to buy them by the box as it cuts the price in half, and you never seem to run out.

If your Temple is indoors, then you can still use the Charcoal Blocks inhouse, but it will set all fire alarms off as it gets filled with a heady atmosphere of smoke and the aroma of the incense you place upon the charcoal. It is preferred to use just Incense sticks in the house as this is not so toxic and does not wreak throughout all your furnishings.

Chimes

In Traditional Covens we sometimes use a Triangular metal chime hung on a tree as a toll to call the Spirits or Elementals, and sometimes frighten them away, depending on what purpose you are using it for. Sometimes it is nice to open the Magick Circle and to call your Coveners to the Circle perimeter ready for the Creation of the Magick Circle.

Chimes are great at Festivals also for tolling different stages of the Ritual, also to commence with the start of something important, which grabs everyone's attention, it is better than yelling out to shut up. In Traditional Covens we all enter according to Rank, as the Magick Circle is Properly Prepared, and Cast before the Elders arrive. One Chime calls all Wicces and Seekers to the Circle who are then welcomed and anointed before being brought in for meditation. Two Chimes summon the Priesthood, and three Chimes welcome the High Priesthood and elders of the Covenstead.

Compass

Everyone should possess a compass, as everything we do in Magick is about directions. All of our rituals or ceremonies are about directions of our Magick Circle. In fact if you look at the Magick Circle it is a form of a compass and we are the magnetic arrow that works its Magick in the 360 degrees of the Circle and the myriad directions including the 365 degrees of Magick.

With our compass we must work and know where true magnetic North is so that our Altar is placed in exactly the right place. East is the Element of Air, South is the Element of Fire, West is the Element of Water and North is the Element of Earth. These points also represent the Four Seasonal festivals, spring, summer, autumn and winter. And the cross-quarters in between are representative of the major Festivals of Samhain, Lughnasadh, Beltane and Imbolg.

The Degrees of the Compass and the Magick Circle also represent key points of Portals to different Tarot Cards and their meanings and uses both Ritually, Meditatively, Magickally and Spiritually. With the Lesser Arcana being placed in specific places around the perimeter of the Magick Circle, check out my book (Tarot Magick and Journeys of the Magick Circle of Thoth). All the Pentacle cards placed from North-East around to North-West. Then the Cups or Chalices being specifically placed between the North-West and the South-West. Then we have Swords being specifically placed between the South-West and the South-East, and the Wands being specifically placed from the South-East to the North-East.

On the Inner Circle of the Magick Circle which is where we perform High Magick we place the Major Arcana Tarot Cards in specific places to signify their powers through Magick. Starting with the 1st Tarot Card The Magician in the North followed by the rest of the Major Arcana Widdershins around the inner circle, excluding 0-The Fool and XXI The Universe which are placed in the very centre for specific dimensional purposes.

In my Covens we actually get the Initiates to tie the Compass to one end of their Singulum, so it is always with them Magickally, and they usually place a Pentagram on the other end or a magnifying glass.

Crystals

Everyone is into crystals these days, and New Age stores are filled with them in every size and shape. I am not really into crystals in such a way. Due to the fact that I believe by listening to people in the know that crystals each have specific powers and abilities. So when we remove these sacred stones from the Living Earth, maybe we are taking from her, her very energy that is sustaining and healing her life. As we take, we never seem to give back, this is where I see the rape of Mother Earth as wrong. If we take something from her, we must in kind give an offering for what she has given us. But that is just my opinion. I have never paid for a crystal in a store but have been lucky enough to travel and discover my own precious gems. Even on my farm land I have large pieces of crystal quartz and many Sapphires, garnets, Zirconia, ruby's, etc. As we live not far from the Gemfields of Central Queensland.

A dear long-time friend of mine Adam Barralet is an expert on crystals where I am not, and in his book "Crystal Connections – A Guide to Crystals and How to Use Them" he writes: "Crystals have been used around the world for thousands of years to attract love, promote luck, banish evil, ensure protection and restripe health. The structure, chemical makeup, colour, shape and place of origin all affect the crystal's energy and its beneficial properties. Some crystals will lead you to new and exciting adventures, while others will protect and build upon what you already possess. One thing is for sure though, there is a crystal perfect for every hope and dream you hold."

His book is so incredible and very in-depth as it holds every aspect that is needed to know about crystals their powers and their uses. It is written in such a profound and spiritual way that is simplistic in its understanding for the lay person who is not educated in this area of expertise.

In my Covens we use Crystals to magnify certain energies that are needed in our Magick. My High Priest – Asherah had the most beautiful Phallic Crystal that we used as a Phallic

Wand for invoking the Goddesses Lunar Consciousness (Drawing Down the Moon) at Full Moons. It was an incredible experience and something I shall always cherish.

For your Magick and your Magick Circle you can place the crystals around your Circle or on your Altar, and if you have a variety of them then they will always be ready when something unexpected comes up that needs a little boost of energy on top of your own.

I was gifted from a friend of mine a very large 40 kilo slab of rare rutilated mushroom crystal. What happened was that he was a manager up in Telfer mining camp where they mined gold in a huge open cut mine. When one day he was called to come down to the pit and when he got there they had a discovered a massive cave of crystals. Which they then had to inform C.A.L.M. to come and take a look. Whilst waiting their operations were on hold.

When CALM arrived they looked at the crystal cave, and decided they were not worth keeping, and so the company then went ahead and bulldozed the entire cavern. My friend decided to venture into the cave before its demise and took out a ute load of crystals. He then brought it down to me and I was given several large pieces and the rest he kept for himself. We later found out that they were very rare Mushroom Crystals and not found anywhere in the world except one other place. But alas they too are gone and destroyed at the hands of man.

Cushions

As much of our work is done standing or sitting in the Magick Circle, these come in very handy when the ground is a little damp or too much moisture. We use them for meditation, journeys, trances, also Astral travel. If you have several members in your Coven, then maybe as a workshop get everyone to bring along some of their own favourite fabric and a cushion to be covered. I also would place on the bottom some type of tarp material to keep moisture or dampness out of the cushion.

Your cushion can be as small or as large as you like. For our cushions we bought some large blue plastic tarps and cut them to size for the bottoms of the cushions, they were so cheap it cost about $10 for about 10 cushions. Even if you don't want cushions you could make a large comfortable blanket and ground sheet in the same way with plastic tarp material on the bottom and maybe just an old blanket stitched on the top. If you make them well and individually then they will gradually over time harness your own energies and the energies of the Magick Circle, which can make them a type of healing cushion.

Goddess and God

Understanding
The Goddess and God

We are all familiar in the Western World with the creative concept of a male God or saviour, whether the idea comes from Christianity, Judaism, or Islam. When we think of God, at the back of our minds is a picture of an old grey haired and bearded man in the sky, or on a hilltop or in a cave who has a certain set of laws; rules and regulations that we must all obey at every cost. If we follow his rules we will be loved and accepted by God, our Father, but if we disobey, we will be condemned and punished, (thanks dad).

Even today when the power of this belief has been weakened, and many do not even believe in a God at all, the image of Jehovah from the Old Testament is still very strong though we may consciously reject this view of God, subconsciously and within the structures of our society, this idea exists. When we feel guilty or unworthy in some way and expect punishment. It is so ingrained in us, that to a large extent the "Jehovah" figure is the only way we can envisage God. We appear to have only two choices; either this male God exists or there is no God at all?

Jesus Christ, through his teachings of the New Testament, tries to offer us an alternative, by describing a God of Love, who loves all, no matter what we do or who we are. Unfortunately, even though Christianity attempts to uphold Jesus' teachings, we find when we discuss the Nature of God with many Christians, that they will and are still heavily influenced by the Jehovah of the Old Testament, and see God as wrathful, judgmental and punishing unless you 'get it right'.

However, in the second half of the 20th century, another concept of God has appeared. This time God is not male, but female. Her devotee's talk about the Great Goddess or the Great White Mother, who existed in our ancient World long before the domination and take-over of male centred religions and before Christianity achieved its dominance of the world. Many books have been written on the need for our society to turn towards the Great Mother Goddess who has been forgotten and ignored for millennia. She was one part of the divine duo throughout all of history as the most potent and well-loved of all religious paths. On the face of it, assessing the idea of a female Creattrix, is a purely intellectual way, it seems quite ridiculous. Why should it matter whether God is male or female? Surely a supreme deity is beyond gender at all.

Eastern religions like Buddhism and Taoism already accept the genderlessness of God. In Taoism, we are presented with the concept of the "Tao", which means "The Way". There is no entity or image which can be worshipped or appealed to, Buddhism is similar, but since its ideas were taught by an historical man Gautama Buddha, he is the one worshipped, despite the fact that he insisted he was not a God.

If we were assessing the Nature of God in an entirely logical way, the concept of "Tao" would be the true representation, since it perceives a supreme entity as pure energy, beyond all ideas of human form and character. The trouble with this idea is that human beings find it hard to grasp what the Tao is really like. It is ever mysterious and beyond the comprehension of our limited minds. We need an image that we can relate to, that we can understand in human terms, so give it a human appearance, but the truest representation of God which we can grasp, and which fits in with our growing ideas of deity, is of God as the Great Mother. A masculine God is omnipotent, but judges us, condemns and gives only limited love if deserved. His power is used to punish transgressors and reward the faithful and obedient. Man does the same.

However, when you think of a Mother, the picture is different. An ideal mother gives her children unconditional love which never waivers nor lessens no matter what her child does, it will always be loved, supported in its growth, and nourished by the Mother. Even if the child abuses her, or commits horrendous crimes within society, this love never alters and changes. A wise mother obviously encourages loving behaviour, and discourages mistakes, but her love never changes. When we think of the Great Mother, we are thinking of a Mothering entity that will unconditionally love us all, forever, whether we believe in Her or not is not relevant, as She believes in us; Because we are Her creations, Her children, the Children of the Gods, to use the Earthly metaphor. This is a completely different picture from the one drawn by the belief in a male God, which relies on the threat of punishment, or withdrawal of love and rewards to keep us in line and afraid, and in control. Since it is now time for the Matriarchal side of our Creator to be accepted and valued by mankind, it makes sense to worship a Female Goddess. Only in this way will we begin to balance our imbalanced society, which has denigrated and denied the Great Mothers gift for millennia, we will raise the Mother but also honour the Great Father as in a balance needed to this time of equilibrium.

As we all aware in our society there are many people who do not obey the rules of the Christian faith, and still seem to escape all punishment. Some of them seem to flout all the laws of society and religion, and yet still prosper and thrive, laughing at the laws of God. Others obey all the rules, behave in a very humble and loving way, constantly devout in the behaviour yet seem to receive no reward for their actions. They are often despised and taken advantage of because of their weakness.

The Christian Church avoid the implications of this by stating that such people are rewarded in Heaven, and the others will go to hell. Since this is only a speculation, and not a **FACT,** it is of little physical help to those suffering on Earth in the present. The priests of the One God can only offer a better life when we are dead - Heaven after Earth. In contrast to this, the Devotees of the Great Mother can promise peace, joy, and Paradise on this Earth as in Heaven, while we are living. To be in Paradise does not require us to be disciplined and sacrificial for the sake of future rewards; all it requires is a small change in attitude.

In the world of the One God, whether it is one reflected to us through Christianity, Judaism, Islam or Science (which is our latest religion) we are offered a Patriarchal world of conflict and fear. We must accept the masculine world of aggression and conquest, whether it is conquest of others or ourselves. We as individuals have also become more aggressive and frightened in our present world. All harmonious ideas of Joy and happiness are looked down upon, as impossible, or just too hard, leaving us with only suffering as the route to all our salvation.

In this ignorant worldview, we learn to succeed only through struggle and pain, so it becomes an inevitable and necessary part of life. When we look to the feminine and the Great Mother, there is a different perspective, one of ease and comfort. The Great Mother will always look after us, no matter what we do and no matter what we believe, say or think. There is no requirement to subscribe to a religion or way of behaving to "Earn" Her love. She shows us all equally no matter. The feminine is a concept of harmony, of bringing together Joy and Peace. The priests of the One God see a world that is out of harmony with itself, where only the strongest survive and the weakest fail, this is not necessary.

The Mother worldview shows us harmony in everything on Earth, and in the whole of creation. This idea is the essential harmoniousness of all creation and was recently brought out very clearly in the book "Gaia" by James Lovelock. His book is named after the ancient Earth Goddess, who was worshipped as the original Earth Goddess. Though She was eons ago acknowledged as the first to emerge from the primordial state of chaos. Later male-dominated cultures devalued Her and placed sky God's like Uranus and Zeus above Her. The Truth of existence is how we see the Earth that we live on, and our fellow man that shapes our lives. Our desires and fears, act as magnets, drawing towards us the reality which we feel is the "True" one, (Like attracts Like). If we believe in this conflict and limited love, if we do not behave in a certain way we will not be loved or rewarded, then this will be the reality that we create. We will become aggressive or defensive to words and ways of other people because we expect them to hurt or exploit us. This in turn like a magnet attracts us to the very aggression we fear and confirms our beliefs, just look at ISL, their destructive and murderous path founded by the very belief.

Mankind seem to believe that the strongest, most powerful and the most ruthless continue to survive, and somehow it is by divine order, in believing this we have no problems in exploiting everything in and on this world, especially the very earth we live on and our fellow man. But we know that deep within the hollows of our mind we have the fear that there will always be someone stronger and more ruthless that can literally take everything we own away from us.

In living like this and allowing ourselves to judge others by seeing them as higher or lower, stronger or weaker, then we will continue to live in fear of us always being judged ourselves.

This new religion has created a god who does this at the end of our life when we die, sending only a few chosen to heaven and the rest as sinners to their hell, based on their scale of balance judging our very worth, devoutness and being told what to do and believe. The sad history of our patriarchal and indoctrinated species for the last two thousand years has been centred on being controlled and living with fear and conflict. Our stupid idea of 'Right' is always based on patriarchal power and force. Just look at the situation with North Korea and America, two stubborn leaders who believe they are right because "might is right". Each of them individually believing that they are right, and nothing can sway as the rest of the world are ignorant morons who do not have a clue as the realities of what is going on. Cause we know what's going on we have all grown up in schools with bullies, this is no different. Each side of this conflict believes that justice will prevail and is on their side, but we all know that it is superior strength that will prevail, but to what extent. Remember they each have their finger just above a red button that may see the demise of mankind and the end of our planet, as we know it.

It is always about people crossing boundaries, about wealth, and differences of beliefs and opinions, and it is the people who suffer the most because of this brutish ideology. We all know that the unwritten law is that the more powerful you are the more you can ignore the rights of others who are less powerful. Look at the world's most powerful countries USA, China and Russia, they have each accumulated such incredible wealth and power by their use of aggression, and so too has the Roman Catholic Church through two thousand years of aggression in the name of love, created armies of powers, a wealth beyond ridiculous, and the total control and domination over a billion souls continuing to fill their coffers. The silly thing is that the British Commonwealth actually has and owns over a third of the world through their domination, even though they are one of the smallest nations in the world, yet the most powerful.

In such a sad and frightening world, we wake up each and every day worrying about the events of the day, thinking that we have to go to work to pay the bills, we have to pay the bills, we have to except the very world we live with all its factories that are destroying our Natural worlds environment, we are afraid of being alone, of losing what we have. Instead we should be happy to go to work, happy to pay our bills, happy to be loved, and happy at what we have in this world, by acknowledging it all and trying to better ourselves, and our very world we live in, with a positive attitude to starting each day as an adventure to find Light and Truth at the end of our journey.

In a Matriarchal world there would be absolutely no reason for anyone to feel unworthy, because we know that no matter what we are and will always be loved by the Great Mother Goddess. Even though our lives are filled with mistakes and errors, Our Great Mother will change Her unconditional love towards us Her children. As She is always prepared to help, defend, protect and support us at any cost. Being at one in a Matriarchal world means there should be no more inner conflicts, regrets, remorse, fear, distrust, and inner torment. As Her Light gives us peace in this life, but sadly we have only ever known a patriarchal world in our recorded history, but there is evidence and documented proof that an ancient civilization known as the Golden Age existed with a complete Matriarchal society which were guided by women. All knowledge of these existences shows a world of harmony and tolerance. But this was later wiped out and destroyed by the patriarchal ruling world as it grew and changed.

The power of the dominating male structures changed the world to what we see and know today. But we again in this changed and enlightened world of the 21st century can lift the Veil and welcome our Mother back home, we can again have the true Garden of Eden, and a Golden Age of Matriarchy filled with peace, harmony, tolerance, beauty, understanding, contentment and the removal of fear. There would be no place for conflict, nor any rules, except the laws of the land and Nature. Today we are again changing, and slowly waking up to the reality that the true spirituality and faith of the world lies in an ancient concept of what is termed religion today. If we bring to birth this Matercentric society filled with unconditional love of the Great Mother darkness will surely fade and Light will engulf the world and our lives.

There are many who believe that the ideal society is one in which both men and women rule and are equal. But this is NOT POSSIBLE, even if we could define what the word 'equal' means. As recent research has shown (in "Brain Sex", by Anne Moir and David Jessel), "there is a fundamental difference between the male and female brain, which manifests itself in the way men and women think and feel. Whilst men can ignore their feelings and rely on 'logic' to make decision, it is necessary for our evolution to move into a female—centred society, one in which men can learn to care for others. It is probable that in the far future we will have societies in which neither sex is dominant, but at our present stage of evolution to move into a matriarchal centred society, one in which men can learn, and it is spiritually necessary and inevitable that we move into a Matercentric society, as I will explain at a later date. This will benefit both men and women. Now our patriarchal society, with its rules and regulations, intolerance and aggression, gives immense advantages to men, because it reflects their way of being masters of the world.

There is no real way that women, or men for that fact, can achieve equality in such a society. We are seeing a drive for freedom within many countries of the world, and a growing acceptance of other ways of living. Many patriarchal structures, which restrict freedom, are being eroded or destroyed slowly. In this climate, women will be far less advantaged than before, because they have to be able to use aggression and logic in the same ruthless way they are accustomed to.

As men see that women's ability to mobilize both intellect and feeling in decision making leads to a greater stability, they will no longer wish to develop and dominate. They will see clearly that they will be happier directed by women than by other men, and gladly allow them to guide society. Women can rule as a mother figure but not by taking on masculine though processes to control, in a butch attitude or way. Women have become more masculine in their views in our world because of having to be heard, the sad thing is that men have also become softer and more feminine in their world views, this is not balance but disharmony of the Natural order. Both men and women have their powers of attainment and authority, when in balance will create a harmony the world needs before it is too late."

Herbs

THE DR BACH SYSTEM OF WILDFLOWER MEDICINE
THE RESCUE REMEDY – THE FIRST-AID OR EMERGENCY REMEDY

This Magickal blend is of five different Remedies, which Dr. Bach uses in all cases of emergency. No first aid kit is complete without it. I always keep a bottle in the draw of my bedside table and in the first aid kit. It is used for a myriad of purposes, even just to keep a patient relaxed and comfortable whilst the doctor has been sent for. It has a genuinely strong effect and used in cases of shock, stress, anxiety, fractures or falls, acute illnesses, fainting, dizziness, cuts, sprains and bruises, strong pain, nightmares, even aids in panic attacks. I believe that anyone over the age of 50 should have this close by as it acts strongly as a relaxant and carminative. All midwives will also find it invaluable for mothers and their infants.

THE FIVE REMEDIES ARE:

- **ROCK ROSE** for terror, extreme fear, panic, either in the patient or in those around.
- **STAR OF BETHLEHEM** for the after-effects of shock, mental or physical.
- **CLEMATIS** for unconsciousness, coma, fainting, giddiness, all of which indicate a temporary lack of interest in the present.
- **CHERRY PLUM** for the fear of the mind giving way, insanity, brainstorms, hysterical conditions, suicidal tendencies.
- **IMPATIENS** for extreme mental tension and irritability resulting in muscular tension and, hence, pain.

PREPARATION OF THE RESCUE REMEDY:

To prepare the Rescue Remedy add two drops from each of the five remedies above to a half or one-ounce bottle of Brandy or Vodka. This will keep potent and remain clear indefinitely, even if not used for quite some time. Label the bottle "Rescue Remedy", or "First Aid Remedy" and cork tightly.

DOSAGE: Three drops in a cup of cold water to be sipped very frequently, as the patient improves, every quarter of an hour, every half hour, every hour or as necessary.

If the patient is asleep or unconscious, then place a small drop of the rescue remedy on the lips, gums, behind the ears and even on the wrists. If there is no water available just place a few drops into the palms of their hands for them to suck up.

FOR EXTERNAL USE: Add six pints to a pint of warm water if possible but if not cold will do. Then with a cotton ball bathe the part that is affected, or even use as a compress. Rescue remedy is also helpful with Bronchial chests by placing on a swap onto the chest. If severe back pain places a compress of it on the lumbar region or the region where the pain is.

FOR ANIMALS: Three drops in a little water given by mouth, or three drops in the drinking water or sprinkled over the food.

Introduction to Herbs as Medicine

The ancient tradition of herbs and their properties is based on verbal traditions that have been passed down from Shaman to Shaman, Sage to sage, Wicce to Wicce, then later with the knowledge of writing it was written down in powerful artistic manuscripts. But through much translation, certain factors have been lost. It was only instinct, intuition, and pure luck in some cases, which created the histories supply of medicines both herbal and even the pharmaceutical allows its essence to be in their many medicines of today, even though they are a hundred times more expensive, and have lost the original spirit of the Natural life of the Plant.

Contemporary herbal medicinal practices are based on ancient Shamanic and Pagan traditions, and a more recent understanding and knowledge of healing and health. The uses of some herbs have changed considerably, while others have changed very little over the millennia. Nearly all the Herbs in use today are native to the lands, which border the Aegean and Mediterranean Seas. Most of them come from the original Persia, which sadly has been lost today due to the warring in those lands. Some from India and Pakistan, Much from China, even Australia has plenty of Herbs and plants used for healing. Most of the common weeds (Herbs) are of Europe and America. Many practices follow the European customs of Herbalism.

History of European Herbal Medicine:

To place herbal medicine in the context of the 21st century, a brief study of its history will help connect traditions to current usage. Ever since Neanderthal man we have used flowers, leaves, barks, twigs and roots as a conscious use for medicinal and fragrant purposes. Even the Chinese have recorded their herbal culture for over 5000 years, as did the Sumerians and Persians. One of the oldest recorded documents describing herbal medicine is the Pharmacopoeia "between 2730 - 3000 B.C."

The ancient Egyptians and their Magickal Priest/Herbalists were admired worldwide and respected for their advanced knowledge of healing and Magickal skills. An ancient Papyrus of 2000 B.C. Documents that they believe that disease and injuries were not caused by Magick and Curses but due to natural causes. Within this ancient papyrus were hundreds of ancient formulations of ancient herbal medicine and Practices. The most famous to come out of Alexandria was not only their magnificent library but the Medical College of Thoth which was established in 332 B.C. Within its confines were learned Priest/Physicians including Galen, but sadly due to the great fires of Alexandria not only was the most elaborate Library the world has ever known been destroyed but also nearly all the archives of the Medical College.

When we look at Greek medicine we always hear the name Hippocrates, his great botanical knowledge and skills of Natural Medicine was taught in his great Medical Colleges which were only available to males as females were never permitted to learn or have knowledge of any form. Throughout thousands of years it has been the Greeks that took the ancient arts of Herbal medicine through the ages to the present Pharmaceutical evaluations and remedies. Hippocrates influenced the whole world with his attitudes to healing and good health but the usage of herbals. He believed strongly in the certain properties of Herbs elevated the Immune System and protected man against ill-health and formulated herbal diets to help the natural body fight against all forms of illness both within and without.

With the introduction of printing with presses in the 15th century, many became learned readers, which established more and more books of knowledge, as man became hungry for knowledge and books gave him the ability to learn from home. Many of the first books that were ever printed were the classic Herbals of Hippocrates who lived between 460 B.C. - 370 B.C., which meant he lived to the ripe old age of 90 years, which was unbelievable in that day and age, he must have been taking his own advice on herbs. His first book published was called "The Materia Medica of Diorscorides".

With the discovery of the Americas, the Europeans discovered many new and exciting botanicals, both edible and medicinal. These great finds started the explosion of Botany and the plant, herb; spice trade became the biggest money-maker of the time. But in the travel many plants lost their original meanings and explanations as they did in translations from one language to another.

Herbalism changed drastically due to a Swiss-German Paracelsus (1493 - 1541) who was a chief Physician, Herbalist and Botanist. He introduced to the world chemical research and defined what is now termed the 'active principal' of a plant. But in doing this he changed the Natural energies of the down to earth Herbalist into a chemical Pharmacist. Where medicines became empty of spirit and fool of negative side effects. He extracted basic substance from the plant that Mother Nature took millions of years to formulate; he then formulated new ways to prepare the plants. This rapid development of Chemistry made them drift apart from natural to unnatural.

Natural Botanicals last for millions of years but then they were thrown out the window when the first synthetic drugs were formulated in the mid 1850's. From here it basically tried to destroy the herbalist and Natural practitioner where it took over the world in the latter years of 1945. Now huge pharmaceutical companies are trying to destroy Herbal medicine and Naturopaths by debunking their remedies as "Old Wives Tales" and dangerous. But they could not stop man seeking the Truth, as Truth always comes out, and many Natural Medicines and Herbalism have continued. We now see the Pharmaceutical companies having their huge lines of Natural medicines on shelves in Chemists covering all aspects. But with a difference, the Herbalist charges for the Herb usually ($2-$5) for the Natural herb, more for tinctures. But the Pharmacist charges a small fortune for the same thing because they are placed in capsules etc.

In my new book *"Complete Encyclopedia of Herbal Medicines of the World"*, covers all known Herbs of Europe, Britain, Africa, Polynesia, Australia, North and South America, Middle East, India and Asia. It shows you what they look like through beautiful artistry and explains in every detail their benefits and uses.

Remedial Herbal Classifications

Abortifacient These are most likely to induce miscarriage, it is considered highly dangerous during pregnancy. Know Abortifacients include Blue Cohosh, Ergot, Golden Seal, Parsley, Tansy (oil), and Valerian.

Alterative Their function is as a tonic to aid in renewal and healing some' Burdock, Elder and Red Clover.

Anaesthetic Cause the nerve endings to lose sensation, making them less aware of pain include; Birch bark, Clove (oil), and Mandrake.

Anodyne Also alleviates pain but may be narcotic including Belladonna, Coca leaves, Henbane, White Willow Bark, and Wintergreen.

Anthelmintic deter the existence of parasitic worms, common in undernourished people include Flax Seed, Tansy and Wormwood.

Antiemetic these are carminative's and stomachic, they alleviate nausea and can stop vomiting; Clove, Frankincense, Nightshade, Spearmint, Ice crushed and taken internally may also be useful.

Antiseptic prevents the wound or sore from becoming infected: Basil, Eucalyptus, and Thyme.

Antispasmodic calm the muscles, stopping spasms and convulsions: Blue and Black Cohosh, Chamomile, Eucalyptus, Lobelia, Skullcap and Valerian.

Aperient similar classification to Laxative, reducing a natural movement of the bowels; Dandelion and Rhubarb.

Aromatic a pleasant fragrance. Allspice, Anise, Catnip, Cinnamon, Clove, Coriander, Elecampane, Ginger, Lemon peel, Peppermint and Yarrow.

Astringent these cause the tissue to contract and tighten pores. Agrimony, Alum Root, Bayberry, Blackberry, Comfrey, Nettles, Sage and White oak Root.

Bathing Herbs	Lovage and Heather.
Cardiac	a distinctive effect on the heart. Foxglove, Lily of the Valley, Rosemary, Tansy, and Yarrow.
Carminative	good for digestion, gas cramps and tension: Allspice, Aniseed, Angelica, Catnip, Cloves, Dill, Elecampane, Fennel, Ginger, Peppermint, Spearmint, Valerian and Yarrow.
Cathartic	for a dramatic release of the bowels. Boneset, Broom, Castor (oil) and Mayapple.
Constituents/Vitamins	Vit A-Dandelion and Alfalfa, Vit B-Bladderwrack and Okra, B12-Alfalfa, Vit C-All Citrus, Vit D– Watercress, Vit E-Alfalfa.
Demulcent	soothing herbs. Arrowroot, Comfrey, Liquorice Root, Marshmallow Root, and Slippery Elm.
Deva	to describe the energy field of an herb.
Diaphoretic	to perspire used in mild fevers. Angelica, Boneset, Camphor, Catnip, Marigold, Pennyroyal and Yarrow.
Diuretic	to aid in the flow of urine, and cleansing the kidneys. Agrimony, Asparagus, Burdock, Dandelion, Elder, Fennel, Piper Methystum and Uva Ursi.
Emetic	cause the stomach to contract and induce vomiting. Boneset, Elder Root, Lobelia, Mustard and Vervain.
Emmenagogue	stimulates the menstrual flow. Blue or Black Cohosh, Ergot Motherwort, Pennyroyal, Rue and Tansy.
Emollient	for external use will soften roughness. Linseed, Liquorice, Marshmallow and Comfrey.
Expectorant	to loosen phlegm, which collects in the lungs. Boneset, Benzoin.
Febrifuge	treats fever and lowers temperature. Boneset, Sage, Tansy and Wormwood.
Fixative	used primarily as a carrier of another. Elder Flower.
Haemostat	quicken the coagulation of blood. Corn Ergot, marigold, Sage and Cobwebs.
Hepatic	works on the liver to function easier; Agrimony, Celandine, Dandelion, Peony and Tansy.
Irritant	Irritates the skin. Bryony, cayenne, Poison Oak, Mustard, Nettle.

Laxative	stimulates the bowels. Boneset, Dandelion, Liquorice Root, Mandrake, Mountain Flax and Rhubarb.
Liniment	making of oils or creams. the mints.
Narcotic	self-explanatory.
Nephritic	Herbs that affect the Kidneys.
Nervine	calming of the nerves and soothes emotions. Chamomile, Cinquefoil, Fennel, Hops, Lavender, Marigold, Rosemary, Tansy and Verbena.
Nutrient	high in vitamins and minerals. Comfrey, Dandelion and Nettles.
Pectoral	works upon the lungs and chest for congestion. Aniseed, Coltsfoot, Irish Moss, Marshmallow, Mullein and Wild Cherry.
Purgative	strongest of the laxative herbs. Bitter Apple, Black Root, Boneset, May Apple, Mandrake and Senna Leaves.
Refresherant	relieves thirst, and sensation of coolness. Aconite, Catnip, Chickweed and Wormwood.
Rubefacient	for painful joints, arthritis etc. Cayenne and Nettles.
Sedative	a tranquilliser relaxes nervous tension. Black Cohosh, Chamomile, Jasmine and Valerian Root.
Stimulant	to quicken the pulse. Bayberry, Cayenne, Cinnamon, Eucalyptus, Horseradish, Mustard, Peppers, Tansy and Wintergreen.
Stomachic	helps the stomach with poor digestion. Angelica, Chamomile, Dill, Pennyroyal, Peppermint, Sage and Wormwood.
Styptic	similar to Haemostatic to stop bleeding. Avena, Nettles, Sage and Cobwebs.
Sudorific	to induce sweating; Cayenne, Germander, Marigold, Vervain and Yarrow.
Tonic	a sense of well-being. Agrimony, Bayberry, Blackberry, Boneset, Catnip, Cayenne, Chamomile, Dandelion, Nettles, Peppermint, Sage, Tansy, Wormwood and Yarrow.
Volatile Oil	their ability to evaporate easily.
Vulnerary	effective in treating wounds. Comfrey, Marshmallow and Tansy.

Incense

Since the Dawn of man we have burnt incense, who knows how it started. I think probably by accident when they carted timber for the fires and realised the different fragrances, and from here we started using them for funerary fires to cover the scent of human flesh.

But eventually it turned into a ritualistic concept where different gums and resins were used at different times of the years at ceremonies and festivals. We have since these ancient times discovered thousands of different fragrances from flowers, plants, herbs, woods and gums and resins that come from them. The ancient Wicces and Shamans used to send their prayers rising upon the incense smoke, this was symbolic, that is why you see Medicine Men and Shamans with the Ceremonial Pipe where they burned Tobacco which they took into their bodies and with their prayers sent the smoke out and up to the ears of Great Spirit.

The Pagans of old have always burnt incense as an offering or ritual sacrifice to the Gods and Goddesses of old. Then the Catholic Churches followed this concept and placed the swinging Thuribles filled with charcoal blocks and gum resins of sacred trees to bless their Churches, Temples and Shrines etc. Here in Australia the Aboriginals collect lemon scented Gum leaves and branches to perform their sacred Fire and Smoke ceremonies to cleanse and purify and also to banish all negative influences as well. They also use traditionally in certain Magickal Ceremonies a sacred Gum taken from one of their trees after fires have burnt through and these trees weep a black resin, which has the fragrance far superior than most you could ever find, it is similar to Dragons Blood and Ambergris mixed together. It is called Rainbow Serpent Blood. But it is easy for you to collect whatever is required to make your own incense by using a blend of either essential oils (do not use normal blended oils as some of them can be quite toxic), herbs, flowers, wood bark, resins, berries and fruit. There are hundreds of recipes all over the website, but use items that are non-toxic, remember it is you that will be breathing it in, so keep it clean and pure.

Why Make Your Own?

You can buy incense everywhere these days, but there is nothing more exciting than smelling your first lots of incense that you have made yourself. It is gratifying not only to yourself, but your friends and the Gods will love the energy you put in making it a part of you. I love granule incense for when you are working outdoors and even indoors if it is a large area so as to not choke by the fumes. But sensibly it is better to burn stick incense indoors as it dissipates quite quickly.

Making your own is quite simple these days as you can buy already prepared wood dust incense sticks, and all you have to do is add a colour if you wish and an essential oil, then lay them flat on a tray and let them dry by the sun. That makes it easy and less complicated and mess free.

Full Moon – Esbat Incense

Ingredients:

As you mix and blend your incense, focus on the intent of your work. In this particular recipe, we're creating an incense to use during a full moon rite, or Esbat. It is the time we connect with our Goddess and the Divine Feminine in all of Nature and revere her through the Moon that shines over our heads. It is when she is at her peak and the power flows from Her to us. Mix your ingredients in a Mortar and Pestle completely so they are all mixed together.

You'll need:

- 2 parts Juniper Berries
- ½ part Marigold Flowers
- 1part Moonflower
- 1part Mugwort
- 2 parts Myrrh
- 1part Rose petals
- 1part Sandalwood

Meditation

Meditation is a means of achieving an Inner Peace, a transcendental experience, a deeper insight, which can help in daily life, and in the search for meaning. The technique of Meditation was devised and still exists to assist man individually, to uncover within themselves that deeply hidden centre of the One Creative Life, that is the birthright of every man and woman. From that centre, much can be understood that is obscure; and from that level much can be done for the world.

Meditation is a means to create a man of conscious enlightened WILL. Meditation is not an exercise in itself but a means of achieving a higher use of consciousness through commitment.

Meditation is composed of several activities:

RELAXATION - The ability to just be in the now and quiet your mind to a state of calm.

BREATHING Breathing helps take us to different level of being away from the normal to the Spiritual.

FILTRATION Filtering outside thoughts, feelings and pictures so the mind becomes a blank canvas.

COMMITMENT regular times of meditation and relaxation.

The following points aid meditation:

Avoid answering questions automatically with solutions from memory rather rely on meditation.
Avoid disputes only leading to form, instead of idea and formation.
Train you in the perception of the invisible within the visible.
Search for analogies and comment on their broadest sense.

Always, seek knowledge of harmony, and fineness of form - the Arts are very ideal for this purpose.

Anyone can meditate, even you. It's not a secret arcane science, nor is it a mysterious esoteric process, although some of you may have heard that it was. It does not involve a lot of discipline or a lot of discomfort. All it takes is a little commitment and a little practice, and a little perseverance to learn to use the fundamental tool for self-expansion and personal growth.

Meditation is easier than walking through a meadow, easier than driving a car, or even easier than cutting a sandwich in half. All of these things and everything else we do require an incredibly complex degree of coordination between mind and body. Millions of neural, muscular and cellular connections must be made, and maintained. And the degree of energy control and precise channelling of your life force into action is almost impossible to imagine. Yet we have learned to do everything that we do, almost automatically without even thinking about it.

To meditate, you don't have to do anything; you simply just have to be in a settled and quiet state. In fact, the whole idea is to stop doing whatever you are doing, consciously or unconsciously and focus completely on the subject of your meditation in a relaxed, flowing and non-controlling way and relax your breathing until it actually becomes you. That is all meditation is. It's the most natural thing in the world, and you are not strangers to it as you have been meditating for most of your life. Although you may not have realised, that this was what you were doing.

For instance, when you watch TV, and drift into the scene, or lose yourself in a spontaneous race between two drops of rain sliding down a windowpane, you are meditating. In each case, you are submerged in a process that takes you out of yourself and your normal stream of consciousness and beyond your ordinary sense of time, thought and space.

The problem is what you meditate on, which can profoundly influence, program and direct your energy, your life cycle and all the space around you. So, when you focus on your breath, a leaf, a stone, a crystal, and a candle flame; a sound or a positive thought; you end the experience feeling more perceptive and more alert. And when you focus on your energy and state of being you re-enter completely refreshed, revitalized and recharged.

In the beginning when you were a baby, you spent all of your time meditating on your growth and development and expansiveness. That is why time was so much more timeless then. You were in a state of harmony with the universe all around you, so when you focus on needing something, you knew just how to materialize it, but since being a baby we have forgotten how to breathe properly and just be.

You begin to lose your meditational harmony as you began to develop your sense of Self, your Ego, which separated and differentiated you from everything else, and you lost even more of it as you developed a rational analytical ego, which kept you trying to find logical ways to shield and protect you from your inner sense, alienation and dissociation from everything else that is; and which hooked you into books, TV, computer games, computers, Facebook, internet, newspapers, teachers, and other authorities as the only way to gain knowledge and understanding of yourself, your world and your Goddess and God.

As far as creature-hood goes, on a physical level, life ends when growth ends. The point is, that now you have grown separated from your macrocosmic universe, as you are in the next phase of growing, which needs to include reintegrating and re-harmonizing yourself with all that is around you. Opening channels to that process, gaining intuitive knowledge and inner understanding, and creative expansiveness out of anxiety and chaos through meditation are the results you can expect from further study and training in this field. We need to do this to widen out connection with the universe and everything in it, or we just become selfish, fearful creatures on a self-delusional path to nowhere.

Taking it a further step, meditation is the word that describes your state of consciousness, when you have become so totally emerged in an object, an event or thought in a relaxed manner. You become so completely involved and centred in what and where you are, that your mental chatter fades away your body tension, emotional anxieties disappear, and time flows at an altered rate of speed. As you begin to more fully experience who you are, how you are feeling, where you are tense and blocked, and what you are asking for out of life, you will develop more and more control over your health, over your wants, over your creativity and self-expansion, and over your actual physical involvement. The more a harmonious meditative relaxed state you are in the more connected and the more creative you will become.

By practicing meditation often not just spasmodically when time allows, and being completely who you are, you will become more than who you are now, you will be able to cross the next evolutionary bridge, being able to develop the full potential of your creature hood. It is the most exciting journey there is, and hopefully I can make it easier, by helping you discover the inner avenues that can take you all the way you choose to go. From wherever you are coming from, to here and to now, and to what lies beyond.

Beginning Meditation!

To meditate you need only two things that are essential outside yourself, a place and a time. Everything else in the Outer World is optional. From time to time you may choose an external object, person or event as a meditative subject. But for now, the right place and the right time will start you on your right way. At this stage, the right place will be anywhere your little heart desires, any place you like and feel relaxed and away from being disturbed.

If you have made yourself an Altar or Shrine to the Goddess, or even a Temple at your home, or even a Magick Circle; any of these places are perfect for your meditative adventures. In that place you might like to include a chair or a large cushion, a soft rug, or whatever warms your spirit. Like a candle, a flower, crystal, familiar, or favourite object, or a picture, or as I said before, even an altar with a statue of the Goddess and God on it.

Whenever you choose to turn inward. At this stage the right time will be any time that you specifically set aside for meditation only. Between 10-30 minutes every morning and night before or long after meals will be ideal. You will not need to be rigid about it, and you don't have to meditate the exact time every day, whether you choose to use it or not. Other than the place and time, everything else you already have is on the inside of your very being.

Alignment

When you are in alignment with the magnetic axis of the Earth, you will yourself flow more freely with the space around you. Getting aligned is easy; always meditate facing North, like a needle of a compass you use to check your direction. Magnetic alignment is the Path of least resistance to meditating, and to interphasing your life energy with the energies around you, on a microcosmic and macrocosmic level.

(Record your Progress and exercise in your Magickal Diary)

Standing in Pentagram

For thousands of years the Pentagram Position has been the primary posture for energy exchange and for recharging and rejuvenating your body. In his sketches, Leonardo da Vinci immortalized it. In your meditation place, it can immortalize you, by helping you maintain a radiant inner glow and an easy access to complete meditation.

Stand with your spine straight, your pelvis aligned under you, your feet further apart than your shoulders or as far as you can place them without locking your knees. Tip your head slightly back, keep your eyes open for balance, but allow your gaze to lose focus. Raise your arms keeping them straight until your elbows are just above your shoulders, and your hands are in line with the top of your head. Turn your left palm down and your right palm up. Breathing deeply into your diaphragm, and experience filling your lungs to capacity then overflowing with newfound energy.

(Record your Progress and exercise in your Magickal Diary)

Meditation Positions

Any position that keeps the right and left hand side of the body in equal balance, and that you maintain comfortably without moving for the length of your meditation, is the right position for you. But always keeping your back and neck straight. Of course, make sure that you are totally comfortable and relaxed. You are constantly taking energy in from your universe, storing it, and discharging it back into the universe again. Converting energy into life and matter, and life and matter into energy is every creature's fundamental role.

When you meditate, the energy exchange is amplified and greatly heightened. Which explains why complete meditation is so truly enlightening and invigorating. To smooth out the energy amplification and make it easier on yourself, your meditation position must ultimately allow you to lose whatever sense of separation or alienation you experience in your universe. That is why you keep both sides of your body in balance. By not crossing one leg over the other, and not folding your arms protectively in front of you. That is also why as you harmonise yourself within your space through your position and your breath, you expand your personal energy and your inner power base to remarkable degree's. Experiment with the meditation positions to find the one's that help you flow into expansiveness with a minimum of effort.

Sitting Position

My favourite traditional position for meditating is sitting. Sitting in a straight-backed chair, or on the floor. In a chair, sitting erect with your spine straight. Keep both feet on the floor a comfortable distance apart. It is better to remove your shoes, loosen your collar, your belt or anything else that prevents you from breathing freely, easily and naturally, and deeply into your diaphragm and abdomen. If you have a robe, then wear this. Allow both hands to fall loosely on your lap. Tilt your head slightly back so that your neck and spine form one continuous vertical line.

Then close your eyes gently and look up at the inside of your forehead. For now, just experience how it feels to sit like this. Notice where you are touching the floor and where you are not. Sense the floor under your feet and the solid support it offers. Connect with the sensuality of the Air Element on your skin, experience it, that's all, and just experience it!

(Record your Progress and exercise in your Magickal Diary)

Lying Down

Let your legs spread slightly apart with your toes and feet hanging loosely from your ankles. Let your hands fall to your sides, palms up. Sense how straight your spine is, notice what parts of your body are in contact with the floor, and what parts are holding up, like the small of your back, just lie there and feel the Air moving over, around and throughout your body. As you breathe deeply and quietly into your diaphragm! I dislike this position for some people as they can get too relaxed and fall asleep. Snoring can be a problem if you are in a group.

(Record your Progress and exercise in your Magickal Diary)

Creative Visualisation

Creative Visualisation is the technique of using your imagination to create what you want in your life. This chapter is about learning to use your natural creative imagination in a more conscious way. As a technique to create what you truly want; such as love, fulfillment, enjoyment, satisfying relationships, rewarding work, self-expression, health, beauty, youth, whatever your little heart desires.

In Creative Visualisation you use your imagination to create a clear image of something you wish to manifest, seeing the end result not the process. Then you continue to focus on the idea or picture regularly, giving it positive energy until it becomes objective reality. In other words, until you actually achieve what you have been visualising. Creative Visualisation is Magick in its truest and highest meaning of the word. It involves understanding and aligning yourself with the natural principles that govern the workings of our universe and learning to use those principles in the most conscious and creative way.

FOUR BASIC STEPS TO MAKE IT EFFECTIVE ARE:

Set your goal.
Create a clear idea or picture.
Focus on it often.
Give it positive energy, continuously.

You do have to try, for creative visualisation to work effectively, you simply put it out clearly to the universe where you would like it to go, and harmoniously let the flow of the river take you there. Visualisation is very important in Magick and Wiccan rituals and ceremonies, as we need to see the end result to make it manifest into reality.

We will now do a simple visualisation technique, designed to get energy flowing, to dissolve any 'blocks', worries, etc., and to keep you firmly connected to the physical plane so that you don't space out during meditation and get to light headed.

Meditational Exercise

SIT COMFORTABLY WITH YOUR BACK STRAIGHT ... EITHER IN A CHAIR OR ON THE FLOOR ... CLOSE YOUR EYES AND BREATHE SLOWLY AND DEEPLY ...

COUNTING FROM TEN TO ONE, UNTIL YOU FEEL DEEPLY RELAXED ... IMAGINE THAT THERE IS A LONG CORD ATTACHED TO THE BASE OF YOUR SPINE ... AND EXTENDING DOWN THROUGH THE FLOOR AND WAY DOWN INTO THE EARTH ... IF YOU WISH, YOU CAN IMAGINE THAT THIS IS LIKE A ROOT OF A TREE ... GROWING DEEPER AND DEEPER INTO THE GROUND ... THIS IS ALSO CALLED THE "GROUNDING CORD".

NOW IMAGINE THAT THE ENERGY OF THE EARTH IS FLOWING UP THROUGH ALL PARTS OF THIS CORD ... AND UP THROUGH YOUR FEET ... AND FLOWING UP THROUGH ALL PARTS OF THE BODY ... OUT AND THROUGH THE TOP OF YOUR HEAD ... PICTURE THIS UNTIL YOU REALLY FEEL THE FLOW WELL ESTABLISHED ...

NOW IMAGINE THAT THE ENERGY OF THE COSMOS IS NOW FLOWING IN THROUGH THE TOP OF YOUR HEAD ... YOUR CROWN CHAKRA ... THROUGH YOUR BODY AND DOWN YOUR GROUNDING CORD, AND YOUR FEET INTO THE EARTH ... FEEL BOTH THESE FLOWS GOING IN DIFERENT DIRECTIONS AND MIXING HARMONIOUSLY IN YOUR BODY ... WHEN YOU HAVE DONE THIS ... JUST RELAX ...

(Record your Progress and exercise in your Magickal Diary)

THE NEXT FORM OF MEDITATION IS DESIGNED TO KEEP YOU BALANCED

BETWEEN THE COSMIC ENERGY OF VISION, FANTASY AMD IMAGINATION, AND THE STABLE EARTHY ENERGY OF THE PHYSICAL PLANE ... A BALANCE

THAT WILL INCREASE YOUR SENSE OF WELL-BEING AND YOUR POWER OF MANIFESTATION ... ONE TECHNIQUE THAT I FIND VERY EFFECTIVE IS TO CREATE A SANCTUARY WITHIN YOURSELF ... WHERE YOU CAN GO ANYTIME YOU WANT TO ... IT'S AN IDEAL PLACE OF RELAXATION, SAFETY AND HEALING, AND YOU CAN CREATE IT EXACTLY ANYTIME YOU WANT TO ...

KEEP YOUR EYES CLOSED AND RELAX IN A COMFORTABLE POSITION ... IMAGINE YOURSELF IN SOME BEAUTIFUL NATURAL ENVIRONMENT ... IT CAN BE ANY PLACE THAT APPEALS TO YOU ... A MEADOW ... ON A MOUNTAIN ... IN A FOREST ... BESIDE THE SEA ... IT COULD EVEN BE UNDER THE SEA OR ON ANOTHER PLANET ... WHATEVER IT IS, IT SHOULD FEEL COMFORTABLE, PLEASANT AND PEACEFUL WITH YOU ... EXPLORE YOUR ENFORCEMENT ... NOTICE THE VISUAL DETAILS ... THE SOUNDS ... THE SMELLS ... ANY PARTICULAR FEELINGS OR IMPRESSIONS YOU GET ABOUT IT ... NOW DO ANYTHING YOU WANT TO DO TO MAKE IT MORE HOMELIKE AND COMFORTABLE ... AN ENVIRONMENT FOR YOU ... YOU MIGHT WANT TO BUILD SOME TYPE OF HOUSE OR SHELTER ... OR PERHAPS CREATE A TEMPLE DEDICATED TO YOUR GODDESS AND GOD ... OR CREATE A LARGE STONE CIRCLE ... OR PERHAPS JUST SURROUND THE WHOLE AREA WITH A GOLDEN LIGHT OF PROTECTION AND SAFETY ...

CREATE AND ARRANGE THINGS THERE FORE YOUR CONVENIENCE ... AND ENJOYMENT ... OR DO A RITUAL TO ESTABLISH IT AS YOUR SPECIAL PERSONAL SANCTUARY ... MAYBE YOU COULD DO THE LESSER BANISHING RITUAL OF THE PENTAGRAM OR A SELF BLESSING RITUAL ...

FROM NOW ON THIS IS YOUR OWN PRIVATE SANCTUARY ... TO WHICH YOU CAN RETURN AT ANYTIME JUST BY CLOSING YOUR EYES AND DESIRING TO BE THERE ... YOU WILL ALSO FIND SPECIAL POWER FOR YOU ... AND YOU MAY WISH TO GO THEIR EVERYTIME YOU DO CREATIVE VISUALISATION ... YOU MAY MAKE CHANGES AND ADDITIONS TO IT AT ANY TIME ... BUT JUST REMEMBER TO RETAIN THE PRIMARY QUALITIES OF PEACEFULNESS AND A FEELING OF ABSOLUTE SAFETY AND HEALING ... EACH OF US HAS ALL THE WISDOM AND KNOWLEDGE WE EVER NEED RIGHT WITHIN US ... SOMETIMES WE FIND IT DIFFICULT TO CONNECT WITH THIS PART OF OUR MIND ... BUT ONE OF THE BEST WAYS OF DOING SO IS BY MEETING AND GETING TO KNOW

OUR INNER GUIDE … OUR INNER GUIDE IS A HIGHER PART OF OUR SELF … THIS FOLLOWING EXERCISE WILL HELP YOU MEET YOUR INNER GUIDE … STILL WITH YOUR EYES CLOSED AND RELAX AGAIN DEEPLY … GO TO YOUR INNER SANCTUARY AND SPEND A FEW MINUTES THERE, RELAXING AND GETTING ORIENTED …

NOW IMAGINE THAT WITHIN YOUR SANCTUARY YOU ARE STANDING ON A PATH … AND AS YOU DO SO, YOU SEE IN THE DISTANCE A FORM COMING TOWARD YOU RADIATING A CLEAR BRIGHT LIGHT … AS YOU APPROACH EACH OTHER YOU BEGIN TO SEE WHETHER THE FORM IS MALE OR FEMALE … HOW THEY LOOK … HOW OLD THEY ARE … AND HOW THEY ARE DRESSED … ARE THEY YOUNG OR OLD … GREET THIS BEING … AND ASK HER/HIM WHAT THEIR NAME IS … TAKE WHATEVER NAME COMES TO YOU FIRST AND DO NOT WORRY ABOUT IT!

NOW SHOW YOUR GUIDE AROUND YOUR SANCTUARY AND EXPLORE IT TOGETHER … YOUR GUIDE MAY POINT OUT SOME THINGS THAT YOU HAVE NEVER SEEN BEFORE … OR YOU MAY ENJOY JUST BEING IN EACH OTHERS COMPANY … ASK YOUR GUIDE IF THERE IS ANYTHING SHE/HE WOULD LIKE TO SAY TO YOU … OR ANY ADVICE TO GIVE YOU AT THIS MOMENT … IF YOU WISH, YOU MAY ASK SOME QUESTIONS … YOU MAY NOT GET AN ANSWER IMMEDIATELY, BUT IF NOT, DON'T BE DISCOURAGED, THE ANSWER WILL COME TO YOU IN SOME FORM LATER … WHEN THE EXPERIENCE OF GETTING TO KNOW ONE ANOTHER AND BEING TOGETHER IS COMPLETE … THANK YOUR GUIDE AND EXPRESS YOUR APPRECIATION … AND ASK HER/HIM TO COME AND MEET YOU IN YOUR SANCTUARY AGAIN … OPEN YOUR EYES AND RETURN TO THE OUTSIDE WORLD, AND RECORD YOUR PROGRESS AND EXPERIENCES IN YOUR DIARY …

(Record your Progress and exercise in your Magickal Diary)

Do not worry if you did not perceive and see your guide precisely and clearly. Sometimes they remain in the form of a glow of light, or a blurry, indistinct figure. The important thing is that you serve their power, love and their importance. Especially their presence, if your guide should come to you in the form of someone you know then that is fine, unless you do not feel comfortable. Do not be surprised if your guide seems eccentric or unusual in some way, the form in which they don't express themselves in words, but instead through feelings or intuitive knowledge. She/he may even change form at some time or may stay the same for years to come. Whatever, as long as you feel safe and comfortable, there is no need to think you are doing something wrong. Because it stems from your own mind, then how can it be wrong? Your guide is there for you to call upon anytime you need.

This last form of Creative Visualisation I wish to discuss is a very simple, but wonderful technique. It is called the "Pink Bubble Technique" and is designed to start you off slowly in the Art of Creative Visualisation, and to lead you into more and more effective and better things. I have thought that sometimes the simplest things are often the most effective, like this exercise. It does no one harm to become stronger and much more adept with more complicated techniques, which I will cover at a later date.

SIT COMFORTABLY AND CLOSE YOUR EYES AND BREATH DEEPLY … SLOWLY AND NATURALLY … GRADUALLY RELAX DEEPER AND DEEPER AND IMAGINE SOMETHING THAT YOU WOULD LIKE TO MANIFEST … IMAGINE IT HAS ALREADY HAPPENED … PICTURE IT AS CLEARLY AS POSSIBLE IN YOUR MIND … NOW IN YOUR MINDS EYE, SURROUND YOUR FANTASY WITH A PINK … BUBBLE … PUT YOUR GOAL INSIDE THE BUBBLE … PINK IS THE COLOUR ASSOCIATED WITH THE HEART …

AND IF THIS COLOUR VIBRATION SORROUNDS WHATEVER YOU VISULAISE IT WILL BRING YOU ONLY THAT WHICH IS IN PERFECT AFFINITY WITH YOUR BEING … THE THIRD STEP IS TO LET GO OF THE PINK BUBBLE AND IMAGINE IT FLOATING OFF INTO THE UNIVERSE … STILL CONTAINING YOUR VISION … THIS SYMBOLISES THAT YOU ARE EMOTIONALLY 'LETTING GO OF IT' … NOW IT IS FREE TO FLOAT AROUND THE UNIVERSE ATTRACTING AND GATHERING ENERGY FOR ITS MANIFESTATION … THERE IS NOTHING MORE YOU NEED TO DO … WHEN YOU HAVE DONE THIS … GET BACK INTO YOUR NORMAL BREATHING AND SLOWLY OPEN YOUR EYES AND ALWAYS REMEMBER:

(Record your Progress and exercise in your Magickal Diary)
"THE DIFFERENCE BETWEEN POSSIBLE
AND IMPOSSIBLE IS ONE'S WILL!"

Sensing Group Energy

The energy that we talk about in Wiccecraft is real, a subtle force that we can all learn to perceive right now, as we are sitting in a Magick Circle, be aware of the energy level in the group. Do you feel alert? Aware? Excited? Inquisitive? Calm? Anxious? Tense? Or Relaxed?

Energy travels up and down the spine, this is called Kundalini or serpent energy, but before we do any forms of Meditation or Magickal work, we must first Earth or ground ourselves, this will be done now. Please close your eyes … focus on your breathing and relax with each breath … completely relax … imagine a warm energy glow at the base of your spine … feel it growing like a root from a tree searching deep down into the Earth for water … but yours is searching for the Earth force … feel it stretching down deep into Mother Earth … deeper and deeper and deeper … Now just Ground yourself and feed from the life-force of the Earth … just sit there as erect as you can without straining … just notice how the energy level has changed … do you feel more alert … more aware … more nourished … more at peace …

Your breath moves energy in and out of your body … it awakens your body's centres of power … so take a deep breath … breathe deeply … breathe all the way down and breathe from your diaphragm … from your belly … from your womb … loosen your pants or belts if you need to … fill your belly with breath and feel yourself relaxing … recharging …

Now notice how the energy of the group has changed … now let's reach out and take hands still keeping your eyes closed … with your right hands facing up and your left hands facing down (this is called the serpent hold) … linking ourselves together around the Circle … it may seem like a subtle tingling … or a low heat … or even a sensation of cold … or a bright whirling light of energy circling around and around and around.

(Record your Progress and exercise in your Magickal Diary)

The Tree of Life Meditation

Now begin by sitting erect and breathing deeply rhythmically in a 4 x 4 breath ... as we breathe remember to sit erect but comfortable ... and as your spine straightens feel the energy rising ... imagine that your spine is the trunk of a giant Tree ... and from its base are roots extending deep down into the Earth ... into the centre of Mother Earth Herself ... and you can draw up power from the Earth ... with each breath ... feel the energy rising ... like Mana or sap rising through a tree trunk ... feel the power rise up the spine ... feel yourself becoming more and more alive ... with each breath ...

And from your Crown Chakra at the top of your heard ... you have branches that sweep up and back down to the Earth like a Weeping Willow ... feel the power burst from the Crown Chakra ... and feel it sweep through the branches until it touches the Earth again ... making a circle ... making a circuit ... returning to its source ... and breathing deeply, feel how all our branches intertwine ... and the power weaves through them ... and dances amongst them like the wind ... feel it moving ...

Now just focus on your breathing as you inhale in that energy ... and as you exhale make a sound you like ... a moan, a sigh, hum, vowel, note, etc. ... and continue this for a few moments.

(Record your Progress and exercise in your Magickal Diary)

Robe

Each level within the working coven has a specific coloured robe that is worn for all Magickal and Spiritual work, especially within the Magick Circle. For the Seeker it should be an earth colour such as green or brown, but never black. The length should be made above ankle so as to not trip and if possible have a small slit at the bottom of both sides of the Robe to give more room for when you are dancing or raising energy in the Magick Circle.

You can have a hood if you so desire, that is a personal choice, they are sometimes great when it is cold, and for when you are meditating. The sleeves should be loose but not swinging free, as large sleeves get in the way and when reaching across your altar for tools, they catch everything and cause more problems than their good looks. I believe we should each have a summer robe (lighter fabric to keep us cool on those summer nights) and a winter robe (heavier fabric to keep us warm).

If you want to make it a little more elaborate, don't as this takes away the look of commonality and uniform appearance within the Circle, as at this level ego has no place. And that is what new Seekers love to be noticed, so hold back the glamour and keep it simplified as it is a working uniform for ritual and Magick not as a glamour aspect of the obvious.

Singulum

A Singulum is a ceremonial Girdle or Cord that is tied around our waist to hold our robe in. Traditionally the Seekers Singulum is green and on the ends of the cord are a compass and a pentagram. The Seeker usually has after they have been Wiccaned (Baptised) a green or brown robe with a 9' Singulum which has had the ends either burnt and dipped with beeswax or sown with the compass and pentagram at either end.

When a Seeker after a year of dedicated training has been Initiated as a Wicce, they then change to a white Robe with Green trim, a green cape, a green Tabard, and they change their Singulum from a green cord to a 9' white cord, which traditionally has 9 knots placed at specific points of the Singulum which represent the Ladder of the Goddess. Again on the ends is their compass and a magnifying glass.

After a couple of years of dedicated training the Wicce who has chosen their selected path to serve the Wiccan community and decided to enter the Priesthood and become a Priest or Priestess. Here again The Priestesses regalia changes to a white robe with red or burgundy trim, a red or burgundy cape, and a red or burgundy Tabard, her Singulum also changes to a burgundy or red Singulum. But the Priest wears a white robe with blue trim, a blue cape, and a Blue tabard and also changes to a blue Singulum. Again after a couple more years of dedicated training if the Priest or Priestess decide they wish to form their own coven, they are then Ordained as a High Priest or High Priestess, here they now wear the same colours of the Priesthood but when they form their own coven the High Priestess wears white with silver trim, the High Priest wears black with gold trim, but their Singulum at their ordination is then a combination of all three Initiations with the white, red, and blue being intertwined. But again it still must measure 9' after being entwined

Tools of
the Wicce

The First Degree – Wicce – The Temple of Lunar – The Moon – The Goddess

The Thurible – Purification, **Athame** - Illumination, **Pentacle** – Perfection, **The Altar** – Faith, **White Robe** – Freedom, **White Singulum** - Umbilicus and Ladder of the Goddess.

The Wicces Altar

The altar is always positioned somewhere safe in your home, so people can (Or if you prefer cannot) view it. But make sure all your Tools are safely put away, so people do not touch any of your consecrated Items. Below is my personal altar in my home. Which is decorated and changed seasonally to suit that time of the year. I always have a candle burning in respect of the Goddess and God, and usually upon awakening light the candle, and some incense and meditate for however long I feel is appropriate, whether it be 10 minutes or 1 hour. It depends on the time I have to spare.

An altar is very personal and should be not too low, so you do not have to bend down to it, or too high. The perfect Altar should be the width of your arms wide, and no deeper than you can safely reach. It should be as high as your waist, and if possible have two levels. One level the bottom - to represent everything in Nature physically, and the top Higher Level to represent the invisible within the visible, other-words the spirit of all life, thus representing the Goddess and God.

Flanking each side should be an altar candle, in the west of the altar should be a black candle representing the Feminine Spirit - the Goddess; and in the east a white candle representing the masculine spirit - the Horned God. In the centre at the back it would be nice to have a statue of your chosen Goddess and God. Everything else is personal, I always like to have fresh flowers and usually once a week put flowers on my altar. My mother always had a living plant in the centre of her shrine with a statue of the Virgin Mary in the middle this was her Goddess. The altar can also be made of anything you want, Oak is preferable, but not a requirement, as it is better to choose a local wood. It is always nice to have an altar cloth on the altar, different colours for different seasons or times of the year, again it is personal choices that make your altar as grand as you wish or as simplistic but respectful.

Altar Cloth

These days you can buy altar cloths at most occult or New Age Stores, Azure Green has a massive variety at good prices, but it is preferred that you make your own. All you need is the right coloured fabric, some nice trim to place around the outside of the altar cloth. If you are artistic you can hand paint a design or picture on the altar cloth.

I find it beneficial to have several altar cloths for differing uses such as Full Moon altar cloth traditionally white or silver; New Moon altar cloth red. Other altar clothes are:

Summer Solstice – reds, golds, oranges, yellows.

Winter Solstice – white, green, gold and silver.

Autumn Equinox – browns, oranges, russets, blacks, and green.

Spring Equinox – multi colours.

Samhain – black, orange, white.

Imbolg – white, cream, grey

Lughnasadh – all earthy colours

Beltane – red

In all honesty the shape, style and colour of your altar cloth are all personal choices and you may make them as simple or as elaborate as you desire. Your altar is your altar and the Gods and Goddesses will love it in any way that is sincere and respectful.

Altar Candles

Altar Candles are very important Spiritually as they represent the Light of the Goddess and God. The Goddess candle is always placed on the west side of your altar and should be black representing the night and women's mysteries of the night, where the Light of the Full Moon shines her light upon us, in the darkest hours. Showing us that Light conquers all darkness. The God altar candles is at the east of the altar and is white. They are just a simple 7-9 hour tapered candle and should be anointed and new every time you commence with a new day, ceremony, Esbat or Sabbat. Never use an old candle as each altar candle must be virgin, anointed and blessed for the purpose it is meant for. These two candles should never change colour, and must remain the same colours. Again it is best if you can make your own candles.

Altar Spirit Candle

The Spirit Flame or Spirit Candle is the central flame that all other lights are lit from. It is traditionally carried into the Magick Circle by the Man in Black as a symbol as the Strength of the coven, and keeper of the Sacred Flame of the Covenstead. This candle represents the Light of all the Coveners, it is the essence of Light drawn from the Solar Light of the Sun. It is masculine in essence and when the Hearth Fire is lit becomes a beacon to the Gods and all those who seek the Knowledge of the Craft.

When carried into the Magick Circle it is already ceremonially lit by the Man in Black (The Principal Ritualist under the High Priest and High Priestess), he is also the Keeper of the Law within the Coven affectionately called by us as "The Coven Cop". He walks into the Magick Circle and carries the Flame in front of himself with arms outstretched as a symbolic gesture, and slowly walks around the Circle three times where he presents it to the centre of the Circle and to the Sun and then continues walking around to the altar and lights the altar candles.

He lights the Goddess candle first, visualising a beam of light coming down as he lights the Goddess candle and says:

"May the Light of the Goddess illumine this Candle as a symbol that the Great
Mother is with us in our sacred Temple. To watch over us and illumine our Circle
and our souls with her divine Light which is from her heart of hearts!"
He then lights the God candle at the east of the altar and again visualises a beam of light descending and lighting the candle as he touches the flame to it and says:

"May the Light of the radiant God illumine this Candle as a symbol that the
Horned God is with us in our sacred Temple. To watch over us and illumine our
Circle and our souls with his divine Light which is from his heart of hearts!"

He then presents the Spirit candle above the altar to the God and Goddess and says:

"As Above, So Below, As Within, So Without!"

He then places the Spirit candle in the Centre of the altar, ready to light the Hearth Fire when needed and also the Akashic Candles of the Four Quarters.

Altar Statues

Although you have the altar candles you still have a statue of the Goddess and God at the back of the altar and if possible at a higher level than everything else. I have many different statues of Gods and Goddess of different pantheons as I always tend to honour all deities at different times and rituals. The Goddess statue is at the rear of the altar to the west and the God statue is at the rear and to the east.

I always place my altar candles aside each statue on the outer of the altar to illumine the Statues. But you do not need to have statues if you so desire, and many people do not acknowledge the physical representations of a human looking deity as Goddess and God, as they prefer seeing the Goddess and God within Nature.

Akasha Quarter Candles

The Lesser Tools of Fire are the Four Akashic Flames/Candles. The altar also represents the microcosmic Element, the Wicces call forth from within the Magick Circle. This they use within the Magick Circle demonstrating the Hermetic Law, "AS ABOVE, SO BELOW, AS WITHIN, SO WITHOUT." Flanking the four Cardinal Points of the Magick Circle, they are the Four Akashic Flames of the Four Elements, the macrocosmic forces of earth, air, fire and water, expressive also of the Four Planes; Physical, Mental, Emotional and Spiritual. This is always a reminder to the Wicce', that the work is always effective on all Planes.

In my Covens we perform the preliminary Ritual, which I call the "Warming and Awakening of the Temple". Our Man in Black, the Principal Ritualist under the High Priest and High Priestess usually carries out this ceremony and get new Seekers to assist and learn this aspect of ritual. He is also a character called "Lucifuge" and carries a flame "Spirit" into the centre of the Magick Circle and onto the altar. From this Sacred Flame all other Lights are ignited. The Magick Circle is opened in the name of the Goddess; Hecate, Aradia, Diana or Isis; and the Horned God; Pan, Cernunnos or Osiris; demonstrating that Deity is the source of all Light/Knowledge/Power.

The Athame

Where the Thurible is the Element of Air and represents **PURIFICATION**; the Athame is of the Earth forged in Fire and represents **ILLUMINATION**. On the Path to Illumination or Enlightenment, the Wicce learns that there is much to cut and free themselves from; and that there is much to UNLEARN'. Superstition and ignorance cloud the Wicces consciousness. It is the Will of the Higher Self that is eventually to be awakened. We then set to work developing clarity of Will in the consciousness through the practices of concentration. This step is for the developing Wicce, is a formidable one. It is not merely that attainment of powers of concentration, but mastery of emotional power over the Self. The formula for this is expressed in the Universal Wiccan Rede; "AN IT HARM NONE, DO WHAT YOU WILL." Or phased in modern terminology, "LOVE AND DO YOUR WILL", or more simply, "LOVE UNDER WILL".

So, the Athame is to become a key to the expression of the Wicces Will and depends on their Magickal maturity. In any Magickal Ritual you cannot act on your Will and authority alone. You must awaken within the consciousness the Will of Deity. This is done by Invoking the Goddess or God, and so uplifting your consciousness into the Akashic Plane of Spirit, being the Goddess and God. The importance of the work of the Thurible which is used to 'Raise the Vibrations' of the Magick Circle, is paramount if the Will is to change on all Planes. The Athame is therefore an implement that no Wicce is without, well from a ceremonial point of view anyway. From a practical point of view, one does not venture forward in Magickal operations without a Willed Intention, which should come from the Will of the "Higher Self" and not the Mundane mortal. It is very important that the Athame, as a symbol of Will, be well planted in your consciousness, the faculties and corresponding powers symbolized by the Tool.

Thereby you have complete control to Banish that, which has been invoked or evoked. Remember the plight of Disney's 'The Sorcerer's Apprentice', who upon splitting the broomstick he had brought to life, found he had two problems to tend with and so on'. Such is the fate of the badly developed Will of the Wicce.

How and where did the Athame come into being? The Truth is that during the period known as The Burning Times, where an estimated 9 million men, women and children were forcibly taken from their homes, imprisoned, starved, tortured and finally and horrifically murdered; the Athame had a more horrific purpose, but as horrific as it seemed, it was a necessity in the saving of many lives. The Inquisition proclaimed that anyone who had any exterior markings or protuberances such as birth marks, moles, tumours, warts or any odd markings, these were the markings of the Devil. They believed that these markings were signs of the devil, and in fact were used to suckle the Familiars known as "Succubi and Incubi", to give them life and power in the physical forms of animals or even Wicces themselves. So, the Wicces in defence, upon hearing that they may be taken and questioned by the local Inquisitors, would take their dagger and cut the markings from their bodies. Preferring the slow bleeding, and sometimes blood clotting, to the slow torture and eventual death of the Inquisitors. We today, who have reassembled Wicca, reclaim this Tool, as a symbol of Hope and Freedom. It is now used as an added extension to the practicing of Wicce.

The Traditional Athame is black hilted with a double-edged blade, the handle is preferably made out of wood or antler, or even stained bone. It should not be a sharp dagger, as it will never EVER cut anything physically. It is an Astral Tool only! Its length should be from the tip of your finger to the base of your palm. It should be as plain as it can be, with no markings whatsoever upon it, and nothing added to it.

It should be clean and virgin. After Initiation certain Magickal Sigils are placed on the Athame, but only during the Rite of Initiation. It is used to direct, and to absorb the electro-magnetic energies within the Universe. It is the same with all Tools of the Craft. They are all specially Prepared and Consecrated in the Magick Circle; they are awakened to the connectedness of the Inner Wicce. It takes a long time in being Properly Prepared to hold such a sacred relic that helps us to remember the pain and suffering of our ancestors during the Burning Times. And as we reclaim the Athame and the title Wicce, we will respect both and so the Powers of the Wicce will unfold. When the time is right, the Athame will seek you out and find you.

Book of Shadows

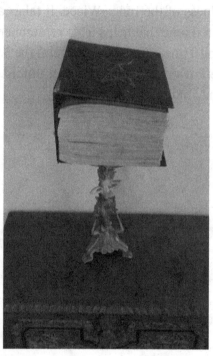

Every faith or religion that has ever existed on our planet has a sacred or Holy Book, a Bible as such that teaches about life and a set of rules and stories to help guide their followers on their Spiritual journey. The Book of Shadows (BoS), as such was never an ancient written truth of our ways as it has always been an oral tradition, passed from Sage or parent to child but is our ever growing and ever-changing bible, and more than that it is more of a Spiritual Diary a Sacred book that holds all of your Magickal thoughts and spiritual rituals. Whenever you come across a book that has information that you feel is beneficial to you and your journey then write it in your BoS. When you do this always put the date, as your journey changes so too will your BoS, and new truths will reveal themselves to, the deeper you go and become aware of your Wiccan journey. The term Shadows is quite important as shadows change and grow too.

When you have a Full Moon or New Moon or just celebrate life and Nature in general writes it down in your BoS. But always put the date to keep everything in order so as to know where you were at that stage in your journey, and mostly to know if you are moving forward or going backwards. Start your BoS as an introduction to your belief system, and sayings that can keep you firm in your belief. Add important data about what you follow or believe in such as Meditations, Dreams, Trance States, Spells, Rituals, Luna and Festival Celebrations, also initiatory processes as you grow and feel wiser and more Magickal, especially being more connected to Nature and the Great Mother Goddess. Write into your BoS a set of self-disciplines, a set of instructions that you must know and learn by heart. As you must know your BoS completely so as to never go off track. Always go by your inner gut feelings, as your soul knows what is right and what is important, more than others tell you. Know your own Truth, and don't let anyone sway you or lesson your ability to be who you really are and put a pause on your Spiritual Quest for that inner reality of what Wiccecraft is!

I myself over 5 decades have had dozens of BoS's and have kept my original one's but have also re-written them and added much to my personal BoS. I now would have in excess of 25 different BoS. My last one (maybe) is a huge handmade BoS with over a thousand recycled pages that I am slowly adding to and making complete of all that I have known and learnt. Not only from this life but also what has been awoken in my previous incarnations. Enjoy your journey, as your BoS will become so important and sacred that it will be your greatest Magickal Treasure, and maybe by handing it down to your children can become all that it is meant to be.

Making Your Own Book of Shadows

- Buy yourself a blank journal and make sure it has many pages, as this will fill up very quickly if you're serious. Add decorations such as pictures, drawings, and leaves from nature, and feathers.
- Start with a Prayer blessing your writings and your journey that it is true, and that the Goddess is with you always guiding you on your journey. Write your own dedication or Self-Blessing Ritual and like everything in your Shadows learn it, know it, and believe it.
- Then write in an Index of all the pages to follow so that you may find them quicker. Keep this next part as an Important Message to yourself stating that "Properly Prepared I Must Always Be". Then write a Consecration or Blessing ritual to bless your paper pages, pen and Book, so they are dedicated only to the Magick of your sacred BoS.
- Add in the Wicces Rune, a chant that you must say and perform every-time to enter your Magick Circle, this is used to raise and build power for your purpose. Next pages write your own Consecration of Water and Blessing of Salt. We Consecrate Water as it is impure, and we Bless Salt as it is pure.
- Next write about the Elements and their Elemental Beings, these you work with on a daily basis, these help you to keep in balance so that your Magick is in balance.
- Next write about Candle Magick, as this is the easiest and simplest form of Magick that you can start using and doing with great success until you gain more confidence.
- Then write your own Magick Circle Preparation and how to cleanse and banish negative energies, and invoke Positive natural energies.
- Now it's time to write down how to form and cast your Wicces Temple or better known as the Magick Circle.
- Write your own New Moon and Full Moon ceremony include the invoking of the Goddess and God and call in energies to assist you with your Magickal Spells or Rituals.

- Write and prepare your own Rite of Dedication, which we call a Wiccaning, this is where the Goddess and God bless your soul and you dedicate your spirit to Wicca and the Goddess and God.
- Prepare and create your own Initiation Ceremony, which will take you eventually from being a Wiccan Neophyte to an Initiated Wicce, take your time and do not rush elevation to this level.
- Write about Spells and how they should always be in rhyme as being in rhyme speaks for itself.
- Learn to raise energy and Do the Witches Rune as a Spiral Dance within your Magick Circle to aid in raising Power.
- Collect and learn about each of your Magickal Tools that will be used in your Magickal studies such as; Thurible (incense burner), Altar, Altar pentacle (To bless and Consecrate things on), your Athame (the Wicces dagger), Chalice for Water, container for Salt, Incense container, charcoal blocks for the incense, 2 Altar candles representing the Goddess and God, Statues of the Goddess and God, robes to wear only for ceremonies and Magickal work.
- Learn and write about the Eightfold Paths of Wicca and what the Wicce must learn and follow.
- Know the symbolism and meaning behind the Wicces Pyramid and the Magick Circle.
- Write your Seasonal and Sabbat Festivals; Blessing of the Animals 4th January; Lughnasadh 1-2nd February; Betrothal Day (Valentine's Day) 14th February; Autumn Equinox 21-23 March; Samhain (Halloween) May Eve; May Pole Day 1st may; Winter Solstice 21-23 June; Imbolg August Eve; Spring Equinox 21-23 September; Beltane November Eve; Summer Solstice 21-23 December.
- Learn the Laws of Nature and of Magick so as to not go wrong "An it Harm None, Do What you Will".
- In the back of your BoS write all your poetry, prayers, songs, Invocations and Evocations.
- Also add all the books that you have read, loved and recommend.

This then makes it complete; keep a second BoS for all the rituals and ceremonies that you do including meditations and their outcomes. Good luck and Goddess Speed.

Clay

You should always have some clay at hand for making of Fif-faths (dolls), if not clay, then something else that can be moulded like beeswax (when warmed to soften), plasticine, or poppets (fabric). It can be used for a lot of different Magickal purposes even making Pentacles of Clay, Dolls, Images, your own Goddess and God Statue, Life Masks (death masks), body moulds which I prefer to use plaster Paris and dipping cut strips of gauze into the liquid and then wrapped around the person.

I love doing this with pregnant ladies, so they keep an image of their full belly with child, and can decorate it later even with their child, by placing hand prints and footprints of the end product to show through its growing stages. You can also decorate them with anything you desire.

The Ceremonial Drum

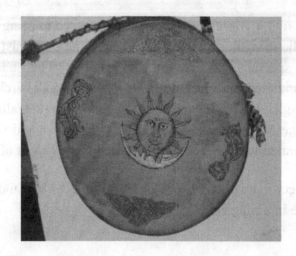

This is used in our Magick Circles only because of my Shamanic Training in South America. The Drum represents the heartbeat of Mother Earth and is used for tuning into Nature and for Awakening certain energies. It is also used for Cleansing and raising one's vibrations, and on a deeper level it is used for Healing. We sometimes use it to drum people into our Magick Circle, as it raises their vibrations in readiness for the Ritual.

You can also use larger drums for ceremony and ritual. We incorporate a lot of music in our Circles which add to everyone being more joyous and free of spirit. I also teach people how to make their Medicine drums as well which they make and then hand paint and decorate to reveal the energy and spirit of their drum.

Magick Cords

When we are Initiated into a Traditional Coven we are asked to bring four 9' cords, one is to be our Wicces Girdle (Singulum) which is worn around our waist over our robes, it is White and has several specially spaced knots and is called "The Ladder of the Goddess", it is used to trace out and mark the circumference of the Magick Circle. The other three 9' cords are to be our Magick Cords that are used in Binding and Healing Rituals. They are white - representing the Maiden, red representing the Mother and blue representing the Crone. Each is Consecrated with special powers of the triple aspect of our Goddess.

Each Cord also has specific healing powers and should never be handled by others unless you allow it, or you are in a Magick Circle.

Medicine Pouch

A Medicine Pouch is exactly what it sounds like, it is a pouch that has an accumulation of items that you have collected that you class as Magickal and Healing, such as crystals, shells, keys, herbs, salt, sand, stones, teeth, claws, fur, flowers, blood, etc.

I have a collection of 40 in my Medicine Pouch and take it into the Magick Circle to be charged every time I enter. They are special items that I treasure, especially the Shells as I have worked with the Magick of shells most of my life as in Gypsy Magick they each symbolise a specific type of Power or Magick that can be used or drawn upon for my personal Spells and Ceremonies. I find that they are great for many things from divination to Empowerment.

In my pouch I also have my Initiatory Acorn that we are each given on the night of our Initiation as a symbol that we, like the Acorn can grow mighty and strong if we grow correctly and honestly with the Goddess at our front and the Horned God having our back.

Moccasins

When I was young I was always barefoot in the Magick Circle, as I was always taught to feel the living Earth beneath our feet. In this way we could ground ourselves and draw up energy when needed from the Mother Earth. It also meant that with every experience we were connected to Mother Earth and Her Divine energies.

But as I got older I became more of a softy and a sook, and so when it was cold I wore a specially made pair of moccasins that I use just within the Magick Circle and when doing Magickal work for the Goddess and her Community. I love my Moccasins as they keep my feet protected from the Elements, warm and I know then that I will not get a chill going through my body.

I also decided instead of getting people sick in my Covens that they could also wear some form of protection on their feet, and I found that the kung-Fu slippers (from most market stalls) were perfect as they had a rubber sole, and were comfy and protective. But when we did higher forms of ritual or Magick we had to go bare foot no matter what the weather, as being connected completely is what Magick is all about.

The Sacred Pentacle

Ruling the Higher Mind over the lower Elements of our being of human Nature. It signifies the Awakening of the Cosmic Consciousness and the beginnings of human consciousness, manipulating its environment beyond the Realms of the physical form and perceptions limited into 5 senses. The origins of the Pentagram go far back to remotest historical antiquity, as far back as Pre-Babylonian Sumer. It has been venerated by nearly every culture and civilization. To the Jews is symbolizes the "Pentateuch" - the five Books of Moses. Early Judaic recognized it as pointing out the '5 Stigmata' - the 5 wounds that Jesus suffered whilst on the Cross. It has since survived a variety of titles such as; The Druids Foot, Mirror of Venus, Penta-labrys; Talisman of the Sun; Talisman of Mars; Macrocosmic Man; Shekinah of YHVH; Star of Isis; Celtic Star; The Endless Knot; Pentacle of the Virgin; Star of Knowledge; Pentacle of the Templars; Medieval Churchmen; Wizards Star; Goblins Cross; Devils Sign; Baphomet's Seal; and to the followers of Pythagoras, called it the Pentalpha, being composed of 5 interlaced A's, or Alpha's. Alpha being the first word of the Greek alphabet, we can perhaps view it as shadowing forth unity in the midst of multiplicity.

"Those involved in Occult practices could be certain that wherever the Pentacle was displayed, evil had no power at all. Traditionally each of the 5 angles has been Attributed to the metaphysical Elements of Wicca."

This becomes a graphic betrayal of Spirit ruling over the Elements, and when the Pentagram is placed within the Magick Circle (a symbol of Eternity, totality and unity) its energies are focused and directed. The Inverted Pentagram with the single point buried in the depths of matter, has for many centuries been misinterpreted by the ignorant and those of ill intent, as emblematic of the powers of evil and darkness. However, for the true student of Wicca, it represents Spirit submerged and bonded into the material Elements. Whilst the Inverted Pentagram is representative of Spirits Descent into matter The Pentagram aright, to those of Spiritual Perception represents the redemption of Spirit from Matter by ruling over it. This High Magickal Tool is to be used as a Paten for ritual consecrations, especially of salt and water in preliminary Banishing's of the Magick Circle. It is represented as a symbol of authority to the Guardians of the Wicca. All-important Tools may be charged upon this pentacle, for consecration before group or solitary consumption. As in all Magick work, ask that you're Magick be correct and for the good of all.

The symbols placed upon the Pentacle are placed in a set sequence to represent an ancient Key to unlock the ancient Epagomenes, and the knowledge of the Ancient Ones, when used correctly by those trained properly.

THE GREAT MOTHER: - The Breast of the Goddess - Womb of the Worlds - The Lunar Goddess.

THE HORNED GOD: - Consort of the Goddess - Lord of the Earth and all Nature - Lord of the Magick Circle.

CENTRAL INVERTED PENTAGRAM: - This represents infusion and bonding of the Spirit into Matter, through control of the Earth'.

THE PENTAGRAM: - Power over the Elements - Spirit Rules.

THE KISS - The successes, joys and all the pleasurable experiences in life that encourages us to strive towards perfection.

THE SCOURGE - The pains, sorrows, trials, and difficulties that is essential in the process of self-mastery in the life of a Wicce.

○

THE MAGICK CIRCLE - The powers and protection of the Magick Circle, the gateway between the Worlds, and enhancer of all True Magick.

INFINITY/ETERNITY - The never-ending cycle of death, birth, life and rebirth. The duality and polarity of manifested existence contained within all-encompassing Unity, which is ever in motion.

TRIANGLE OF DARKNESS - Symbol of the Seeker, the Child of Darkness.

TRIANGLE OF LIGHT - Symbol of the Wicce, the Child of Light.

The Sacred Pentacle is Traditionally made from Bee's wax and Dragons Blood, of which our Coven makes exclusively for Wiccans.

Perfect Love and Perfect Trust!

Most Wicces are aware that the Age of Aquarius began in 1829 and will last 2000 years. Many Seers have predicted great changes and upheavals that will take place in the history of mankind. In fact, if we are to believe recent translations, Nostradamus predicted almost total destruction. The ancient Egyptians of almost 4,000 years ago predicted that during the Age of Aquarius, when the Planets have lined up, there would be a great explosion of psychic power - some good and some evil.

As R. Lewis said in his book, "The Thirteenth Stone", "The planets follow the Sun in a great cycle which as I have said takes 25,920 years to complete. During this time the Sun appears to be in a particular part of the zodiac for a period of 2,160 years. Roughly speaking, from 4,000 to 2,000 B.C.E. The Earth was in Taurus; when the Shamanic and Horned God's were around. It then moved on to Aries for Another 2,000 years, when the major wars started, and at the time of the Spreading of the Christian Gospel, it had moved into Pisces, the fishes which is the true symbol for Christianity."

According to our Astronomer Priests, Pisces was going to be an Age of Iron, and a time when the Sun would dominate the Moon. It would be an Age of masculine material science rather than a balanced era; the coming world would turn its back on the Priest and all this hard-won wisdom. The tree would be cut down. All this was to happen within a Great Month, a twelfth part of the 25,920 years in which day and night, light and dark, good and evil alternate. Pisces is to be followed by Aquarius, which is governed by Saturn. This according to our Astronomer Priests would be the beginning of yet another Golden Age. In this Age the tree would again bear fruit, and mankind would come to live in peace, harmony and justice.

The main concern of the ancient Priests was that their Spiritual heirs should not have to start from scratch, as they once did. With them in mind, a vehicle was prepared which would carry all that they had learned through the stormy seas of the Piscean Age. The Christian Bible was built as a Trojan horse, which would meet the religious needs of the people of

Pisces. Wicca was and is prepared for to take people through the Age of Aquarius and to suit the religious needs of the people of Aquarius. And so it was that the SCRIPTURES WERE WRITTEN, giving the materialistic, male-dominated people of Pisces a Material God to worship. At the end of that dark time, God/dess would send an Interpreter of the Law, who would reveal to the Children of Aquarius all that hard-won wisdom. In John 4-22; Jesus in the role of teacher is heard to say; "Ye worship, ye know not what!"

This could cause destruction and then a new beginning. This prediction is in the sacred care of the Inner Temple of Isis in London. It is my personal opinion that there was a slight miscalculation, as twenty years here or there are infinitesimal, when you are dealing in thousands of years. I felt it was a little premature and more likely to commence at the turn of the last century, also one must bear in mind that our calendar dates from the birth of Jesus and may or may not be worth consideration.

The prediction which is written on a clay tablet in the script of the ancient Temple, states that there will be a Universal use of Arcane Sciences, the discovery of resources available but not yet identified and finally Chaos, followed by rebirth.

If one studies the headlines in the newspapers of this day, one could easily believe that this psychic Chaos is well under way. Man is becoming more selfish, cruel, greedy, radical, and indifferent. In America there was 9/11, in Indonesia the constant bombings. In the USA many years ago a young man from a rural Australia, whilst on a visit to LA was mugged twice, stripped naked and chased to his death on an electric railway line in the subway, by a jeering crowd who stood and watched and did nothing whilst he died. In Melbourne, a young girl staggered from a train into a crowd of people her nose was broken and bleeding, she had been assaulted. She pleaded for help, but not a person slowed down to help her. They all through fear looked the other way and did not want to get involved.

This is a description of the obvious, but the more ghastly and insidious attacks are the psychic attacks being inflicted by EVERYONE!!!!! Yes everyone, as we do this without even realizing what we are doing. Know and remember; that everything starts from a thought, and if infused by intense emotion, becomes more realistic, and is created on the Astral counterpart into the physical; so, we do well to remember, do not wish ill on anyone or anything; never boast and never threaten; and the Goddess will smile upon us. Remember the Karmic Law; "Whatever you do good or bad, will come back to you, threefold!"

We of the Wicca all have one thing in common - love and concern for the Mother Earth, and ALL life upon and within Her. Our aim is to free our people from the fear and promote Love and Trust. In Wicca we have what we call the "Wicces Rune", and a couple of the lines are "Queen of Heaven, Queen of Hell". For me these words mark the knell of fear, separation, and illusion. Wicca is not puritanical sweetness or a hellish diabolism.

It is the essence of life, encompassing all Nature; by the wisdom of our Goddess we are made into the creation by a design, and not a chance. The design, our very being must have a purpose, what is it? From day one we become magnets that surround us with situations that bring us experiences s placed into good and bad. Surely the purpose of our very existence is to ensure that we gain as many life experiences by finding both good/bad; pleasure/pain; success/failure. Surely, we should strive always to live our Highest Ideals and live by the words; "An it harm none." We are aware that we will have our failings; most of us know upon awakening, that we will meet failure and success to varying degrees.

Our Goddess and God rule a Holistic Nature through all aspects. When we stumble through lack of Inner Strength, immaturity, ignorance or stupidity, we are not condemned or judged by our Gods, we merely learn from our mistakes, and must learn to be all the stronger and wiser for that experience. Good/Pleasure and Bad/Pain are hidden teachers; but they are not the real lesson. The true lesson is in which we react, adhere and grow. Our Goddess abides in every extreme of our consciousness, always ready to give the gifts of the Cauldron of Cerridwen to Her needy Children. So, when we fail, we are not cut off from Her, as She allows us to make our mistakes so that we can hopefully learn from them.

We all need to go through light and dark cycles, as everything in nature does, even in Christian mythology Jesus descended into the Underworld. The great strength of our Goddess is in that we are inspired and loved and always uplifted that we may grow and understand our total individuality. In this awareness we learn to harmonise with Nature in all Her deepest Mysteries. So, once we have learned this, we become a true child of the Goddess and God and know that we have arrived home. With each Rank or Degree in the Wicca, we have many in-depth Mysteries that can only be taught and passed on from Traditional Covens, but with each solid and devout step we get a lot closer to the Oneness we seek with Deity.

The Goddess is the Soul of the Living Earth, and a Divine link with all things primordial, dark, still, and warm as if in the Tomb or Womb of Eternal Time. The Goddess has many thousands of names; She is the Inner Reality, manifested in all Life. The Goddess is not separate from the world; She is the world, and all things in and on it. She is the very essence of everything, the very breath we take is of her, and every heartbeat is by her loving grace. She illumines our souls and awakens us to the Mysteries of Nature and of ourselves.

After a millennium of Herstory, the Goddess is reawakening, not to conquer or master the masculine forces, but to affirm, the two great life principles, the electrical-male and the feminine-magnetic polarities, which are active in the Universe and to affirm that together they form a Unity, a Unity that affords us a vision of harmony and balance of the Human Spirit. By reconnecting the opposing yet connected forces of the Universe, the forces of Light and Dark, Night and Day, Masculine and Feminine, Yin and Yang, Consciousness and Unconsciousness, Birth and Death, Form and Energy. The continual Spiral Dance of life eternal, always giving and in return always receiving.

To truly understand the Goddess and gain a deep insight into an Initiation of the Mysteries, you need to go back, back to the time thousands of years ago, when all of mankind's survival depended upon an intimate knowledge of aligning their intuitiveness with the forces and cycles of Nature. A transformation of personality was implied in every Initiation, from the Mundane Plane to the Fool Stool of the Gods. Women needed a female Initiation and men needed a male Initiation. For each gender, what was a sacred Mystery was largely determined by their attempt to understand their own primordial sexual essence.

Ancient female Initiatory Rites were supposed to imitate the maternal birth process, as well as the process of eternal Rebirth. The Initiation was a way of contacting deep levels of awareness; theirs is a realisation that this that makes up the obvious physicality of the world is not true and real. There is a realization of the real and the eternal, which are a different kind of reality. Plutarch, the early Greek Historian describes an inscription about Athena, one of the archetypes of the Goddess. The inscription says: "I AM THAT WHICH HAS BEEN, AND IS, AND EVER WILL BE. AND NO MORTAL HAS REVEALED MY HOLY ROBES." This inscription speaks of the eternal never-changing, ever-changing reality of the Goddess who was and is and shall ever be the same but different. Initiation also represents FREEDOM from the world as it frees the spirit. But the price of that freedom is the willingness to face one's own true dark and light self. To perceive the unconscious rather than the conscious, to touch the Inner Abyss of our own Being, and those parts of us that are a part of our totality. We need to become TRUTH and know our TRUTH. As long as those areas are distorted, we will not be free!

Initiation is also a process of confronting the Guardian of the Threshold, the Dread Lord of Shadows. The Initiate must be willing to be completely trusting and uncomfortable and face the Shadows. Death and Rebirth are the themes of Initiation, and death is the root of our deepest fears, and the true face of the Shadow, it is the terror behind VULNERABILITY, and during Initiation you are in your most vulnerable state of your entire life, blindfolded, bound, naked and at one with the elements and a lot of strangers.

Rainbow Coloured Ribbons

An assorted collection coloured ribbons are important in rituals, especially for bindings, creating web and weaving Magick, making Dreamcatchers, building Maypoles, tying to Festival Coronets, and for also sealing Magickal letters etc. Like everything else nothing should enter the Magick Circle unless it has been Consecrated (Blessed and Charged), as all objects must become sacred and holy relics for the Arts.

If you get the men to fetch the Pole for the Maypole then the women and children can make the Chaplet of Flowers for the very top, and place 7, 9 21, 40 coloured ribbons around the ring that should be 1 ½ times the length of the Maypole. As they will be woven and weaved around the pole to help in bringing Fertility to the land, such as crops, orchards etc.

We never unwind the ribbons as they remain on the Maypole and get sealed onto it, this Tool is then offered to the God and Goddess at Beltane and placed in the ritual fire called the Bale Fire.

All the other ribbons are kept securely away for when they are needed.

Raw Wool

Traditionally the Elders would collect the wool from the newly Shawn sheep and then stretched on a wheel over and over to make it thick and strong. When they have reached a certain length of 9' for each length, it is then either bleached or dyed according to the colour of your advancement within the Coven.

This was how the originally Singulum's were made but these days it is much easier just to go down to the haberdashery and collect from a myriad of cords that are available, I love the pyjama sized cords as they are easy to work with and seem far more practical. But we must never forget our past and the Traditional ways that we made our sacred items and Tools within the Craft.

Rattle

A Rattle is a symbolic Tool from ancient Shamanic practices that change the vibrations of certain objects in readiness for Magick. They stimulate our senses and change the very energy that is around us, by either awakening or removing certain fields. The Rattle is also used to Awaken the Soul in healing and ascending. It is used to aid one when going into Trance State.

Rattles can be made from many items, I have Shell Rattles to move the cosmic tides within us; Tortoise Rattles to ground us; Deer Toe Rattles for ceremonial lifting; Bell Rattles for changing environment as with music; etc.

Rattles can be made from almost anything, whatever the imagination can create, as long as it makes a specific rattle sound, that vibrates with each of our Magickal vibrations such as our Chakra's. The baser the tone the Earthier is the Rattle, the higher pitched the higher Airy aspect etc.

Rock Salt

We all need to carry with us a small bag of rock salt, pure salt of the sea. As this is used to Consecrate Water which in turn aids in Consecrating all our Tools and Regalia. It is important to always have a small dish or container of Rock Salt on your Altar.

For High Magick we also soak our Three Magick Cords in Consecrated Salt Water so that it absorbs the purity of the salt and water as a blessing, when these Magick cords are used they are already pure. I also have a long white cord which has been soaked in Consecrated Salt Water that can be laid around the perimeter of the Magick Circle for higher ceremonial uses. As it creates a protective barrier instead of having to cut a barrier with your Athame or sword if time does not permit etc.

Consecrated Salt has the Power to do many things, to cleanse, heal, charge, ward off evil, bless, purify, anoint, along with many other charges.

Singulum of a Wicce

The Initiated Wicce wears a White 9' Singulum which is called the Ladder of the Goddess and has 8 ceremonial knots which are placed in a ceremonial Spell which represent different stages of training that have to be learnt by the Initiate. It is used to measure the traditional Nine Foot Magick Circle which represents the microcosm of the macrocosmic Moon.

It is used in keeping us bound to the world of mortals until such as a time as we can be freed by the mortal toll of life and become one of the Shining Ones and be a Guardian Light Angel to teach and guide man. We also wear our Sheaths for our Athame's so our Athame is always by our side.

By knot of One the Wicce has begun, By knot of two all Spells will come true,

By knot of Three your inner sight is open, so you can clearly see,

By knot of five you are welcomed into the Hive and where all Magick is alive.

By knot of six all power is Fixed.

By knot of seven you are grounded and leaven.

By knot of eight the Goddess through this cord has sealed your fate.

Shells

Shells are a beautiful creation of the Sea Mother; all creation comes out of the primordial oceans. Shells are the Magickal vessels that the ancient Wicces and Shamans used to hold messages, charms and spells which were rolled up and placed inside the shell then sealed with beeswax and gifted back to the sea, chanting at the same time that the great ebb and flow of the oceans tides would take away all negativity and darkness and with the incoming movement of the tide gift to us the Magick that we have requested and petitioned for.

At one time In ancient history Cowry shells were so prized that they were worth more than gold, and even today the rarest gold cowry is worth millions of dollars. Also when a friend or sister gets pregnant and is about to deliver her baby give her two tiger cowry shells for her to place in each hand, this makes for an easy delivery and blesses the mother and child.

Caracoles, giant sea snails have been used for containers and drinking vessels, I have an elaborate Shell Chalice decorated with sterling silver and covered in precious gemstones, this is my sacred Water Chalice.

You can also make talismans with shells, by writing your Magickal Spell on parchment rolling it and placing inside the shell, get a long piece of leather strip as a necklet and place ends in the shell and then seal with beeswax. This can then be charged and Consecrated and then presented to who you made it for or kept for yourself.

Spirit Bottle

A Magickal Spirit Bottle is different to a Wicce Bottle as they are used for different reasons. Firstly it is used to trap evil forces or powers which will within time dissipate. Or to trap good powers to be used for a Spell or any Magickal Operation.

Or it is used as a Bottle for Magickal Spells, as you would place a small parchment inside that has your request written on it, and then added to it would be some Anointing or Magickal Oil or Potion, just a drop is all you need. Some herbs or a small Talisman of sorts, then make sure it is sealed tightly and securely. Do your ritual and then either bury it or throw it to the sea and lets the tides of life decide where it ends up

I love doing this with a Blessing Bottle, so you bless it and Consecrate so that whoever finds it is blessed with Love and Magick.

Spirit Candle

The Spirit Candle or also known as the "Eternal Flame of the Goddess" is the first Light that is brought into the Magick Circle, usually by the Maiden on Moon ceremonies or Man in Black at festivals. It is brought into the Magick Circle and presented to the Quarters and placed in the Centre of the Altar. It is then taken to the Centre of the Magick Circle and the Principal Ritualist holds it high and invokes the Light/Life of the Goddess and God and imagines three streams of light descending into the centre of the Hearth Fire which is placed in the Centre of the Circle as they visualise and Invoke, they slowly light the Bale Fire, representing the bringing of Light and Life to the Magick Circle. After they have done this they then go to the Altar and acknowledge and welcome the Goddess by lighting Her altar candle first, and then acknowledge the Horned God and light His altar candle. The Spirit Flame is then placed in the centre of the altar again, prior to the cleansing and preparation of the Magick Circle in readiness for the High Priestess and the guests.

> "BE TO ME THE FIRE OF MOON,
> BE TO ME THE FIRE OF NIGHT,
> BE TO ME THE FIIRE OF JOY,
> TURNING DARKNESS INTO LIGHT.
> BY THE VIRGIN WAXING COLD,
> BY THE MOTHER FULL AND BOLD,
> BY THE HAG QUEEN SILENT OLD.
> BY THE MOON, THE ONE IN THREE,
> CONSECRATE THIS MAGICK CIRCLE - BLESSED BE!"

Tabard

A Tabard serves several purposes, firstly it keeps the robe protected and clean. Secondly it keeps your front and back warm; thirdly it distinguishes between the ranks when we do not wear capes. For the Wicce the tabard is a green velvet or white and black with either silver or gold trim depending on whether you are a male or a female. At the chest centre is a Labyrinth of the Goddess Seal or the Seal of the Wicce which is a gold triangle inside a silver circle.

When our covens are at open festivals they all look unified and quite smart, with Wicces all wearing their white and green with their symbols of silver triangle inside a gold circle, Priesthood wearing burgundy/red and white with the seal of the Priesthood being an inverted gold pentagram inside a silver circle, and High Priesthood wearing white and silver and black and gold with a seal of the High Priesthood being an interlaced hexagram incorporating an upward pointing triangle and an inverted gold triangle. The Arch Priest and Arch Priestess can wear whatever they desire but traditionally purple and silver for the Arch Priestess and purple and gold for the Arch Priest wearing their seal of 40 stars in a circle.

Theban Runes

The Theban Alphabet

Language of the Wicces

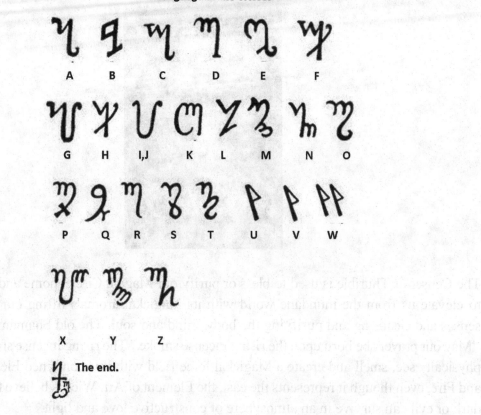

This is the traditional alphabet of the Wicce and used for writing specific petitions to the Angels and for ceremonial purposes. You can if you feel clever also write out your Book of Shadows in Theban as well. But traditionally it is for Magickal petitions and letters.

The Thurible

The Censer or Thurible is used to bless or purify our Magick Circle, home and us. It helps to elevate us from the mundane world with its Magickal aroma's lifting our old factory senses and cleansing and purifying the body, mind and soul. The old Shamanic saying is; "May our prayers be born upon the rising incense smoke." The rising incense smoke we can physically see, smell and create a Magickal force field with this combined Element of Air and Fire, even though it represents the east, the Element of Air. Wicces believe that nothing dark or evil can survive in an atmosphere of constructive love and light.

I see many people fighting invisible forces all the time but do to this only increased its Power. Therefore, we should always arm ourselves with Love and Light, combined with the faith in our Goddess. This not only dissolves negative energy but also paralyses any evil force or entity. If we focus and concentrate on the negative forces within and without ourselves, we realise that it only serves to enforce them and give them more energy, more life. We should always be aware of them, keeping them in check, but never give them the gratification of feeding them with our minds giving them too much attention. We have to starve these forces, to release ourselves from them. If we are working 100% on the focus of the good, then all other energies will just fade away.

Our first task then is to Thurify our Magick Circle, this then helps to clear our mind and elevate and insulate us from the outer mundane world. The Incense in the Thurible does this by distracting our consciousness by the mere association of the specified Magickal aroma that is being used. So, our Magick Circle then becomes purified of all our outer thoughts and emotions. The Thurible represents Air and is the Symbol of Sacred Space. It aids in contacting certain energies or forces that we need for our Ritual of Spell. It raises our own Vibrations and this part of our Ritual is called; "The Awakening and Raising of the Temple".

No Spell or Word of Power will draw down Cosmic Light but are Tools to aid in raising our Consciousness to enter the World of Magick. Even the phrase *"Drawing Down the Moon"*, is very misleading, as we do not draw down the Moon but instead open *"Manifest Lunar Consciousness"* and ourselves. When we are working within the Magick Circle we attempt to impregnate this sacred space with certain forces, energies started.

"FOR MY PRAYERS SHALL BE BORN UPON THE RISING INCENSE SMOKE".

Since the beginning of man's awe with Magick, we have used and burned offerings to the Gods. We are not sure how it exactly came about, but I gather it was by mistake. Maybe whilst collecting some wood for a fire, one of our ancestors found either a scented piece of wood, or some aromatic herb or plant, and decided to just throw it on the fire. From here it is a logical step to see how it grew into the beautiful and many varied types of granular gums and resins that we now call incense.

My first Thurible was a "pearl shell" from Broome; I filled it with beach sand to absorb the heat from the burning charcoal blocks. But my next Thurible I purchased at a 'swap meet', it was an old antique silver cake stand, which cost me $3, and for $2 more, I purchased a brass dish to go on top. I put beach sand in that too. The one I used in my Coven (as pictured above) is very special as I brought it in New Orleans at the French Quarter at a friend's Voodoo shop, I paid $160 US and I love it. The Thurible itself is associated with the Air Element, and the incense is associated with the Earth Element and the Charcoal block is associated with the

Fire Element. These fire blends are a way of releasing the aroma of incense, the energizing properties of Earth, Air and Fire, plus the grounding and cleansing powers of mineral salts. These Traditional Magickal blends come together in a Natural and effective technique that purifies and Charges any area with Air and Fire, and an aroma to help change the sacred spaces vibrations. Negative energies are drawn into the salts, and the Air and Fire Elements release the Magical scent clearly and positively.

Resinous blends of incense burned on a charcoal block are stronger and more resinous than regular incense, so use less. This method of releasing fragrance is to be used with caution, and never to be performed unattended, always use care and common sense whenever dealing with an open flame, remember Wicces and Fire do not go well together (Ha, Ha excuse the pun). Do not use in windy areas, or near flammable substances - to be used with caution and respect.

Here in Australia I discovered many years ago the beautiful aromatic scent of a Grass tree Resin. But there have been over the centuries many different substances used for incense such as Asafoetida (Devils Dung), for evil Rites and Banishing's; Wormwood for Necromancy; Musk for seduction; Myrrh for embalming and funerary rites. In general, the extracted oils or gums were used instead of the actual plant or wood, the more common of these oils being; Cinnamon, Lavender, Rose, Ylang Ylang, Lime, Cloves, Frankincense, Copal, Myrrh and Benzoin. When you find your perfect Thurible, for static use, rather than to Thurify (perfume) a Magick Circle area, the bowl without the chains is best. The Thurible should be well cleansed and Consecrated, and then a Spell of dedication should be recited like this one I wrote years ago:

"AS I LIGHT THEE PERFUME MAKER,
GOOD-SPIRIT CALLER AND EVIL BREAKER.
AS I KINDLE THIS EARHTLY TOKEN,
POWERS MIGHTY FROM WITHIN ARE WOKEN.
TOOLS OF EARTH, AIR AND FIRE, FOREVER BE,
CONSECRATED NOW BY ME AND THEE!"

Practical - Thurible

Light some incense in your Thurible, using the above suggestions or choose your own, for this experiment, perfumes used should have emotionally wearing associations to you. The atmosphere should be darkened, lit by candlelight. Sit in a comfortable position, in the Centre of your Magick Circle, with your Thurible just before you. Concentrate just on your Thurible … just before you. Concentrate on your breathing … inhale … hold … exhale … and continue to draw the vital force from your surroundings … When placing incense upon the lit charcoal block in the Thurible in devotional rituals, it is customary to always offer a prayer to the Goddess, or power that is being invoked. My original Coven use to say this one;

"WE BRING OF YOUR GARDEN, O MIGHTY HORNED GOD,
THE FRAGRANCE ABOUNDS THEREIN.
WE BRING OF YOUR GARDEN O GRACIOUS MOTHER,
THE MAGICK AROMA ABOUNDS WITHIN.
WE FILL THIS AREA OF YOUR PRESENCE.
WE SPEAK YOUR SACRED NAMES,
AND THEREBY SUMMON THE WHISPERING VOICES OF WONDER
FROM ALL THE REGIONS OF YOUR FIELDS
AND ALL YOUR WOODLAND TREE'S.
COME, MIGHTY FATHER, GRACIOUS MOTHER, COME!"

Water

All Magickal, Spiritual and occult practices need to have clean pure water at hand. It should either be from a stream, spring or purified water in some form. We need to always have water in the Temple and the Magick Circle for several reasons.

Firstly and importantly a ritual container of Spring Water for using in ritual that is placed in your Ceremonial Water Chalice ready to be blessed and consecrated for cleansing and washing the whole Temple/Magick Circle. It is used to anoint ourselves, sprinkle around the perimeter of the Magick Circle (mixed with consecrated salt), to anoint and re-bless all our working tools. I also leave a small dish of water out for the Elementals and also some Luna or Sabbat Cake as an offering.

We should also have a container close by for drinking if needed, and a hose or water supply to keep the fire at bay, and to put out at the end of the night.

Wheel of the Sabbats

Originally the Wheel has been reused in modern times by many Pagans and Wiccans the world over, but this was a torture device used against women, Wicces and Pagans who were all called Heretics. So we should not be incorporating this Catherine's Wheel into our Covens at all. But to have a Wheel of Light, a Wheel of the Sabbats, Wheel of the Year, Wheel of the Magick Circle, Wheel of Dreams, Wheel of Change. These are far better terms that we use throughout our Wiccan Calendar.

At certain Festivals we roll a Flaming Wheel down the hillside to bring back the Light of the Sun, it is used as an offering to Light the Traditional Bale Fires. I prefer instead of destroying a great wooden wheel and doing this to either make a smaller version with recycled wood or even get the creative to make a Paper Mache wheel, and then decorate it. We also make a micro wheel of the macro wheel to represent the Seasons and place this on or before our Altar, it is decorated with all the beauty of each Season and as the yearly seasons change we turn our micro wheel to be in balance (As Above, So Below, As Within, So Without).

It is great to also have a Wheel in the form of a Seasonal Wreath to place on our front door to distinguish and let all know that we are celebrating the Seasonal Round of that time of the year. It lets then known how connected we are without actually let them know we are Wiccans, Wicces or Pagans.

Wine or Fruit Juice

At the end of the Esbat, Sabbat or Magickal Ritual we always share with the God and Goddess a toast to them and each other with our Ceremonial Wine Chalice filled with either red or white wine (depending on the ritual), I prefer Port (white or red) as it is real heavy and warming especially in the colder months. But during the Winter Season I love making a warm spicy mead in the small Cauldron. All you need is some wine (red or white) some fruit and spices and honey, warm them over the Hearth Fire and partake at the end of the night.

This adds a great deal of Magick in making and preparing in the Magick Circle. But there are many Covens who prefer not to have alcohol in the Circle, so they make their own Fruit Juice to have instead of Wine. Also if you have children attending this means that they can also partake of the Toast to the Gods and each other. But do not buy shop bought juices make your own, this way you can have a different blend each gathering. Maybe even get a different member to make it each month.

If you know a wine maker you may be able to get them to help you make a ceremonial wine, but you are picking the grapes ritually and blessing them before the process of fermentation. You can then also make special labels for them and sell them at your Festivals or just store them away to a later date.

Wicces Hat

I have only worn my Wicce Hat on very few occasions. As they were a ceremonial object that were used at special Magickal Rituals. But let me take you back to the beginning of hats, and we have always had a history of pointed hats from the tapering Hennins, the Cone Hat with a trail of light flowing fabric, which were favoured by many medieval noblewomen through to the soft Phrygian Caps that were adopted by the French revolutionaries (and please do not forget the famous Smurfs). But throughout history there have been a great number of different style pointy hats.

But the earliest representation of this ancient conical headdress was uncovered when they found three mummified women found in the region of Subeshi in China, who were known as the "Witches of Subeshi", they were famous for covering their long flowing hair with these large funnel shaped hats of black felt and allowing their long black locks to flow out through the open end of the cone.

But anthropologists are not exactly sure when conical hats actually became associated with Magick and Wicces and sorcery. It is strange but most medieval artworks of Wicces drew them as naked and hair flowing quite free and long, as though dancing like the flames of a fire. It was not until the 1600's that artists pictured Heretics and spell-casters in these common conical shaped hats. Then again, they were shown in the 1700's but in children's story books that also illustrated fantastical creatures, supernatural tales of Magick and Sorcery in these large conical hats worn by hagged old Crones with big noses and hairy faces. It was from this debasement that European artists fuelled this image and began to modify the beautiful appearance of Wicces as these ugly old crones with large black capes and pointed hats. They always made the point erect and stiff as to symbolise an evocative way to represent dark magic. This imagery travelled far across the globe and started to appear on postcards from the American Colonies. Legendary figures of Mother Goose and La Bafana-the Italian Mother was so deranged by the death of her infant, that she was said to fly through the night air on a Broom delivering nice gifts to good children and lumps of coal to bad children. She was also given the Pointed Conical hat like Mother Goose.

The Victorian era also saw these hats used in storybooks and during the Salem Witch Trials a large tall black negro was pictured with a high crowned hat representing the devil and the dark forces. But there is another theory that pairs the Witches with their peaked conical hats from the anti-Quaker prejudice. As they were a minority sect in colonial America, the Quakers were believed to consort with demons and devils and dabbled in Wiccecraft. This is when they were pictured with the conical hats as Wicces and Sorcerers.

But in mid European Countries like Germany the Wicces Hat symbolised something far more Magickal and real. The rim of the hat represented the Magick Circle the outer circle and the inner circle. The Cone represented the Mystical Magickal Cone of Power that Wicces of the raised within their Magick Circle as a spiral of Power going up and sometimes coming down. This was traditionally done by The Sacred Circle Dance with chant and music to raise great Power traditionally on the Full Moon.

Tools of the
Priesthood

The Second Degree – Priest/ess - The Temple of Sol - The Sun – The Horned God

Boline - Love, **Wand** - Will Power, **Chalice** – Fertility, **Tabard** - Shield of Faith, **Cloak** - Power of Invisibility, **3 Magic Cords** - Sacred Space and Healing.

The Altar

East Altar

The Eastern Altar is placed in the East and is dedicated to all that this realm represents, the rising Sun, the Air Element, winged creatures such as Sylphides and Faeries, birds, flying insects etc. It was also the doorway to the mind, of the intellect and the Portal to the Great Library of Thoth where all the knowledge of the world was hidden and learnt by the Priest and Priestess Isarum of Thoth, for this ancient Temple Library had all the knowledge of the world, filled with parchments from great philosophers, astrologers, mathematicians, alchemists, astronomers, Magick, medicines, navigation, maps, sorcery, Wiccecraft, occult sciences, and a million other forms of knowledge.

The altar was simple with a blue and gold altar cloth with a rising Sun painted on it. On the altar in the centre was the Thurible for burning the Incense. An Air Wand, feather, bowl of Incense, a rattle, and a flute.

South Altar

The Southern Altar is placed in the south and is dedicated to all that this realm represents, the noon day Sun, the Fire Element, crawling creatures such as Salamanders and Dragons, snakes, beetles, etc. It was also the doorway to the Heart, of the Emotional and the Portal to the Great Temple of Aset where the Holy of Holies was created and hidden from all but the Isarum Priests and Priestesses of Thoth, for this ancient Temple concealed the Heart of Hearts which was the Light and Love of the Sun God Ra.

The altar was simple with a red and gold altar cloth with a noon day Sun painted on it. On the altar in the centre was the Spirit Flame which is the Light of the Sun, and illumines all other Lights in the Temple, there is also an Athame ritual Dagger known as the Dragons Tooth, a Fire Wand, bowl of charcoal, a drum, and a Staff.

West Altar

The Western Altar is placed in the west and is dedicated to all that this realm represents, the Setting Sun, the Moon, the Water Element, swimming creatures such as dolphins and Undines, mermaids, fish, crabs, etc. It is also the doorway to Magick, of the ebb and flow of all Magick and the Portal to the Great Temple of Aset where the Holy of Holies was created and hidden from all but the Isarum Priests and Priestesses of Thoth, for this ancient Temple concealed the Cauldron of Creation and the Holy Grail of Immortality which was the Life and Love of the Moon Goddess Aset.

The altar was simple with a green and silver altar cloth with a setting Sun painted on it. On the altar in the centre was the Chalices one for Water in the west and one for Wine in the east which is the Life Blood of all life, and illumines empowers and charges all Magick, there is also a dish of pure water, a Cauldron, Water Wand, Aspergilla's, a large shell like a Conch for summoning and Awakening all.

North Altar

The Northern Altar is placed in the north and is dedicated to all that this realm represents, Midnight and the Moon, the Earth Element, standing creatures such as trees and plants, Picts, Gnomes, herbs, walking animals, etc. It is also the doorway to the Living Earth and Nature, altar to the Goddess and God, of the ebb and flow of all that is Physical and the Portal to the Great Temple of our Ancestors where we can awaken and connect.

The altar was simple with amber, green and silver altar cloth with a Moon painted on it. On the altar in the centre is the Sacred Pentacle which is the key to the ancient Mysteries of the Epagomenes, and key to all the Gateways of the Magick Circle and awakens and empowers all Truth, there is also a dish of pure rock salt, a Book of Shadows, Earth Wand, dish of earth, a bunch of herbs, you can also have your two altar candles representing the Goddess and God or actual statues of your Goddess and God.

Central Altar

The Central Altar is placed in the Centre of the Magick Circle and is dedicated to all that this realm represents, the Divine Feminine and Divine Masculine as One, it is symbolic of the Spirit Realm. The altar is bare, but represents the Moon and the Sun as One, fire and ice as one, male and female as one, life and death as one, light and dark as one, fear and hope as one, love and hate as one. This realm represents the Invisible within the Visible. The Portal to the Great Temple of Aset and Asar where the Holy of Holies was created and hidden from all but the Isarum Priests and Priestesses of Thoth.

The altar was simple with a black, gold and silver Altar Cloth with a hexagram painted on it. On the altar in the centre is nothing as it is kept bare out of respect.

The Boline

The Boline is a Traditional Tool of the Wicce and I have two, one which is only used, within the Magick Circle for cutting, etching, carving, and creating. It has an antler handle and a strong steel blade.

This one I purchased from a store and use it specifically for the ceremonial cutting of my Herbs for ritual use. It is a small sickle or scythe that is used during harvest time. The Boline does not seem to be mentioned much in the Wiccan world, but is of great importance, especially if you are a Ritualist who wishes to carve candles, make statues of wax or clay, or as in my second one ceremonially harvest your Magickal Herbs and plants. This is a Feminine tool with its Crescent shape, where the Athame is masculine.

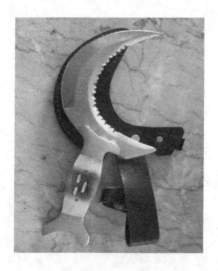

Sickle

This is my Sickle with a stag antler attached to the end, we use it for our farm plants at Harvest time. The Ceremonial Sickles are used at Death and Birth Festivals, that celebrate Life and Death such as Samhain. They are only used by Elders or Crones who have the years to understand and truly appreciate life and the journey that we all take. They are symbols of the Harvest, so they are on display at Harvest festivals but covered with many harvest flowers and fruit.

The Chalice of Water

The Chalice starts out as a lowly goblet for everyday drinking, but when taken and consecrated in a Magick Circle, which is then used only for Ritual as it becomes a Ceremonial Magickal Chalice. The picture of my Chalice above is an 18th Century Chalice from Rome and is engraved with all the Cup Runes around the perimeter. This Chalice is for Ceremonial Wine. There are two Chalices, which are needed in the Magick Circle, One for Water for Blessings, and one for Wine, for giving Thanks and Offering to the Gods.

The Chalice represents the Womb of the Goddess, and because both water and wine are classed as the "Blood of the Earth", they are important in all our Rituals. The Wine Chalice represents the Goddess, and all within it are Blessings from Her, even water which is the most impure substance on our planet, and which is what every species needs, is a must as it is the vital source of life as we know it. 70% of our bodies are made up of water, and when we mix it with consecrated sea salt, (which is the purest substance found on our planet) when they are mingled it becomes Holy Water. Water that is used to cleanse, purify and banish all negative influences. We should even anoint ourselves in the Magick Circle with the Consecrated Water. The High Priestess always takes a sip of the mingled Salt and Water, to purify herself, in readiness to receive/perceive the Goddess.

The Wine Chalice, with red wine or Port in it also represents the sacredness of the Goddess. It is used in all ceremonies associated with Fertility. And when it is co-joined with the Athame (representing the Horned God/Phallus) represents impregnation of Divine Union being called "The Great Rite", and from here all who partake are blessed by the unification of Goddess and God, and Fertility takes place, such as blessings and new beginnings.

The actual Blessing of the Wine in the Chalice is one of the most SACRED OF ALL RITUALS IN THE CRAFT and should always be respected with silence and contemplation when it occurs. Visualising the concept of Goddess and God becoming One for the betterment of all Life, so whenever in a Magick Circle, and the wine is being Blessed, please enter the silence, focus and pay respect, as it is an act of Ceremonial Magic at its Highest Level. Even though some things may happen within the Magick Circle that you do not understand, always honour and respect the Ritual as a Mystery, and in time through your respect, dedication and devoutness, you will gain the Insight to understand the Sacred Knowledge of the Wicces, and the Mysteries of the Goddess and God.

This Chalice is used during Large Festivals with large numbers of people available as it holds 4 litres of wine. It has etched around the outer rim the "History of Avalon and Merlin".

This Shell Chalice above, was made for me in Indonesia, it is set in sterling silver and encrusted with precious gemstones. This is my Water Chalice that is used only on special occasions.

Conch Shell Horn

The Ceremonial Conch Shell Horn is something that I use at festivals to Summon the Elementals and to Awaken the Earth. The Conch has been an ancient tribal item where Shamans whispered their prayers into the shells and when blown would send their prayers to the Ancient Ones, the Gods and Goddesses of old. Both the Conch and Triton Shells have been used in many cultures since the dawn of man. They have always been for sending messages to the Gods and to the Ancestors.

They are also used as a Blessing on all those in attendance. The Conch when used correctly is a combination of all the Elements, Earth – the solid form; Air – the element that carried the message off to the Gods; Fire the sacred breath from the heart that has the warmth of fire and emotion; and the ebb and flow of the tides of the oceans that helped to form this Magickal Tool.

In ancient Greece and even in modern times the Priestess blows the horn to the four directions to thanks the Gods and Goddess for the harvest of grapes, then they do a traditional dance barefoot in the large vat of grapes to break them down to form the first of the harvest to be used as spiritual wine and as an offering of the blood of the Earth.

Coronet

The Coronet is a silver circlet that is worn around the head as a symbol of being a Priest or Priestess. The Wicce does not wear a Coronet as such but may wear just a circlet of silver with no etchings or designs at all, the plainer the better.

The Priest wears a silver coronet with a Triangle of Silver around a piece of Lapis Lazuli which opens his Third Eye to the Mysteries of the Craft, or he can have just an oval shaped silver plate to symbolise the honoured of the Great Divine Feminine. As for the Priestess she wears a coronet with a crescent Moon at the front, and if feeling elaborate can get a Rainbow Moonstone set into it.

A High Priest wears a Gold Coronet with a Hexagram at the front set with a Ruby or a Garnet. The High Priestess has a Silver Coronet with the Horns of Hathor, or the Breasts of the Goddess set with a Rainbow Moonstone or a Diamond.

My Coronet has several attachments which can be clipped into it, I had it especially made for me years ago, it has a Silver Crescent Moon; Horns of Hathor with Lapis Lazuli in the centre; Triple Moon Symbol with a Rainbow Moonstone set in the Middle; a Silver Pentagram with a Star Sapphire set in the middle; and my Coven Symbol in silver with 13 diamonds set into it.

Didgeridoo

As part of our honouring the ancestors and the Spirits of our land in Australia, we traditionally use the Didgeridoo to sound creating a Sacred Space around our Magick Circle, it is used to send a wave of vibrations to awaken the Earth and its ancestors, and to honour and thank them for the knowledge given to us.

My High Priest – Asherah, was one of the most spiritual and dedicated people I had ever met, we had been friends and Craft colleagues working together in our Covens for over 30 years. He brought balance into my Covens with his skills as a Meditator, Crystal Worker, and knowledge of music and the Aboriginal Didgeridoo. We never used the Ceremonial Sword in our ritual much as we kept it for High Magick and for Ritual Initiations. Instead when we entered the Magick Circle he would present the Didgeridoo as though it was his Staff, and then by doing sacred breathing into it, would trace it out around the Circle to create our sacred space and welcome the ancestral spirits of the land.

This connected us to the original people of Australia and to its Magick and to Nature. It brought a certain amount of Grounding for us all as well and taught us to listen to what the Earth was saying to us.

Drum

The Drum also has its place in our covens as it connects us to the Heart of Hearts, for in Magick we believe that all thinks are linked not only by the Universal Divine Light of the Mother and Father that we call God and Goddess but also each heart beats in rhythm with the Goddess and God as well and with the beat of the Living Earth and all life within and on her.

There are a variety of types of drums and it matters not what sort of drum you have but they are connected to the Earth, with their deep base sound that vibrates and awakens our own senses. At festivals we usually have a couple of people with their drums who welcome all the guests by Drumming them into our Circle, this awakens their chakras and Prepares them for the Magick that is ahead, it helps to bring everyone into sync each with the other.

We have a large Festival Drum, but I prefer the individual Shamanic Medicine Drum, as I have taught people how to make them through ceremony and to birth them into Truth by breathing life into them and making them a Power Energy. There are Traditionally several sounds that represent the Elements that can be used singly or as a whole with others each using their Elemental rhythm. 1 beat – equals the Air Element and the Mind; 2 beats – is the Fire Element and the Heart; 3 beats – is the Water Element and of the Soul; 4 beats – is the Earth and of the Physical; 5 beats – is the Spirit and of the Spirit.

Red Cotton Reel

Red Cotton (real cotton) is used in Initiations for the 1st degree level which is that of the Wicce. It is for taking the sacred measurement of the Wicce during the ceremony. I prefer strong linen cotton as it is easier to handle. When the Initiate is Measured, 1. A knot is tied at the end, 2. then there measurement is taken by measuring their height, (then a knot tied in the cotton). 3. Then their arm span, (then a knot tied in the cotton). 4. Then there chest (then a knot tied in the cotton). 5. Then there head (then a knot tied in the cotton). 6. Then there waist (then a knot tied in the cotton). 7. Then around both ankles (then a knot tied in the cotton). 8. Then from their wrist to the tip of their middle finger (then a knot tied in the cotton). Then a knot tied at the other end. Making 9 knots in total similar to the Ladder of the Goddess.

Red cotton is also used in Binding Ceremonies, as long as it is Consecrated and not used for anything outside the Magick Circle.

Robe

Each level within the working Coven has a specific coloured Robe that is worn for all Magickal and Spiritual work, especially within the Magick Circle.

- For the Seeker it should be an Earth colour such as Green or Brown, but never black. The length should be made above ankle so as to not trip and if possible have a small slit at the bottom of both sides of the Robe to give more room for when you are Dancing or Rising Energy in the Magick Circle.
- For the Wicce it should be white with a green trim to represent purity and life.
- For the Priest it should be white with blue trim to represent the masculine Power of Creativity, and the Priestess should wear white with burgundy trim representing the feminine Power of Creativity.
- For the High Priest he should wear white with gold trim to represent the Divine Masculine, and for the High Priestess she should wear white with silver trim to represent the Divine Feminine.
- The Man in Black should wear a black robe with Gold trim to represents the Lord of Shadows and the Maiden should wear a black robe with silver trim to represent the Maiden of the Mysteries.

You can have a hood if you so desire, that is a personal choice, they are sometimes great when it is cold, and for when you are meditating. The sleeves should be loose but not swinging free, as large sleeves get in the way and when reaching across your Altar for tools, they catch everything and cause more problems than their good looks. I believe we should each have a summer Robe (lighter fabric to keep us cool on those summer nights) and a winter robe (heavier fabric to keep us warm).

If you want to make it a little more elaborate, don't as this takes away the look of commonality and uniform appearance within the Circle, as at this level ego has no place. And that is what new Seekers love to be noticed, so hold back the glamour and keep it simplified as it is a working uniform for Ritual and Magick not as a glamour aspect of the obvious.

Tabard

A Tabard serves several purposes, firstly it keeps the Robe protected and clean. Secondly it keeps your front and back warm; thirdly it distinguishes between the ranks when we do not wear Capes.

- For the Wicce the Tabard is a Green Velvet with either silver or gold trim depending on whether you are a male or a female. At the chest centre is a Labyrinth of the Goddess Seal or the Seal of the Wicce which is a Gold Triangle inside a Silver Circle.

When our Covens are at open festivals they all look unified and quite smart, with Wicces all wearing their white and green with their symbols of silver triangle inside a gold circle, Priesthood wearing burgundy and white with the seal of the Priesthood being an inverted gold Pentagram inside a silver circle, and High Priesthood wearing white and silver and black and gold with a seal of the High Priesthood being an interlaced Hexagram incorporating an upward pointing triangle and an inverted gold triangle . The Arch Priest and Arch Priestess can wear whatever they desire but traditionally purple and silver for the Arch Priestess and purple and gold for the Arch Priest wearing their seal of 40 stars in a circle.

Wands

The Ceremonial Healing Wand

This Wand above I designed, and it was made by Shankari, the famous jeweller, and has my mother and grandmothers hair in it, alongside my own. It is made of solid silver and decorated with Angel Hair (Rutilated Quartz) emeralds, pearls, moonstone, and clear quartz. It is used for Invoking/Evoking spirit energies, for Healing, and more importantly Invoking the Matriarchs of my family.

Wands Traditionally are made from different things the simplest and best is the Natural Branch from a tree (that has never touched the ground, as it must never be Earthed). Rose wood Wands for Love; Pine and Cedar for Strength: Oak for Deity Invoking: plus, many more. It depends on personal choice, but the more elaborate does not necessarily mean the better. I have several Wands. The Wand of Isis for Egyptian Workings: Engraved Ceremonial Wand for Ceremonial Magick: Acorn Tipped Wand for Invoking/Evoking the Goddess and God in Wiccan Ceremonies: Pine cone tipped Wand for Full Moons and Festivals again for Deity: No matter what the Wand always remember it is an extension of yourself, and you must always be PROPERLY PREPARED.

Tools of
the High
Priesthood

The Third Degree – High Priest/ess – Temple of Astrum – The Stars – Goddess and God as One

Scourge – Time; **Sword** – Infinity; **Bell** – Harmony; **Cauldron** – Inspiration; **Sceptre** - Control.

Ceremonial Bell

- **The ceremonial Bell** - seems to be used less and less in Traditional Covens, but is of importance due to the fact that it signifies that when rang at the beginning of a Ritual, for all to quieten and ready themselves. It is also used to Awaken certain energies or Elemental energies that are welcomed to the Magick Circle. We use the Ceremonial Bell to Toll the Circle and to Awaken its energies it is rang 11 times to each Quarter. These days there are so many beautiful elaborate bells that can be used. Just remember that all Magickal Tools must be Consecrated and used for a specific purpose.
- **Buddhist Bell -** A traditional Buddhist bell that is used by many because it signifies calm, concentration, Attunement, and readiness.
- **Silver Pentagram Bell -** This is a pretty little Bell with a Pentacle etched on it, used by Wicces in their Ceremonies. It is cute and easy to obtain from many Wiccan and new Age shops.
- **Crescent Luna Bell -** Is the ceremonial bell that I use in my Magick Circle it has been engraved with the Seal of the Breasts of the Goddess, atop with a Crescent Moon? Again this can be purchased easily too.

- **Hathor Temple Bell –** This lovely little bell I found in a store many years ago, and use it for Egyptian ceremonies, it has a deep tone which is quite Earthy.

Besom

The traditional Wicces Broomstick or preferably called the Besom, is used by the HPs to sweep and cleanse the Sacred Space prior to the casting of the Magick Circle. It is done in a Widdershins manner around the Magick Circle to cleanse and remove all negativity in a Deosil fashion to attract and draw in all positivity.

The Traditional Besom has many meanings throughout history, the Negro Slaves adopted it as a ceremonial sweeping of the path ahead of a new married couple, so that their path ahead is cleared. But Traditionally the Besom was just a decoy, it was a distraction from the genuine purpose of what lied hidden underneath the brushes. In ancient times many were too poor to have swords or the such to defend themselves, so they learnt the skill and art of using a Staff. It was this Staff traditionally called a ROAD (ro-ad). It was their ceremonial item as well as one for protection. In these times when many were poor they used what was readily at hand and gifted by Nature. To conceal the purpose of this Staff they tie brush around the bottom to signify just a normal household broom. It is used for other ceremonial uses as well, but this is only for High Magick by the High Priesthood. When placed outside your door in this upright fashion means that all is safe within. If upside down or on the ground then it means there is danger within, do not enter.

My Besom pictured was decorated by my High Priesthood, and they all added their names around the spiral of the Staff.

Cauldrons

The Cauldron is a Tool that no Coven should be without, but is not completely necessary in the workings of every Wicce, as it is used for those into herbal remedies and Potions. We have several Cauldrons that we use;

1. One is for toxic workings, other words for using ingredients that are harmful except for specific Magickal workings and Spellcraft.
2. Another small one for herbal workings, to make ceremonial potions and lotions for ritual work and for healings.
3. Another large clean one for Festivals as a stew pot for all to bring something to throw in for Supper and Feasting. Whatever the purpose they are handy to have, but can be quite expensive for the genuine working Cauldron.

Circle of Stars – Necklace of the High Priestess

Traditionally when a new Coven hives off to form a new coven, they may take any existing Coven members who wish to move across to the new Coven. But before that is done a Ceremonial "Necklace of the Stars" is hand made by the original coven members to hand to the New High Priestess. This is Traditionally made from acorns, but can be of any local nuts that are in season and in your area. This is a circlet of 40 Acorns with a silver bead or a small wooden bead in between each of them, (make sure that the items you use are all natural, no plastic etc).

My beautiful Acorn Necklace was made by my first Coven in the late 70's. I supplied the Acorns from my Oak tree, and had sterling silver beads made in Bali by a jeweller friend of mine, I also placed Garnet beads either side of the silver beads and used resin to coat all the Acorns. On the cap of the Acorn which was glued onto the Nut, I also glued a small ruby. I still have and use this circlet on special occasions, and shall donate this item to the Buckland Museum of Witchcraft and Magick in the US, along with many of my beautiful relics and tools.

The Acorns are divided between each member evenly if possible. Each Acorn is charged and blessed by each member with a certain quality, so that together they embrace all that a High Priestess needs to be the best HPs that she can be. Each Acorn is charged individually with the following Powers and Abilities:

1. The Power to Listen
2. The Power of Unconditional Love
3. The Power of Courage
4. The Power of Individuality
5. The Power of Silence
6. The Power of Intuition
7. The Power of Focus
8. The Power of Awareness
9. The Power of Meditation
10. The Power of Healing
11. The Power of Abundance
12. The Power of Protection
13. The Power of Humour
14. The Power of Skill
15. The Power of Virtue
16. The Power of the Feminine
17. The Power of Imagination
18. The Power of Transformation
19. The Power of Truth
20. The Power of Innocence
21. The Power of Nurturing
22. The Power of Grounding
23. The Power of Communication
24. The Power of Quickening
25. The Power of Balance

26. The Power of Commitment
27. The Power of Sensuality
28. The Power of Dreams
29. The Power of Mystery
30. The Power over Darkness
31. The Power of Harmony
32. The Power of Gathering
33. The Power of Strength
34. The Power of Endurance
35. The Power of Knowledge
36. The Power of Aspiration
37. The Power of Wisdom
38. The Power of Time and Space
39. The Power of Magick
40. The Power of Empowerment.

I also have another for special occasions which was a gift from His Holiness the Dalai Lama, (pictured above) it was his Prayer Beads used for meditation and was made from 40 Amber beads and had also carvings of Jade Buddhas in it with gold tassels at the end.

Coronet of the Priestess and Priest

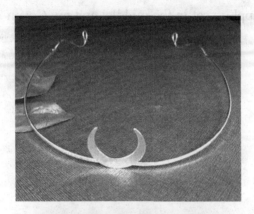

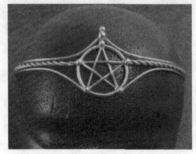

The Coronet is a silver circlet that is worn around the head as a symbol of being a Priest or Priestess. The Wicce does not wear a Coronet as such but may wear just a circlet of silver with no etchings or designs at all, the plainer the better.

The Priest wears a silver coronet with a Triangle of Silver around a piece of Lapis Lazuli which opens his Third Eye to the Mysteries of the Craft, or he can have just an oval shaped silver plate to symbolise the honouring of the Great Divine Feminine. As for the Priestess she wears a coronet with a crescent Moon at the front, and if feeling elaborate can get a Rainbow Moonstone set into it.

A High Priest wears a Gold Coronet with a Hexagram at the front set with a Ruby or a Garnet. The High Priestess has a Silver Coronet with the Horns of Hathor, or the Breasts of the Goddess set with a Rainbow Moonstone or a Diamond.

My Coronet has several attachments which can be clipped into it, I had it especially made for me years ago, it has a Silver Crescent Moon; Horns of Hathor with Lapis Lazuli in the centre; Triple Moon Symbol with a Rainbow Moonstone set in the Middle; a Silver Pentagram with a Star Sapphire set in the middle; and my Coven Symbol in silver with 13 diamonds set into it.

The Scourge

Of all the many Tools in Wicca none is more controversial than the Scourge, the Wicces symbol of Power. Originally it was called the Flail, which separated the wheat from the Chaff, but like many things it has been bastardized down to its present use a whip, a cat of nine tails, etc. It also has some involvement with sexual perversions by the ignorant minds both within and without the Craft. But the true purpose is its original meaning of separating the bad from the good as in the wheat. But on a deeper level, a Spiritual level, it is always used gently for the symbolism of ridding the Initiate of their negativity and awakening their positivity. Many old Monasteries and Convents used this Tool as a symbol of fear and domination, also for chastisement and the gaining of Sight through flagellation. But in the Wicca, it is used for Purification and Enlightenment. Only the older more Traditional Covens use this Tool, as many are not truly aware of its meanings and significance. The High priest or High Priestess makes the Scourge in a ceremonial way, as it is never used by anyone under the rank of High Priest or High Priestess.

The Scourge is made from leather; with the handle being wrapped, attached are eight tails each with 5 knots, totally forty, the number of birth. This Tool is described fully in my next book. But as Douglas Hill comments: "The ordeal of flagellation seems very important in the face of the fantastic life-span of purification or therapeutic uses of a whip. Flagellations are thought by many to be sexual perversions, but even the devotee's, claiming that the mild birching's they endure are intended to stimulate the circulation and not the libido".

Staff

The Ceremonial Staff is used by the High Priest or High Priestess, it was traditionally used in self-defence and for assisting on long walks. Many travellers also tied bags of their belongings on the end of the staff as an easy way to carry them. But the Staff used within Magick was of great significance as it was used as a large form of a Ceremonial Magick Wand.

It could channel the energies of the Magus or Crone to do their bidding. In old movies you see the Priests turning Staff's into Serpents as a Familiar to attack or to defend. The Staff has many purposes and is also used to formally cut a perimeter around the Magick circle to create a Barrier to keep all harm at bay, and to contain all Power within. Children were taught from an early age how to yield a Staff for self-defence by using it to channel their power and energy with an extended length to keep attackers at bay, and eventually were shown the Magickal significance when they were old enough.

Ceremonial Sword

The Ceremonial Sword is only used in working full Covens or Churches, by the High Priesthood and the Man in Black or Maiden who are the Principal Ritualists under the High Priest and High Priestess. It is a significant Tool of the Higher levels of Magick and is used in the swearing of the oath, discipline, severing bonds, releasing Binding Spells, and also in the Blessing of a hand Fasting.

The Ceremonial Magicians Magick Sword

The Sword is the active Weapon of Fire and hence its action is hot and energetic – *"The Phallus of Living Flame"*. Three is the Sword's number because activity requires three Elements – the actor, the action and the object acted upon.

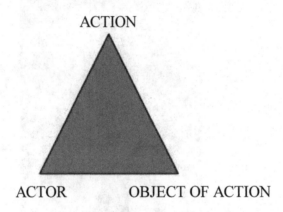

ACTION

ACTOR   OBJECT OF ACTION

Thus, the Red Triangle – Tejas – is Fire.

The blade of the Sword is Iron or Steel, the martial metal. One side of the blade bears the inscription:

SHALOM – (Peace) painted as –
in black on a white background
and framed with gold. The other
side is inscribed in white.

CO-ACH – (Force) painted as
on black and framed with gold.

The inscriptions are close to the hilt leaving the rest of the blade a bare polished metal colour. For coagulating, the SHALOM side is used and for dissolving the CO-ACH side.

The quillons, or crosspiece, of the Magickal Sword is made from two crescents of Silver, the watery aspect of the Sword to contain and direct the fiery energy. Double Crescents also emphasize the duality of the Sword's potential actions. On the crescents are inscribed the names of the Sephiroth of RUACH as shown in the diagram.

The grip is a seven-coiled serpent of copper. Seven is the number of Earth; hence this is an Earth Serpent. With its head resting on the quill ions on the SHALOM side, the serpent winds Deosil into head and tail on the SHALOM side, however, on the other side just the seven coils are visible.

The pommel of the Sword is a hollow silver ball containing Mercury which screws onto the tang to hold the Sword together (SEE DIAGRAM). Two more silver balls containing Mercury are attached between the Crescents. These three balls represent Air, being three in number since this is the numerical attribution of the Sword.

For this reason, also, the Sword is three feet in length from end to end.

The Sword is a macrocosmic Weapon, but for microcosmic work an Athame similar in design can be made. A good overall length for the Athame was explained before, but usually 30 centimetres.

Hebrew Names for the Sword and Chalice:

נֶצַח — Netzach

הוד — Hod

תפ**אר**ת — Tiphareth

גְבוּרָה — Geburah

חסד — Chesed

רְפָאֵל — Raphael

מִיכָאֵל — Michael

גַבְרִיאֵל — Gabriel

אוּרִיאֵל — Auriel

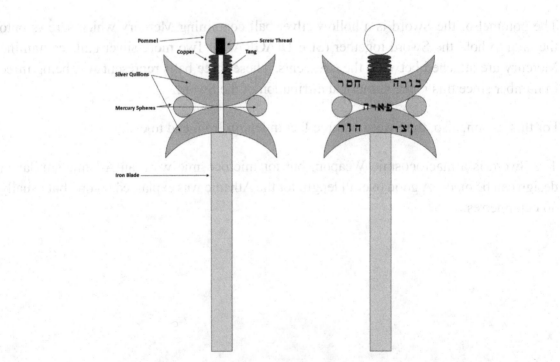

The Magick Sword of the High Priest and High Priestess

The Magick Sword is only handled by the High Priestess, High Priest or the Maiden and Man in Black, and they must all be of sufficient levels in the Priesthood. When I see Covens of untrained knowledge using the Sword, I get annoyed. In ancient times it was forbidden for most people to possess a Sword, so they were in short supply, usually just one to a Coven, and usually held by the leader and at times wielded by the Man in Black, the Guardian of the Coven, or as I affectionately call them "The Coven Cop".

I had my traditional sword made by an armourist, a professional who could make medieval armour and weaponry. I gave him the design and he made it perfectly. The length of the Sword should be from the ground to your waste.

The hilt design is of "The Breasts of the Goddess" or better known as the "Triple Moon" which is two crescent moons back to back with a solid disk in the centre. These represent the New Moon, Full Moon and Dark Moon. Or specifically the Maiden, Mother and Crone. We made these out of solid brass with a bound leather studded handle with the Coven Pentacle and Seal of my Family at the end of the hilt.

It must be kept away and wrapped in pure silk, I had always had ours placed back into a special handmade wooden case that I used for when I travelled so as to take it with me.

The Ceremonial Wand

Traditionally is Magick there are several types of Wands, as each tradition or system of belief differs in their analogies. You have the Ceremonial Wand, the Ritual Wand, the Wicces Wand, the Magick Wand, the Elemental Wand, the Magicians Wand, the Celestial Wand and the Healing Wand. Every single one of them is used for different reasons and purposes. But Traditionally the Wand is the Tool of Air, the intrinsic Element in which Fire, Water and Earth interact.

- **CEREMONIAL or MAGICIANS WAND:** Alchemists call the Air Principle *"Prime Movement"* and Alchemists Gold' representing the beginning and end of the Great Work - which is the same point. As the Serpent eats his own tail, the tail and the head become the same point, like the point at which a Circle "begins" and "ends". The Circle is thus an Air symbol, as also is the number ONE, the first number; so too is YOD, the seed-shaped letter.

  A most useful macrocosmic Wand is the Lotus Wand. The Lotus Flower is the Yoni, while the stem is the umbilical cord connecting all things to the Source of Life with a vital cord. Three whorls of petals, the calyx and centre, make up the Lotus flower. An outer ring of eight petals represents Earth, and Water, in each of the four worlds; similarly, eight petals in the next ring (going towards the centre) are for Fire and Air. Ten petals of the inner ring answer to the Sephiroth of the Kabbalistic Tree of Life and calyx has four sepals for the four Elementals. Air is the centre.

  The petals are made from a thin sheet of silver that is thick enough to hold the petals *'shape'* but sufficiently thin enough to produce a "rustling" sound when the Wand moves. Either the petals can be cut individually, or they can be cut in rings (of 8, 8 and 10 or perhaps 4, 4, 4, 4, 5, and 5). The two sets of 8 petals are painted olive green outside with five veins on each leaf (for the four Elements plus Akasha, the fifth Element or Spirit). The inner surface of these petals is left bare silver or painted very bright gloss white. The ring of ten petals is silver or gloss white on both sides while the calyx is vivid orange inside and out. The centre is gold, conveniently a gold-plated screw perhaps, to fix the lotus flower to its stem. In accordance with its numerical attribution, ONE, the overall length of the Lotus Wand is one unit (one yard or meter is best).

TWO RINGS OF 8 PETALS

White inside and olive green outside - 5 veins on each petal.

INNER RING OF 10 PETALS
White on both sides

CALYX OF 4 ORANGE SEPALS
Centre of God

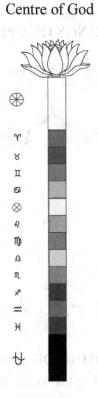

The Lotus stem is a wooden rod painted in coloured bands, that is hollow and has a central core of Mercury, with copper around the outside and a silver disc on the bottom. At the top of the stem is the widest band, white in colour and painted with the symbol (spirit). Slightly narrower, the black band is at the bottom and bears the symbol (Earth). Stretching between are even narrower bands, twelve in number, bearing the zodiacal spectrum of colours and symbols. Note: the order in which the four Elements appear in the colour of the Lotus stem.

In use, the appropriate coloured band is held to correspond to the nature of your work. This makes the Lotus Wand a very finely tuned, versatile Weapon. When working with the four Elements blue, red, green or yellow is used. For Spiritual work, white is appropriate or for more physical work - black. Zodiacal attributions and Imagination will also help you to choose the most effective band for your work. Try to keep the Lotus flower above the level of the stem when using the Wand since inverting the Wand tends to reverse the affects you seek.

- **THE RITUAL WAND**: A Wand for microcosmic use can be made from a hollow rod of wood bamboo which is convenient - one foot long (including tips). At each end are metal tips and a piece of wire (gold ideally, but copper will serve) connects them, which is wound around the Wand clockwise, (I use copper wire as it is readily available and easy to work with and not so expensive.) The base of the Wand has a hole drilled into the end and your blood on a cotton wool bud placed inside then sealed with beeswax. There should be metal-to-metal contact from end to end. Making caps for the top and bottom of the Wand is easy, just cut two circles of copper plate to fit and then mould and bend to fit securely over the tips. The back end of the wand should be flat where the tip of the Wand is rounded.

The tips should be roughly spherical and either gold, gold plated or copper. As copper is also a conductor for energy especially as an electro-magnetic polarised energy that can attract or repel. Round brass curtain ends with thin gold plating are quite effective as well. After plating one tip should be painted black and one white to induce polarity. The shaft is sky blue and could be painted with Sigils or talismans for Air.

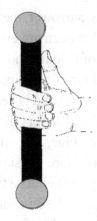

- **THE CELESTIAL WAND:** Has many uses as well but is mainly used for connecting with celestial Beings especially the Shining Ones, the Angels that connect with us and teach and guides us in our spiritual endeavours along the path to finding our Divine Truth.

   The perfect timber for this is a long piece of Bamboo as it is hollow, it must be from the crook of your elbow to the tip of your middle finger. Again, a swab of blood in the back end of the Wand and a Celestial Crystal or better still a piece of Meteorite to be placed at the tip of the Wand. The Wand should be dipped in silver or chrome. After it has dried and hardened you then add the crystal to the tip, making sure that it is secure.

   When using the Celestial Wand, you should be in a hallowed placed such as your Magick Circle. We never demand or summon them, we must always be polite and ask for their company and assistance. Make sure that what you ask is not of greed or of something that time can take care of itself. When thanking them and making an offer it must be of your time and service and not an object, it must be of self-sacrifice in the giving, as this is the only thing they accept.

- **A HEALING WAND:** Is traditionally by individual choice, your Wand must represent you and your Truth as a soul spiritual Wicce. You must take an object of the Earth that has been absorbed and created by Mother Nature as a gift to you. It must have electro-magnetic qualities. But the most important part of this Healing Wand, is you! You must be TRUE to yourself and your abilities as a Wicce, and know that you are only the object of Healing, and it is the Universal Divine Light Force of Goddess/God and All That Is that is the Power behind your Wand.

We cannot truly heal if we need Healing, we must first heal our own wounds physically, mentally, astrally, psychically and spiritually before we can become a true instrument of the Divine Spirit and assist in Healing of another.

Healing is about connecting, absorbing and working with the Magick of the Universe to either remove, or heal what needs to be corrected by working with Nature, and changing it through one's Will-power.

- **THE ELEMENTAL WANDS:** Elemental Wands are created by their own Element, infused by all the other Elements to a lesser degree. Such as the **Earth Element** should be of the Earth such as a Crystal that has certain properties that has been formed and created over a long period of time by Nature's own Magick. The **Air Wand** should be of a branch that has never touched the living Earth, it must be high about the ground as though reaching for the stars. Different tree's give off different Magickal powers such as the Willow for healing sadness, Oak for healing strength, Ash for new directions, Rowan for changes, Rosewood for divine love, Apple for fertility, Birch for courage, Eucalyptus for healing etc.

- The **Fire Wand** should have been forged by Natures power and fire such as the Obsidian Crystal, forged by the volcanic flow of lava sealing the essence of the earth by water and cooled by air. A **Water Wand** should be of the sea such as a Cornet Shell which has a long spiral pattern that is either Deosil for directing healing powers, or Widdershins for removing sickness and ill health.

- **WICCES/PHALLIC WAND:** The Phallic wand is primarily for invoking the Goddess and or God, traditionally ours was a normal length of Oak with an Acorn fixed to the tip. This was called the Phallic Wand. Some other Traditional Covens had similar, but it was a pine rod and a small pine cone fixed to the tip as their Phallic Wand for Invoking deity.

   Only the Ordained Priesthood use the Phallic Wand as it is used on special occasions such as Full Moons for Invoking the Goddess and or God, for Major Festivals such as Beltane, Lughnasadh, Samhain, and Imbolg. We also use the Phallic Wand for impregnating fertility into plants, fields, orchards and crops to give more life to the plants, that they be healthy.

All Wands are Magick Wands, but they each have a specific reason and should never be used for anything else, as this would cause adverse effects and may create a negative result instead of the intended desire of the Wicce. Your Wand should be cut between the season of Spring and Summer when the sacred mana of the tree is flowing faster. I love working with the Rowan or Oak tree. If the branch is long enough it is advisable to also cut a length for your Besom, which is to be used by the Female Elder of your Magick Circle to cleanse and purify the Temple space.

When using a Wand or making a Wand make sure you impregnate the intention of its uses, a Magickal Tool is like a child and needs to be always considered, nurtured, fed with emotional support and love, and taught of its reason for being as a positive amplification of your Divineness. A Wand can be as elaborate or as simple as you desire, but make sure it is NATURAL with no chemical added gums or glues.

Tools of the
Covenstead

Black Mirror

Creating the Magick Black Mirror

"You sit, silent, bare
awareness towards soulless
blackened lens, empty space empty
mind, empty colour sister of the mirror, becoming
substance of Light, melting to form the mirror within a
mirror, slow swirling converse carrying consciousness

gently, tunnels of time, tunnels of space, tunnels
of energy. We enter the blackness of
nothingness to become something
That is far reaching the depths
Of our
inner mind
and soul."

YOU FEEL - sensations of the corners of time.

YOU THINK - your thoughts, orange, expand to the laws of the Universe.

YOU LOVE - the Sunshine's on the reaches of space, sunbeams melt becoming Stars.

YOU SMILE - infinitely.

"Deep in the mountains, a long time ago a Wicces settlement lay in the middle
of a lost and forgotten valley To the East of the valley the mountain Air
enriched in colour by its own thinness, harboured textures and shades of blue
very rarely seen on Earth To the South, a volcano infrequently threw small
embers of Fire into the Air. To the West, a huge waterfall fed the river, which
ran by the settlement. And to the North, the mountains rose ever steeper.

The fog was just starting to lift off the valley and the sunlight barely filtering through, when a door in a building opened and a boy walked out into the gardens. He passed flowerbeds, ponds and rockeries and finally, came to a small clearing where he sat cross legged facing an old tree. The tree was tall and thick giving the appearance that it had grown there for thousands of years. The tree was huge and solid giving the appearance that its roots held the world together. Beneath the tree was another figure even more solid and aged. An old woman sat unmoving, a monolith of rock, hewn and etched by the process of time. A face bleak and barren. The boy having sat still for a few minutes considered the woman's face "Old One, I had a dream last night. I was sitting alone in a darkened room the only light present was coming from me … In front of me was a black box enclosing an even blacker mirror it seemed to reflect the light back towards me. It made me feel very old and I could remember things I'd never known before". A slow smile came to the woman and she turned to watch the Moon hanging over the valley in the bright daylight … Words of stone "Before the floods in the great Mother country the Black Mirror was used as a lens to focus and direct Auric energy. The Lemurians centred it mainly on living matter whereas, after the floods the people of Egypt were using it more for non-living things. It was one of the machines used in the construction of the Pyramids" She looked away from the Moon. "The younger members of Magickal communities found enjoyment in using it for time travel and other spectacular but rather meaningless exercises". A small child stumbled into the clearing and headed towards the old woman who immediately became engrossed in laughing and playing with the child. It was a month later when the boy thought of the Black Mirror again. He had searched all day and finally found the old woman sitting next to the waterfall at the end of the valley. The scene surprised him. The spray from the waterfall was being caught by the Sun and produced myriads of rainbows that seemed to play down into the woman's hair. He sat himself in front of her, a look of contemplation on his face and spoke. "Old One I dreamed again of the mirror last night" Silence - he tried to recall the details more clearly. 'I think I learned how the Mirror was made I was searching for a watch glass I finally found one about twenty centimetres across, it had no scratches or defects. I then found some camphor wood and made a box and lid to enclose the glass I remember I lined the inside of the box and lid with black felt and painted the outside the same colour with a dull paint I think I remember taking the rest of the black felt and sewing a bag to keep the box in I then had to make a Talisman using the four Shining Ones and a Goddess or a God.' He watched the rainbows, "I think that choosing the Goddess or God was the most interesting part of the dream' He laughed.

The rainbows that had been playing with the woman's hair now
seemed to float down into her face it was as though each section of
her face took on a colour giving life and beauty to the form.
"The dream then changed I was sitting in my Temple I had just sterilised the glass
and had fixed the windows and doors so that no light could enter. It was totally
dark, and I was sitting in the middle of the Magick Circle the four Shining Ones
standing around me smiling. I seemed to have a macrocosmic Middle Pillar flowing
around me and at that moment I was invoking the God in the Talisman to come and
help me. I then put a flow through the Talisman and asked the Shining Ones and
God to help me build and use the Mirror I placed my Talisman in the bottom of
the box and lit a beeswax candle this was the only source of light in the Temple. I
then took the watch glass and passed it slowly over the flame so that the soot from
the flame formed a layer of blackness on the outside curve of the glass. It took
many layers of soot to form a film so strong that no light could pass through.
I then gently lay the glass down in the box with the Talisman resting underneath
it. I had to be careful not to smudge the black upper surface of the dome with
my fingers. I thanked the Shining Ones for their help in ritual and them in turn
spoke to me of its use. For one month, I was to take it out in the dark room
every night I was to look at it, think about it, and imagine being it ...
Her eyes peering gently through the rainbows the colours now melting
down over her body so that her dull gray robe became a garment of serene
greens and gold's, every part of the cloth ever changing hue.
"After I had used it for a month in that manner I was to try and see images and scenes
from that day's events in the mirror. Once accomplished, I was to try to see events a
few days previous then slowly work back further into the past. After having spoken
thus the Shining One left amidst glorious sounds and fires and I slowly awakened.
The rainbows were becoming richer and vibrating the Sunlight as they
seemed to engulf her leaving only a vague outline of the woman. A
stone sitting in a mist of rainbows and sparkling water drops. Strangely,
her whisper seemed to transcend the roar of the waterfall.
"My young friend, it appears as though you are to make a Black Mirror". She chuckled,
then more seriously. 'Camphor wood has properties that make it a very dense Astral
material. It is this denseness enclosing the glass that protects it Aurically. The black
felt stops light from entering the box and destroying the Mirror. The Mirror is very
sensitive to light and exposure will harm its properties. Felt also carries an electrical
charge very similar to the Mirror. The Black paint helps to absorb any light present.

The glass must be exceptionally clean for the final step, so sterilising it was a good idea … The soot from the beeswax sets up a layer of district nine over the outer surface of the Mirror the thicker the better as it is this layer of the chemical that sets up the Auric Mirror. The Shining Ones are invoked in the Talisman to control and regulate any adverse effects. At first you must choose the areas of Magick you wish to use the Mirror in, be it healing, communication, Scrying, time travel, introspection, or whatever, and invoke the appropriate God-form into the Talisman. The God will then guide and teach you in these Areas. For example, if you wanted communication with nature you could invoke Pan to help you. If you choose healing, then you could call on one of the Goddesses like Kwan Yin to guide you.

The ritual for the final stage of physical construction consists of firstly a microcosmic banishing of your Magick Circle, then a Banishing of your implements in the Magick Circle. Invoke the Shining Ones, to follow that with an invocation of a macrocosmic Middle Pillar, then sit down in front of your Talisman and call the Appropriate God. When you feel its presence, pass a flow through the Talisman then put it in the box after you have lit the Candle and completely blackened the Mirror, thank the Shining Ones and God then finish the ritual in the usual manner. Do not, after this stage, ever let the mirror meet light. The four-week contemplation and observation of the Mirror will produce an Auric link which will be your means of entering it."

The boy looked up and noticed the rainbows were now engulfing the space between him and the woman, seeming to link the two of them in colour and sound.

'After this stage is finished you will find there are many uses for the Mirror. You must experiment carefully, searching for as many effects as necessary. Find out more about the mechanics of the Wiccetool, become fully competent in the understanding of its workings. You will find, after the first months' work, the mirror will seem to form a whitish dome facing the opposite direction underneath the black dome. This will happen as the Auric link solidifies. Once there, try letting yourself drift through it. Instead of seeing the scene in the mirror, as at first, you will be there in the scene. This whitish anti-mirror is the heart of the machine. She looked through the rainbows at the boy, she smiled - infinitely. Words of stone, laughter of rainbows. She moved the rainbows ever closer around him.

"The mechanics of the Mirror are simple. The Auric energy you give is taken, refined and very finely focused by the machine. It is then sent back into your tree. Example - the time travel, is a refined reflection of the Geburatic memory. As you become more competent with it, my young friend, always remember to use it to help others as much as it has helped you. There are some Wicces who have fallen from great heights by negligent use of the Mirror and Magick.

Hearing this, the boy looked at her. All he could see were rainbows and sparkling water drops in the air before him. Beautiful golden flowers grew out of the rainbows and sang windy songs. The scene then floated upon the ground and became a flowerbed, one of the many lying beside the waterfall. The young boy smiled, said "Thank you", and walked away.

The car pulled up to the curb, a young lady slid out, locked the door and trotted up into the building. She got out of the lift and walked over to the open door. An old man was sitting on the sofa. She smiled and said "Teacher, a friend of mine had a dream last night in which he saw me sitting before a Black Mirror". The old man returned the smile and glanced through the window at the Moon.

Book Reading Easel

When you have gatherings it is hard to be walking around with papers doing a ritual, that is why we try to know the rite off by heart and get everyone to learn their parts. But we do always have a person to act as Orator to guide and for this we have a beautiful metal stand that has been made for my coven to hold the Book of Shadows and any documents needed for ritual and festivals. It looks neater and tidier as well as professional.

It is also nice to have a small book holder just in front of your Altar to display your book of Shadows for all to see. By doing this you are keeping it off the ground away from moisture that may ruin it. It also looks beautiful in front of the altar, and if it is needed urgently during an operational Spell or Ritual it is close at hand.

Chairs or Seating

When meeting in a Magick Circle it is always beneficial to have some form of seating available. As standing and working ritual can take several hours and can get quite tiresome for many. Also when you have elderly people or people with disabilities you will need some seating.

I have around the perimeter of my Temple several concrete garden seats that are situated at the cross-quarters of the Circle, all that is needed are cushions to be placed on them for comfort. If meeting out in a forest or the bush, then fold-up deck chairs can also be quite easy to transport. It also means that each member can bring their own if they so desire, or at least bring their Circle Ground Cushions.

Consecration of Tools and Weapons

As a Talisman needs to be *"Charged"* in order to be truly effective, so Magickal Wiccetool's must be consecrated before their full scope can be utilised. Consecration is the linking of a physical Wiccetool through Ritual, to the source of the energy, which that Wiccetool directs on the Etheric and Astral Planes. To consecrate a Wiccetool, set up an auric flow with the rest of your group while sitting in a Magick Circle. If you are consecrating a Wiccetool for personal use only, by yourself, then sit in a semi-lotus position facing in the direction of the Element used (e.g. for the Athame/Sword, face South). You might like to use incense appropriate to the Element of the Wiccetool (Galbanum for the Wand; Olibanum for the Athame; Jasmine or Onucha for the Chalice, and Storax or Sandalwood for the Pentacle).

Visualise the colour of the Element, its appearance, texture, sound, and taste. When you "feel" the Element, pass a flow from your hands through the Wiccetool. Thus, the Wiccetool is linked to you aurically. In a group ritual, pass the Wiccetool around to each person to see and handle and then place the Wiccetool in the centre of the Circle. Then everyone in the Magick Circle visualises the Element as mentioned above and directs a flow through the Wiccetool.

Remember to begin and end with your rituals with an Isian or Kabbalistic Cross.

In dealing with the Mysteries of Wiccecraft, it is said that no secrets can be ever given away, secrets do not belong to anyone, and knowledge over the years has been lost due to secrecy and superstition. Here is a single main definition of the objects of all Magick Ritual; it is the uniting of the microcosm and the macrocosm. In examining the Working Tools, you will notice I have grouped the Tools corresponding them to the three Degrees of the Craft, as part of a complete formula. I will concentrate a good deal on their esoteric uses rather than the more Elemental associations, although I will make references to these as well.

Coronets

Spring

A Spring Coronet or Chaplet of Spring Flowers are what is worn at the Rites of Spring Festival. Usually we make a special one to be presented to the Maiden who is chosen as the Spring Queen. This is usually by everyone voting for the specific person and then they go through a small ceremony to be made the Spring Queen for a year, until the next Spring Festival returns.

This coronet is made up of all the traditional Spring Flowers that are in season, with a few added herbs and sprigs of Baby's Breath for purity. They are entwined with ivy and rainbow coloured ribbons which fall down the back of the Coronet.

Summer

The Summer Coronet is made with withy and ivy and bound with ribbons of gold falling down the back of the Coronet. It has a large Gold Foil Solar disc at the front of it with a small tapered candle in front to illumine the gold foil Solar Disc to represent the birth of the Sun and the welcoming of the Light and Warmth back to the Living Earth. This is usually presented to a young warrior type male representing the Sun God in his prime.

Autumn

The Autumn Coronet is bound by Earth toned withy and wine, and Autumn leaves, of browns, russets, oranges, pinks, whites, blacks, and a small amount of green. It represents all that has been let go of from the previous year. As the leaves let go of their life force so must we at the end of our journey also learn to accept the inevitable and also let go of our life, so we can ascend to the realm of Dreams and new beginnings in The Summerland.

Winter

The Winter Coronet is about the death and rebirth cycle and so the coronet should represent new life and new growth, with the greens and whites represents innocence and purity. Also the cleansing of the Spirit in readiness for the Spring. It is a Coronet that displays Life and Purity.

This is the time we bring young saplings into our home to represent the return of the warmth of Spring at the end of the restful period of winter. Yule trees are decorated with gold representing the Sun. Green representing new Life. Red representing warmth and sexuality. These are the three Magickal colours associated with Yule.

Crystal Ball Gazing and Clairvoyance

CLAIRVOYANCE = CLEAR SIGHT; the development of the intuition to a level of practical usage. On the Kabbalistic Tree of Life, it is the ability to perceive Hod from Netzach, and Netzach from Hod, to see them as action and reaction respectively.

The use of clairvoyant Tools such as the Crystal Ball will aid in the development of the intuition. The Crystal is a focus point for you to use your imagination in a positive visual way by a concentrated effort of Yesod's artistic energies.

Once you have acquired the Crystal Ball it is necessary to free it of any auric influences that may be attached to it (because of previous ownership or handling, etc.). This is achieved by a Banishing Ritual performed in a salt and water Magickal Circle, followed immediately by covering the crystal with black silk, which will keep it protected until you begin work with it yourself.

The crystal is used on a special Scrying table, which is ideally constructed of ebony with writings of gold, if ebony is unavailable, any heavy grained wood, painted matt black, would substitute. The table after completion would also need to be covered with black silk (to contain no aura but your own). A small holder for the crystal is required; this too should be your own construction, painted matt black and kept covered with black silk.

It is necessary for the preparation of this Magickal equipment to take place during the moons increase, i.e. going toward the full. This is most important to your success; the moons magnetic and perspective aura benefits the crystal.

Further to your success, all crystal gazing, preferably, done in a controlled environment. This is best achieved by the construction of a salt and water Magick Circle, in which you have done a full banishing and invocation ritual. The circle should be set in a clean, darkened room where you will be undisturbed. Take care that it is free of any objects that may reflect in the crystal, and thus disturb your attention. The room should not be dark, but rather, shadowed with dull light, somewhat like a moonlit room. It is necessary to time you're sitting, so set a clock where, though the face is visible, the ticking is inaudible.

Before commencing your crystal work, attention to self-preparation is of prime importance. Fasting for at least four (4) hours before your ritual is most beneficial, in contributing to a relaxed state of body and mind, enabling easy chi production. Before you start, meditate on full relaxation followed by a tree ritual. After this, you may go about constructing your circle, or if using a temple, you may enter now.

The art of crystal vision may be classified as follows:

1. Images of your thoughts, opinion;
2. Images of ideas unconsciously acquired from other by telepathy etc.;
3. Images, pictures bringing information as to something past, present or future, which the gazer has no the way of knowing;
4. The ability to see accurately, the qualities, quantities and distribution of the Elements of any given *'field'*.

Under this fourth (4th) heading, comes true crystal vision.

Do not be disappointed if, when and even after you have completed the preliminary exercises set forth here, you do not apparently perceive an answer to what you are seeking: after the first or even following attempts. On the other hand, if you have a particularly GIFTED POTENTIAL to be a Seer, you may begin perceiving on your very first sitting; you are advised to disregard it, as, continuous success will only come as a growth development and these exercises will secure it.

Commence the first week of your work on a Monday, during the waxing cycle of the Moon. Monday being significant because it is the day of the Moon. Your Magick Circle set, you re-enter with your crystal, table and holder. Place them, after removing their covering, in the centre of your Circle, facing east. You would then sit comfortably, opposite in lotus position, facing the crystal with your back to the west. Fix your eyes on the ball itself, not a pierce - stare out with a steady calm gaze. Concentrate on your breathing (inhale for 9, hold for 2, exhale for 9, will allow an easy even flow). Start projection through the eyes of your hands and set up a flow with the crystal.

This is all you do for the first week, but do not underestimate the importance of this exercise, as the result and sole aim of this is to establish an auric link with your crystal before which no SUCCESSFUL work can be attempted. This exercise should be carried out at a regular time, daily, and should not exceed more than 30 minutes.

The same piece should be used in the second week, and by this time it should be noticed that a rising cloud forms the base of the crystal. The crystal seeming to alternately appears and disappears, as in a mist. This is your signal that you are not linked with it. Go ahead, to use your ability to visualise by allowing images to form in the ball. These images should not be forced, just allow your mind to wander; letting each thought form a picture. Do not try to interpret these images, this is merely an exercise in control, the benefit of which will begin to acquire a feel for CLEAR SIGHT - the difference between what is or was and what may be merely a projection of your own opinion. (1-2 classifications).

Once you have completed these exercises for a full week, you may commence using your crystal for divination. Using the same routine as before, concentrate on what you wish to enquire about. Don't force your query, just softly hold it in mind, by using your imagination in a positive visual way, play with your query, make images while holding your steady gaze on the ball, it. When you see that the crystal is beginning to become dull and the cloud on clouds begin to rise, this is your signal that you are about to see what you seek, for suddenly the crystal will clear to all else but a bluish flame, against which, as if it were a background, the vision will be apparent.

Practice will develop an automatic ability to obtain results in the exploration of any given field.

Doing Oracles for people is a good start, allowing immediate reference points, depending, of course, on what they wish to enquire. When doing this the person should keep silent and remain seated at a distance opposite you, all questions asked should be in a slow and low tone.

Although the Moon is in harmony with the crystal, the days and times you do your work will depend on the nature of your enquiry. For example, if you are enquiring of a past life, then Tuesday would be used being the day of Mars; Mars is the planet assigned to the Sephiroth Geburah, the sphere of memory. A ritual for this purpose done on a Tuesday in the hour of Mars, coupled with an invocation of Geburah would be most successful. Alternately, to enquire knowledge of something more present, this life, the Thursday, being the day of Jupiter, which is the planet of plenty, growth, abundance and gain and assigned to Chesed, would be more suitable.

As you develop, your work will lead you to a kind of astral workshop. This will be your own creation and an art form of the four quarters, in action allowing you to see and use Tetragrammaton in your everyday life.

Fire Hearth

Every outdoor Magick Circle should have a fire pit in the centre of the Circle, not only to keep warm but to represent the Hidden Light that is invisible within the visible. It is representative of the Sun and all that it offers. Fires are great for sharing in any occasion but within a Magick Circle they seem to add their own Magick and Mystery. We use the Hearth Fire as a symbol, a beacon to attract others to the Light.

We also use it for making potions and Spellcraft, also to share in stories. But a Hearth Fire is very important, so much so that if we are indoors, then as a substitute we place the Cauldron in the Centre of the Magick Circle and place a large Red candle in it to represent our Hearth Fire.

Firewood

By having a Hearth or Circle Fire you will also need some firewood, so make sure it is in plentiful supply and close at hand, so you do not actually have to leave the circle to get it, so have it laying just on the boundary and accessible.

Geomancy

Geomancy means literally 'divination by Earth' and is a form of divination, which operates through links with Earth Elementals.

A question is asked, and by the chance throwing of pebbles or random drawing of lines in Earth, an odd or an even number is obtained. This procedure is repeated sixteen times and the results are arranged into groups of four lines, one under the other in their original order. The four lined figures thus obtained are interpreted to provide an answer to the question.

Geomancy figures are not unlike I Ching hexagrams, except they have only four lines. For example, a figure consisting of two odds followed by two even lines would be recorded. There are only sixteen possible combinations, but as four such figures must be obtained initially to answer any question, the combinations number more than 65,000.

Traditional names, qualities and planetary attributions are ascribed to these sixteen figures and when used in the format given later you can expect to obtain a full and qualitative answer to any question you may ask. However, your success with Geomancy will depend on your ability to take an apparently mechanical and inanimate process and make it into a delicate and sentient Magickal operation.

Although it may appear complex and confusing at first, the basic form of Geomancy is simple and concise. The major obstacle to using this and indeed any form of divination is attaining the state of mind necessary for perceiving the simplicity. The following section describes an approach, which in time will allow this simplicity to show itself.

There are four Elements to be considered in the process. They are firstly, the person conducting the divination, the Tools used e.g. Tarot Pack, I Ching sticks, the entities or level of consciousness you aim to communicate with and, fourthly, the mechanical process itself.

To carry out successful divination these Four Elements must be made to function as a unity. They must be set up so that the interaction between them is a smooth flow of perfect communication.

In preparing yourself and your Tools you must aim to reach a level where intuition takes the place of will and reason. However, intuition is a quality of Netzach and will not be recognisable immediately, so you must use the Tools you have in Yesod. These are intellect, emotion and art used on the framework of your imagination. If you approach divination in this way, intuition will just happen by itself.

There are no rules to follow, but you must find out your own balance as you go. You could start by studying the system as it is explained later. See how it fits together intellectually and then let you feel it. Contemplate the Geomantic figures, play with them in your mind and get a feeling for them. Expand their meanings by relating them to your own experience.

The next question that arises is the choice of a method for obtaining your primary figures. Traditionally this is done by tracing random lines in soft Earth with a stick, counting the number of separate fragments in each line and thus obtaining an odd or an even number (you would have to draw sixteen broken lines).

The operation should be completely random and uninfluenced by conscious mental process. This can be difficult as the speed at which lines can be drawn in Earth often allows your mind time to count the dashes you are making - and the more you try not to, the more aware you become. If you choose this method, you could compose a suitable Chant to recite and hopefully keep your conscious mind occupied.

Any method of drawing random numbers could be valid and perhaps it may help you to personalise the system by coming up with one never used before.

It must be kept in mind, however, that the process you choose and the Tools with which you carry it out, contribute to the link you aim to form with the Earth Elementals through which Geomancy operates - the more you become involved with this, the more of an art you make it, the stronger and more functional will be those links. The Tools you use - for example a wooden marker for drawing lines in the sand - should be selected and fashioned as a Magickal Tool, with its purpose held in mind always.

Another method, which I have found quite satisfactory consists of drawing numbers of pebbles or balls out of a bowl designed for the purpose and counting the number, either odd or even. A design for a painted bowl is given here. If you decide to use this method, you should make the bowl yourself. Design it, shape it and colour it as you would when making a Magickal Wiccetool. Be careful not to let anyone touch your work or help you with it. The links you require will be formed initially as you make your Tools - any extraneous links will be difficult to sever without destroying your own.

All forms of divination have a negative or qliphotic function, which must be bound. With the I Ching this is accomplished by having a negative bundle of sticks. In Geomancy, the method of binding the negative will vary according to the method employed. With the bowl method, the snake eating its tail around the base of the bowl, binds negative. This is not the only possible way, but it is quite effective. Once you have your Tools prepared, to perform a Geomancy reading is basically simple. It is best if you make a ritual of it, the main requirement being a Banished Circle.

First you must formulate the question you want answered, make it precise and free of ambiguities: You will obtain an answer to the question asked, not necessarily the question you think you are asking. You should write this down on top of a piece of paper, on which you will also record the Geomantic Figures you obtain.

Then proceed to derive the four primary figures of your reading, by whatever means you have decided upon. These four figures, traditionally known as the "mothers", give an absolute answer to your question. Considered Tetragrammically, they are the intrinsic, the positive, the negative and the neutral - in that order. In terms of the Elements they are Air, Fire, Water and Earth.

This absolute answer may suffice for your question. However, two other sets of four figures can be derived from the Mothers, which as a quality comment on the first four.

If you take the first (top) lines of the Mothers and arrange them in the order of the Mothers from top to bottom, you will derive a fifth figure. Repeating this process using the second, third and fourth lines of the Mothers, you will have another set of four figures. These are called the Daughters and represent the Yang or positive aspects of the Mothers in the order, Air, Fire, Water and Earth.

The Yin or negative aspects, called the Nephews, are obtained by adding together in pairs the eight figures you have already. The first two Mothers added together give the first Nephew; the second Mothers added yield to the second Nephew. Similarly, the first and second pair of daughters give in addition the third and fourth Nephews respectively.

Addition of Geomantic figures is not difficult. The first lines of the two figures when added together yield an odd or an even, which becomes the first line of the derived figure. An odd plus an odd or an even plus an even yields an even; an even plus and odd yields an odd. This process is repeated using the pairs of second, third, and fourth lines to produce the respective lines of the derived figure, e.g.

The four Nephews are the Yin aspects of Fire, Water, Earth and Air, or the second, third, fourth and first Mothers, in that order.

At this stage of the reading you should have twelve Geomantic figures looking rather confusing in columns on a sheet of paper.

CAPUT DRACONIS - literally means *"The upper threshold, entrance"*, *"The Head of the Dragon"*.

Elemental Ruler:	Hismael	and Kedemet
Planetary Ruler:	Venus	and Jupiter
Zodiac Sign:	Caput Draconis	
Element:	Air of Air.	

Comment: This figure and that of *Cauda Draconis* are the most Yang's of the sixteen Geomantic figures. This quality, along with the ruler ship of Venus and Jupiter suggest expansion. It is an action, a beginning or an end, depending on how you look at it.

ALBUS - Literally *"White head"*.

Elemental Ruler:	Taphthartharath
Planetary Ruler:	Mercury
Zodiac Sign:	Gemini
Element:	Fire of Air

Comment: The Latin name suggests the wisdom of age. The Mercurial influence is communication and learning. Fire of Air is the action of Air Which is an active interweaving of macrocosmic and microcosmic forces leading to wisdom.

TRISTITIA - Literally *"Sadness, grief"*.

Elemental Ruler:	Zazael
Planetary Ruler:	Saturn
Zodiac Sign:	Aquarius
Element:	Water of Air.

Comment: Saturn indicates contraction but can also be knowledge. Sadness is a subjective reaction to loss, and true sadness is an expression of love. This figure refers also to the separateness of individuals. The context in which the figure occurs will indicate how it is to be interpreted.

PUELLA - Literally means *"a girl"* or a *"pretty face"*.

Elemental Ruler:	Kedemet
Planetary Ruler:	Venus
Zodiac Sign:	Libra
Element:	Water of Air

Comment: Venus signifies beauty, emotion rather than intellect; also pleasure or fostering. A *"pretty face"* can be the vision that inspires an artist or the beautiful façade that's seen from within a prison.

AEQUISITIO - Literally means *"Obtaining"*.

Elemental Ruler:	Hismael
Planetary Ruler:	Jupiter
Zodiac Sign:	Sagittarius
Element:	Air of Fire.

Comment: Jupiter is associated with expansion and gain. This figure is traditionally taken to mean good fortune. However, he terms expansion and gain has no inherent direction, and as with all the Geomantic figures, the idea of good fortune is not a quality that can be assigned. The direction that the 'gain' indicated by this figure is to take will be indicated by the context in which it occurs.

FORTUNA MAJOR - Literally *"the great fortune"*

Elemental Ruler:	Sorath
Planetary Ruler:	Sol
Zodiac Sign:	Leo
Element:	Fire of Fire.

Comment: The Sun here indicates balance. In one respect it is he externalisation of what is internal.

VIA - Literally a *'street, way, journey'*.

Elemental Ruler:	Chasmodai
Planetary Ruler:	Luna
Zodiac Sign:	Cancer
Element:	Water of Fire

Comment: The figure of Via and that of Fortuna Minor are the two most Yin of the sixteen Geomantic figures. As a street or a journey, it is an action; but an action of opening and allowing things to enter, rather than to attempt to change what is without!

PUER - Literally *'a boy'*, *'yellow, beardless'*.

Elemental Ruler:	Bartzabel
Planetary Ruler:	Mars
Zodiac Sign:	Aries
Element:	Earth of Fire.

Comment: Mars has attributions of discord and war but is also a symbol for strength. The image aroused by the name Puer suggests the strivings of youth or perhaps youthful folly.

RUBEUS - Literally means *'red'* or *'red headed'*.

Elemental Ruler:	Bartzabel
Planetary Ruler:	Mars
Zodiac Sign:	Scorpio
Element:	Air of Water

Comment: Activity, a concentration of forces, to strive for freedom, or build a prison.

FORTUNA MINOR - Literally the *'lesser fortune'*.

Elemental Ruler	Sorath
Planetary Ruler:	Sol
Zodiac Sign:	Cancer
Element:	Water of Fire

Comment: COMMENT: Along with Via this is the most Yin of the Geomantic figures. It is the action of Water. The interpretation of what is external.

POPULUS - Literally *'people, crowd, congregation'*.

Elemental Ruler:	Chasmodai
Planetary Ruler:	Luna
Zodiac Sign:	Cancer
Element:	Water of Water

Comment: COMMENT: This is the effect of Water. Water is contraction; it is the most complex of the Elements. Like a crowd of people, it may represent richness or confusion in its diversity. If considered with the figure Via, Populous can be the effect of the action of Via.

LAETITIA - Literally *'joy, laughter'*.

Elemental Ruler:	Hismael
Planetary Ruler:	Mars
Zodiac Sign:	Pisces
Element:	Earth of Water

Comment: COMMENT: Joy is a reaction to temporal gain, given here with the energy of Mars. As with the figure Aequisitio; the outcome of this gain carries no connotations for good or evil.

CAREER - Literally *'prison bound'*.

Elemental Ruler:	Zazel
Planetary Ruler:	Saturn
Zodiac Sign:	Capricorn
Element:	Air of Earth

Comment: This appears an animus figure, Saturn being cold and contracting. Yet a prison when it applies an external condition, allows the possibility of internal freedom. Saturn is also a sign for knowledge and knowledge is gained by struggling with problems and restrictions.

AMISSIO – literally *'loss'*.

Elemental Ruler:	Kedemet
Planetary Ruler:	Venus
Zodiac Sign:	Taurus
Element:	Fire of Earth

Comment: Earth is solidification, and in the context of Venus *'loss'* is an appropriate name for this action. However, the loss could also be a loss of confusion.

CONJUNCTIO - Literally *'coming together'*.

Elemental Ruler:	Taphthartharath
Planetary Ruler:	Mercury
Zodiac Sign:	Virgo
Element:	Water of Earth

Comment: Mercury is communication and learning. In this present context it could refer to a coming together of formerly unrelated things that result in communication and learning, or results in a closing off channels that inhibits further development.

Grain and Seed Basket

As many of our rituals, ceremonies and Festivals revolve around the seasons and Nature, we need to have a small basket for ceremonial grain and seed that is used in ritual. If not a basket then maybe a large dish with a Pentacle on it, something that can contain the grain and seed so as to be easily attended and shared.

We have many of our ceremonies ritually working with seed, as seed is the first process of continual life. From the seed grows a tree, and from the tree grows fruit, and from the fruit grows the seed, ad infinitum. We traditionally plant our seed ceremonially within our Cauldron and then it is transplanted into the garden and cared for, as it contains all our blessings that we have each bestowed into the seed through Magick.

From the tray we each take a few seeds into our hands and Bless them with life, love and fruitfulness. We place them in our left hand in a clenched fist and hold it up high and say:

"Blessed Be the hand put forth with Might!"

We then place our right hand in the air but open and say:

"Blessed be the hand put forth with Meaning!"

We then mix our hands and rub the seeds together after spitting in them and say:

"Blessed Be what we must do with Might and Meaning, that our hands may hold the Harvest of our Highest Hopes!"

We then separate the seeds and keep just a few and put them into three lots, one lot we discard and throw them out of the Circle. The second lot we plant in the Coven Cauldron, and the third lot we take home to nourish ourselves.

Harvest Basket

This much the same as the grain and seed basket but much bigger and decorated with seasonal flowers and grape vines with grapes attached. The basket is the offerings that everyone brings to the gathering and shares. The basket contains all the seasonal fruit that each feel is appropriate for themselves. They are blessed and then cut up into portions and everyone shared a little of the bounty leaving some as an offering to the Elementals and the Goddess and God.

The Making and Caring of Magickal Tools

All materials used in Magickal Tools or Wiccetool's should be virgin and clean. As far as possible you should make all your Wiccetool's unassisted (except to others who will be using them). Only you should see and touch the Wiccetool's from the moment you begin to work on them; again, except for other Wicces who will be using the Tools in your Coven work. This will ensure that there are no unwanted or uncontrolled links connecting your Wiccetool's aurically with any minds apart from the minds using them. To maintain the auric purity of your Wiccetool's they must be kept clean and in good repair. Also, they should be wrapped in black silk when not actually used, cleaned or repaired. As the colour black absorbs heat and light, so black, and especially black silk, tends to absorb "auric pollution" to protect your Tools from contamination. Store them in a safe place where they are unlikely to be seen or arouse curiosity.

The Magickal Wiccetool's are the Tools with which the Wicce works. Four traditional Wiccetool's - the Wand (or Rod); The Sword/Athame (ritual dagger); The Chalice (Cup), or Crucible or Cauldron; and the Pentacle (or Shield, Disc, or Seal) - are the Wiccetool's used for the Elements of Air, Fire, Water and Earth. Usually these are referred to as the Wiccetool's of the Wicce/Priest/ess; however, do not imagine that only these four are legitimate Tools for practical Magick. Mandala's, incenses, colour, oils, music, the tarot, mantras, mudras, tattwa's, talismans, yarrow sticks, herbs, divination, meditation, visualisation, trance state, these and innumerable others are the Wicces Tools or Spiritual/ Magickal Weapons. In fact, everything you can apply to help with your practical work in Magick is a true Magickal Wiccetool.

Four Elements - four Traditional Weapons - four parts of the Magick Circle you can use in Magick via the Wand, Athame/Sword, Chalice, and Pentacle. How do these Weapons fit into Tetragrammaton (Ceremonial Magick)? Eventually you, the Wicce must discover this from your own experiences but until then I recommend (from my experiences) this arrangement.

Maypole

A Traditional Maypole is created for pre-puberty children and not for adults. As it is a fertility aspect of penetrating the earth with God force and bringing all into all of Nature into fruition. It was Traditionally only danced by boys giving their maleness to the Phallic Maypole.

The Maypole is a freshly cut down tree and Properly Prepared by the boys, the girls are away separately and are making the floral sheath to be placed on the top of the Maypole with the coloured ribbons of the rainbow. The Maypole Traditionally was eight feet tall, but these days the Maypoles are every size that is desired. They should be either 8 feet, 10 feet or 17 feet high. The ribbons that are tied to the floral sheath circlet at the top are usually twelve feet long for the 9-foot pole. They should be about one and a half times the length of the pole.

The boys do a formal Morris style dance circling both directions until the pole is bound with the rainbow ribbons where they are tied off, and fertility flourishes through the land.

Methylated Spirits

To make fire more Mystical and Magickal we use Methylated Spirits which is placed in the Cauldron instead of having a log fire. When the timing is right the principal ritualist throws a light into the cauldron and the flames of blues and greens emanate from the Cauldron for Fire Gazing Magick.

It is used to also throw petitions or letters into that you are asking for something from the Element and the Dragon of Fire. Methylated Spirits does get very hot, so you need to be very careful. Especially with flowing robes or capes as well. Depending on how much Methylated Spirits you place in the Cauldron depends on the timeframe that it takes to burn down.

Music

In my Covens we use music at every gathering, as we all love to sing and dance our way into the circle and out again. We build our power with Circle Dancing and our High Priest is a professional musician and singer, and so he has written many songs for our Coven. Also many of our members have ceremonial drums that they use within the Circle as well.

At festivals we each bring along some sort of musical instrument to enjoy in the festivities at the end of the evening. The one thing about me Is I have always been strict and quite disciplined with the formal Traditional side of the training but when it comes to relaxing I am quite the Fool and love to bring a sense of humour into every situation, this is to help relax Seekers who are a little unsure of their surroundings. Plus music makes the heart sing.

We even open the Circle with Asherah Awakening the Circle with his didgeridoo, as the circle starts with music and ends with music, this helps to bring us closer together as a Spiritual Family.

Tarot

The Tarot Cards are the Book of Universal symbolism compiled by the great God Tehuti-Thoth who gave it to his Isarum (Initiates) of Saiss as the key to the Magickal constitution for learned people. The word Tarot is self-explanatory; TAR - meaning ROAD, and ROT - meaning ROYAL; i.e. Road of Royal Wisdom and Divine Enlightenment.

The true pack was modified by the Hebrews to fit into the Kabbalistic system of Philosophy, which evolved from the Egyptians. The Persians and Assyrians also got access to the Cards, and the Crusaders were the first to be credited in taking the Cards into Europe when returning from the Crusades. The Gypsies (derived from Egypt-as people of Egypt) are the people mostly associated with the Cards, using them for Divination purposes. The pack most commonly used was the Marseilles Pack. And presently today the most popular is the Rider-Waite deck.

There are now numerous packs in circulation with a lot of variations in design and some variations in numerical order or attributions. The bulk of the cards are now based on Kabbalistic concepts. For example, a pack published by the Brotherhood of Light called the "Sacred Tarot" is designed to be an intellectual pack with a variety of correspondences in symbology and interpretation e.g. the concept of card one; the Magus, is described and interpretations are given in numerology, astrology, Alchemy, Bible, Masonry, Magick, and Wiccecraft etc.!

In the Rider-Waite pack descriptions and divinatory significances are given. Waite, being a Magician has designed his pack as a Tool, which can be used in Kabbalistic Magickal work. The pack designed by Aleister Crowley is an excellent pack as a work of art, as symbology and art are useful as meditation and ritual tools. They are also easy to relate to for divination purposes, but better used in Ceremony and Ritual.

To know more of the Traditional Tarot of the Isarum of Thoth please read my book titled "Tarot Magick of Thoth-Journeys Through the Portals".

Royal Sceptre

This Sceptre is a royal Sceptre, which is a 18th Century Arch Druids Sceptre from Britain. It is quite lavish, and I use it only for Formal Occasions where the Arch Priestess side of me comes out, usually large Festival gatherings when there is VIP's from overseas, and High ordinations of the High Priesthood. This has a Twisted Horn as the staff part, with engraved in Celtic design motifs in silver and gold. It has an Amethyst either side, and in the top is a Meteorite rock from the Moon, which is the power source of this Wand, (with the power of the Stars and what lies beyond). This Sceptre is also used as an official Wand for High Magick and for Dubbing of Newly Ordained High Priests and High Priestesses.

Coven
and Circle
Activities

Aboriginal/Native Elder Visit

In Australia as in the U.S. there are so many different Native tribes that make themselves available for people to learn of their ways. They try to educate the truth about their culture and history. They are as varied in their ways and traditions as you could imagine.

There are many stories that they can share to help be aware of there ways, they may even show you some exciting things such as how to throw Boomerangs, hunt for Bush Tucker, in finding Bush Medicine, dancing their Dreamtime, and even how they paint their stories and dance their stories.

Ask what it is that you can do for them, to assist them in getting out their message. Remember like you they are a minority, and they are also the oldest Pagan living culture on the planet with over 50,000 years of history and stories to tell.

If your Coven have the finances maybe you can visit some of their Sacred Sites, and see the oldest art galleries in the world, etched and painted on cave walls that tell of their struggle for survival and hunting, and how they as nomads moved with the seasons to find new sources of food.

Learn of their seasons and how they lived and survived by listening to what Mother Nature was telling and guiding them. Speak to the Elders, the ones with the knowledge and ask of their Magick and their Shamans.

Adopt a Park

Adopting a Park is a great way to be a part of your environment, it means having a place to worship. Adopting a Park was what my Coven did many years ago in Perth, Western Australia. We had a traditional Sacred Site that we held all our Festivals, it was called Boulder Rock. We worked at this place which was about an hour from Perth city for over 30 years. I ended up being in contact with CALM, who were the carers (supposedly) for the area and asked since we often attended there, that we could be the caretakers of the Rock.

They eventually agreed and so a new journey of acceptance by government organisations became quite beneficial. Every time we arrived we were sure that there was rubbish around, and surely there was usually heaps, even broken glass. So, everyone was asked to bring some rubbish bags, so we could walk around and clean up the area as best we could. We eventually showed that we were responsible, and they sent a thankyou letter for our efforts, which I might add saved them a lot of money in the cleaning up of this vast place.

The adage, "Leave it the way you found it", didn't sit well with us so our new adage was "Leave it better than we found it".

This was a spectacular place to hold festivals and other important events especially when the amount of people was bigger that what the home could handle, it also meant that we were away from suburbia, and from prying eyes in a place that was ancient and gave us the energies that we needed under the star lit sky.

Alchemy

Alchemy is the art of perfection, the taking of something that is raw or unbalanced and changing it into a more perfected state. The work you'll do as a Wicce is what is called Personal Alchemy or Internal Alchemy. What you are doing is changing your state of being to a more balanced or perfect state. We call it an ART, because it involves the use of emotion and intellect (the balancing of your actions and reactions). What I am going to talk about is Alchemy as an art of perfecting herbs and metals etc.

Unfortunately, this form of Alchemy has suffered in many ways because more people have refused to treat it as an Art. For many years western society has tried to find its Truth through science, and science, as WE KNOW IT, is not an Art, it is basically an intellectual function.

As we have said before, Alchemy or Art needs BOTH intellect and emotion. We use intellect so that we can be analytical and predict the outcome of any of our operations; and emotion so that we can feel or be sensitive enough to be able to assess what is happening (from an infinite number of possibilities) at any given time. To give an example of this, if we were treating an Herb Alchemically, what we are trying to do is change the herb both physically and Aurically, we are trying to perfect the action that this herb has. Intellectually we assess the possibilities of the herb, we predict the outcome of the operation, and act on bringing about the desired result. (Remember intellect is action). Emotion is happening during the operation both Aurically and physically, and to assess what is happening at any time so that the herb is treated as an INDIVIDUAL THING each time.

This, together with you, make Alchemy an Art (it is creative). YOU are acting on the herb and reacting to it. It is acting upon you and reacting to you. You have made that herb alive. It is by this process that we find the Soul of the herb. We break down its Yin and Yang actions and rebuild it into a more balanced or perfected state (we balance its action and reaction).

Because in Alchemy you are acting on and being acted upon by whatever you are treating Alchemically, whatever you do in Alchemy has a direct effect upon you. You are Aurically linked to the herbs and the process, so in perfecting anything with Alchemy you are perfecting yourself. This makes doing Alchemy an extremely effective tool to use in your own Magickal work as a Wicce, and in finding your SOUL.

To begin your work in Alchemy all you really need is a simple distillation apparatus and a quiet place to work. Sometime later you may decide to expand this into a full working laboratory, but never until after Initiation, because at this stage more knowledge is revealed.

The process of finding the elixir of life is a relatively easy physical process (as shown in the following paragraph), but the difficulty you find will be auric control. To help with this, it is necessary to use whatever tools are available to you. These tools are only limited by your ability to understand them. The tools you use should include:

Astrology   Tarot   I-Ching   Talisman's   Tattwa's Incense   Oils etc.

There is an unlimited number of tools that can be used. Some you may find better suited of more effective than others, depending upon what you want to do.

I will give you a brief description of the simpler form of Alchemy, which you should put into practice during your Neophyte/Seeker stage. Treatment of the herb involves seven basic stages of distillation and coagulation. The first thing to be done is to distil a fair amount of water. To this we add our dried herb and soak for a period of about twenty-four hours (or minimum overnight). After this we can begin our distillations.

In all the distillations you do, you must remember that we are trying to work with Nature, we are trying to help Nature perfect, so we must work as Nature works, slowly and gently. All your distillations should take about half an hour to bring to the boil, and roughly and hour to distil after boiling.

- **First Distillation** – this first distillation is basic and simple. The herb is boiled and distilled, the first distillation having no POSTHEAT.
- **Postheat** – is heat applied once all watery fluids have left the still.
- **Second Distillation** – for the second distillation we join the residue (what is left in the still) with the distillate. Then again, we distil gently (as with the first), only this time we POSTHEAT for 5 minutes.
- **Third Distillation** – same as with the second distillation, only we POSTHEAT for 5-10 minutes. During the POSTHEAT you may find that a white cloud forms in the flask (still), this is the oil rising from the herb that can be collected off the distillate once the distillation is complete. The oil can be removed by using the tip of a piece of wire to pick it off the distillate. The oil is then put aside and saved.
- **Fourth-Fifth and Sixth Distillation** – same as with the third distillation, only POSTHEAT for 15-20 minutes. (It is important to not burn the herb, when this starts to happen, stop the POSTHEAT). During these distillations you will find it helpful to crush the residue with a pestle (before re-joining residue and distillate) and calcifying it. Save the oils.
- **Seventh Distillation** – same as with previous distillations, only after calcifying, the calcified herb should become a redbrick colour. Once this achieved, add a few drops of oil and distillate to residue, this should produce a yellow colour, if you have this, then you have the ELIXIR.

Aliens

There are so many theories as to where and how we arrived at this very destination. Many believe that we came from the Stars, and many also believe that we are part of Mother Nature's evolutionary progression.

It does not matter what we believe, but it is a great topic to discuss, and get your feeling heard and understood.

You might even have some great Alien DVD's that everyone watches and then have a discussion afterwards to see how they feel, or have their minds changed. Talk about nearly every ancient culture documented that they had encountered Light Beings from the sky, even our Aboriginals drew pictures of them on the cave walls as a memory to never forget, and to let those of the future know of their existence.

Many believe that they have been abducted, this is a great topic to talk about, do you have any abductee's in your circle. See if they can share their experiences.

There is so much to discuss on this topic and debate, but remember Ontogeny Recapitulates Philogyny, which means that within our very DNA is the essence of all of creation, whether it is from the Earth or even from the stars. Whatever has been, or is, lays buried within our very DNA awaiting to awoken and confronted as the TRUTH.

Alphabet Learning Goddesses and Gods

I have played this game for decades, as it is the best way to learn about the many millions of Goddesses of the ancient and new Pantheons. What you do is sit around in a circle, with snacks in the middle. Then one by one start the alphabet with A, and then naming all the Goddess names that start with A, keep this going around the circle until someone gets stuck, and then they must pay the price and speak about the Goddess starting with A and everything they know about her and her name and culture. If she can't do this then she is penalised and is not allowed to eat snacks for 15 minutes.

Once this is done you then commence on with the alphabet of Goddesses again until someone gets stumped.

This game can be played by using also God names, herbs, countries, crystals, flowers, oils, etc. It can be a fun way of learning as it brings a bit of light-heartedness into the way we can structure or reconstructive teaching and learning.

Altar Cloth and Regalia Making

Having different Altar Cloths for different seasonal Festivals, Full Moons, New Moons, Wiccaning's, Initiations, Hand-fasting's and any other special event is important. As it shows organisation, respect and the colour help to elevate our psyche.

You can be as elaborate as you desire, you can have black and purple for deaths and for Samhain, Red and Gold for Beltane and Mid-Summer Solstice, Brown and Gold for Autumn, Orange and Yellow for Imbolg, Blues for Lughnasadh, Multi colours for Spring Equinox, White and Silver for Full Moons, Greens and Mauves for New Moons and Initiations, Green for Wiccaning's and Crafting's, Blue or Red for Ordinations into the Priesthood, Bright Blue for Blue Moons, Green on White for Winter Solstice, and Red on White for Hand-fasting's.

If you have someone in your Circle who are creative and can either paint or sew, they could then decorate the Altar cloths with elaborate and beautiful signs of what they represent.

Robes

Robes are different, I believe that they should be as simple as possible as they are your working clothes in ritual. In my Circles we each wear robes in colour difference depending on our position in the Circle.

Wiccan children-white robes
Wiccans-who have been crafted green robes
Wicces-white robes with green trim and green overlays and capes
Priests and Priestesses-white robes with burgundy trim with burgundy overlays and capes.
High Priests-white robes with gold trim, gold overlays and capes.
High Priestesses-white robes with silver trim, silver overlays and silver capes.
Maiden-completely in white
Man in Black-completely in black
Elders-Crones, Sages and Magi-Whatever their heart desires.

If you have a coven seamstress then that is excellent as it will save you a lot of money, and she can have the patterns ready to go for people who are entering your circle. I believe that your robe should be above your ankles with side splits to not trip, and that the sleeves should not be flared as they get in the way and can cause problems when leaning across an Altar.

The sleeves can be a little flared but too much as they can even be dangerous reaching across Thuribles and Candles.

Tabards/Overlays

These are relatively easy to make but make the robe set quite dramatic and beautiful, they look professional, as well as protect the robe from fire sparks, soot, and any other damage that could occur in the darkened night.

Tabards are simple and straight with no hood but are usually a thicker fabric which can also protect you from the elements and keep you warm. Of course, in summer it is time for being skyclad, if you do not have too many delicately nurtured senses.

Capes

Honestly, for me capes get in the way, they look great, but I feel they are only appropriate during the colder months as a form of a blanket. So, get rid of them in the warmer climates as they have no benefit at all. I have also included a design for capes but feel that they are easy to obtain and or make. In my circles we also have our Wardens, who oversee each Quarter, and the corresponding tools and objects associated with that realm. They each wear different coloured Capes to the rest of the circle and they are also elaborately hand-painted.

Brown cape for the North with scenes of forests, pentacles, the Horned God, and gnomes. Blue cape for the East with scenes of clouds, Faeries, winged creatures, wands and the sky and Sylphides. Red cape for the South, with scenes of fire, the Magickal Sword, Dragons, and Salamanders. Green cape for the West, with ocean scenes and mermaids, dolphins, the chalice and cauldron, and Undines.

Archaeology Visit

Archaeology is one of the most important aspects of learning about our past, and the very truth that it reveals. You may have a budding archaeologist in your Circle, if so ask them to prepare some for the Circle as an educational night. If you do not have anyone qualified maybe you can contact your nearest Museum or University and see if there is anyone available who can share their time with giving an information night.

Many museums have tours at their premise, which means that as a coven you can all go and visit and learn from the best qualified and see many artefacts from our history that reveal their story.

You may be lucky enough to volunteer at a local dig if there is one, or maybe when travelling overseas visit and assist in a local dig to give you insight and education the hard work that is put in with the pain staking process of a serious and important find.

The only digging that I have done was for opals and sapphires, and that was exciting enough.

You may be lucky enough to be able to have a University student come to your Circle and share some information with you, (They do not usually charge but remember they are students so having a whip around to at least pay for fuel and giving them a light supper at the end of the night is respectful). I have over the years had many guest speakers come and talk to my Coveners and have always offered them something in return for their time and energy, I have also usually sent them a card and a small token of our thanks.

Astrology Night

This is a very important part of being a Wiccan, is knowing your sun sign and moon sign, and what your astrological chart says about you and your future. You do not have to learn everything about Astrology, but we all need to know the basics, as it will help in our guiding path that lies ahead.

One of my High Priestesses (Lady Sharadon) was an Astrologer and she use to do charts for all who entered the Wicca, as this was there guide. She was very good at it too, sometimes a bit too good. So, if you have a budding Astrologer in your Circle, get them to do everyone's charts, and maybe teach a little about Astrology. It is easy to download charts on the internet to fill out your basic details, they are readily available.

What you will need, is definitely day of birth, and time of birth if possible, the rest is up to your Astrologer. If you do not have an Astrologer then maybe you can contact one, and hopefully discuss a good financial arrangement to come and do your entire Circle, if they would like this of course.

In my Circle I have a questionnaire for all new members, so I can get to know a little about them and see if they fit within the mind frame of my Family Circle. This way I can hopefully have a full circle of equal number of elemental energies such as:

Water signs – Cancer, Scorpio, and Pisces.

Earth signs – Taurus, Capricorn and Virgo.

Air signs – Libra, Gemini and Aquarius.

Fire signs – Sagittarius, Leo and Aries.

So, learn what you can about this very important knowledge source.

Author Meet and Greet

An author "meet and greet" is quite remarkable, it firstly shows support for them and educates your Circle. Many authors are quite busy doing their tours, but if you are lucky to have an author in your town, just ask, as they too need the platform to speak to people and get their writings out there. It also gives them a chance to promote their writings and maybe sell a few more books.

If you cannot get an author to speak at your home, then keep your eyes open for when one maybe attending your local Wiccan or New Age store for their new Book release and their Meet and Greet. If this happens then ask your Circle members straight away and as a group visit and show your support to this author who has worked tirelessly on their writings.

Many people do not see nor understand the amount of behind the scenes work that is involved in the publication of a book. It is hard work and can take many years not only to write the book, but then to promote and market your book is extremely costly and time consuming. With myself when given the chance I prefer to attend small book stores or groups to discuss my books and Oracle decks and get the work out there. It is a hard process but worth it in the long run if you stick to it.

There may even be an event such as "Body, Mind and Spirit" festivals, New Age Festivals and even local Pagan Festivals where you can attend as a supporting group to your Wiccan sister or brother and Meet and Greet them on a grander stage.

Support your local author's as they need it!

Bio-Booklets

This is a great way to get to know your fellow Wiccan better and more personally. Get each Covener to prepare a small or large Bio-booklet, make sure it covers their Zodiac signs, birthdates, place of birth, where they have lived, their history, skills, Magickal skills and interests, likes and dislikes, dreams, guiding principles, Family members, are they open about their Craft involvement or keep it personal.

What do their family and work colleagues think of their involvement. What are they wanting to learn, and how far are they wanting to go within the Craft, are they wanting to be a healer, teacher, guide, or remain as a Seeker.

Only the author knows what they wish to be revealed and placed in the Bio-Booklet. Do they have college transcripts, skills qualifications, Magickal or spiritual qualifications?

What are their favourite colours, foods, Goddess and Gods, animal, plants, books, clothes. Are they married or single and seeking true love?

What is your vision for five years' time? Ten years' time?

When you have everyone's then it is time to bring them all together into your Coven Bio-Booklet. Place them in a special or alphabetical order, photocopy them and bind them, and at a special Festival or event present them to each member. This then will help each member learn more about and understand each person, but hopefully will bring them together to have "Perfect Love and Perfect Trust".

Blessed Bee Honey Bee

If you are lucky to have someone in your Circle who has a farm in a rural setting, then that is perfect. If you don't then maybe you can ask a farmer if you could keep a Bee Hive or more on their land. They usually don't want payment but accept some honey in exchange.

If you have someone who is open to taking control of this venture, that would be an excellent way of making pure honey for your Circle members, (which they could purchase from the Coven to raise funds), or you could sell it at the local markets, and at Festivals.

Even if you don't have a farm or cannot get to use a farm then your suburban backyard may be big enough even just to have one. But make sure there is plenty of plants, herbs and bushes or tree's around you, as they will keep them healthy too. Try to keep your garden free from all pesticides. If you wish to make natural pesticides then view the recipes in my "Complete Teachings of Wicca-Book Two-The Witch", and my "Complete Encyclopaedia of Herbal Medicine and Magick".

Remember that we need bees for our survival as they are part of the creation life chain, without them-nothing exists, and without frogs-nothing exists, without humans-everything thrives!

Blessed Be Sewing Bee

We all have so much in our homes that need to be mending sown or made. So, someone must have a sewing machine and hopefully the ability to be a budding seamstress. If so make a day of it, get everyone to bring what they need mending, fixed or made. To bring their patterns, designs, clothes with buttons missing, zippers broken.

So, bring it all, especially threads, needles and whatever else is needed even fabrics. Just do not get too carried away wanting a full wardrobe to be made at the Covens or seamstresses expense. This is to empty your house of those clothes etc that are just pushed aside because you are not skilled enough to fix them, or too busy, or maybe just too lazy!

This also a good way for people to learn some sewing skills, for future mishaps.

It is also a good time to maybe make some Coven Pouches, Amulet bags and bags for the Coven Tools. As each Tool should be cleaned after being used and then placed carefully away inside their own Magick Pouch to keep them safe and clean until next used and needed. I have another section listed later for the making of Ceremonial Robes, Tabards, Capes and Altar Clothes.

Events like this not only teach you to sew but also give special together time for all the Circle members, and maybe even include extended family members who ay be interested or qualified.

Blessed Be Book Binding

Blessed Be Book Binding, this is a great time to get together and do some Coven Book Binding of Festivals, Books of Shadows, Coven Song Books and more.

Its about putting all your notes together, maybe you are holding an Outer Court Class for Seekers who are interested in Wicca and joining your Coven. My Circles hold these Outer Courts which usually last for about 6 months, this is an education process that allows both parties to see if they fit in the mind of your Circle, and for them to see if it is truly for them.

You may just wish to put all your teachings, or even a Coven Calendar together for all to enjoy. It is best not to give them to your Circle members but to charge them whatever the cost is to the Circle. This at least keeps the coffer's full as a Circle does cost quite a lot, especially when you have lots of open gatherings.

You may wish to Bind copies of the Rituals or festivals and sell to those who are in attendance, so they have a memory of their gathering in your Wiccan Circle. Many people love the idea of having a souvenir or token of their involvement.

Book Launch Author Meet and Greet

As I stated before a lot of work goes into writing a book, and sometimes it takes years of hard work to write and complete a manuscript that is both attractive and professional, and that also offers a little something new to the Seeker of Wicca.

The great asset is having an autographed copy of a book which will always be very special. All my books that I attain I try to get them autographed. Sometimes it is very hard, as they have either passed into the Summerland's or at the other end of the world. But even if they are not famous, try to support them and give them your time and they have shared their knowledge with you.

Many book stores are sometimes lucky enough to hold Author Meet and Greets, if not there are many Festivals you can attend as a group, to meet the author, even many New Age events, but in all cases, try to support them even if you do not know of them. Get to know them as they could be a great learning in the pagan life.

This author could be a great asset not only to yourself or your Circle but to the hold Wiccan community with some information that is very important on our journey. Sometimes as special Book Fares, there may be many authors at the event, but it is unusual to have many if none Wicca or Pagan authors. So please check and support them and they are the teaching foundation of our Faith.

Book Club Share and Exchange

This is an excellent way to share our favourite books with likeminded brothers and sisters. Talking about them and your favourite author really helps to keep everyone connected. Also, it is good to read out your favourite passages from the book.

I would even go to the extent of having your own Wiccan Book Club, where you can get together every two to three months for an open discussion and share and or exchange.

Book clubs are great especially if the whole Circle focuses on one book, they each purchase the book, where sometimes as a group purchase from an author will sometimes save you up to 50% off the retail price of the book. If it is a genuine Coven and if they order 6 books or more, I will autograph my books and then send them at wholesale prices, so they can save a fortune. Or I can even recommend a Book store that is selling my books.

Get everyone to read the books and along the way take notes, and then when you all come together you can speak openly and honestly about the book, its writings and the author.

A book club is great to also have an exchange on books, because usually when we have read the books, we hardly ever pick them up again. So, allowing them to be borrowed or exchanged allows everyone in the circle to have a good read and then pass it on.

I feel that as a Circle we should also recommend certain books that are beneficial and maybe have a specific Recommended Reading Booklist. Grade each book as well from 1 star up to 5 stars. This then shows what you prefer and do not prefer.

Boomerang

Boomerangs have been a part of Aboriginal culture for over 50,000 years, and they are used for several purposes. One of course is the Killer Boomerang (which does not come back) is used to throw and kill their Bush Tucker, such as goannas, wallaby's, kangaroo's, possums and anything else that can be eaten.

There are also the returning Boomerang which if it does not hit its target does return in a semi-circular fashion. These Boomerangs are the main tool for hunting.

These days you can buy inexpensive Boomerangs from local souvenir shops, that are usually made in Asia and decorated with Aboriginal artwork, but they are fakes. If you want the real thing (which I recommend) go onto any Aboriginal website and get a genuine hand painted artefact from them, this supports the maker, the artists and the Aboriginal community.

You can even find some Aboriginals that teach you how to throw Boomerangs as part of their deal, and you can sit with them and decorate them yourselves guided by their elders. This makes the day not only informative with an ancient tribal elder but enjoyable as something to take and remember.

Along with Boomérangs, there are many other artefacts or tools that you can acquire or make such as Gidgee's (spears), Woomera (message stick), Shields, Didgeridoo's, and even tap sticks for making music and tribal dances.

Bragfest

Bragfest's can sometimes bring out the ego, or the reverse show the insecure souls. But a word of caution does not let the ego's soar, remind everyone that sometimes-humble pie is best. But sometimes we can dump humility and shoe our self-esteem and all the glory that comes with it

It is always good to speak of your Truths, and share your experiences, and your larger-than-life abilities, exploits and adventures.

Gather the Coven as in a theatre and have them all sit, be an ancient auditorium and speak as a theatrical artist would speak, even add a few thee's and thou's if you must, but make it interesting. Speak of your adventures and if you have video's or photos to back up the display of prowess then do it, as it adds to the colour of the Bragfest.

Remember it is not about boasting, well yes, it is, and the more coloured the story the better the audience. Your audience is looking or a storyteller, and a great yarn if it's got a little truth in it (wink wink), as they are not going to get too picky about adjectives.

So, speak of your adventures at work, home, the street, travels, dating, event at a Pagan festival. But be brave, elaborate if you must, but do not fly too high as you may fall. You are brave! You are strong! You are eloquent!

Know that you can accomplish incredible feats and huge obstacles, just be weary of the heckler in the audience, and know they are your foe, and give what they give in return. Tell your story, you may feel like a fool at first, but could end up being the hero.

Bumper Sticker Design and Making

When I had my store in Fremantle, (The Alchemist) I literally had hundreds of bumper stickers as they were so popular, and every month I would have some new ones. Just so people would pop in the read them for a laugh.

Bumper Stickers can be symbolic of your feelings about Nature, your spirituality, or just for a joke. But in all they do get the point across.

I remember my good friend Liz got stopped for speeding, and when she wound down her windows to hand the officer her driver's license, he said "You weren't listening to your angels, were you?" And she thought what a strange thing to say, she then asked what do you mean, and he explained, that she had a bumper sticker on the back of her car saying, "Never drive faster than your angel can fly", she cracked up laughing, and so did the officer who let her off with a warning.

If you have some Coven funds, it is also a inexpensive way to make some more funds for the Coven, by making and selling bumper stickers especially if they are relevant to our present situations in society.

Camping with the Coven

Camping is so much fun, whether it is just your family or with friends, but it is especially fun with your Coven, as it can also be not only a relaxing time but an enjoyable and educational time depending on where you camp.

All Covens should go camping, or at least Glamping to get everyone out of the city and touching a bit of the raw Earth. There are so many places to camp that are remote, you could even pick a time when it is the Full Moon or a festival and combine the both together, this way you can all see the sun rise together (if you are well enough too that is).

The more popular parks may be a bit too occupied, so find somewhere away from viewing eyes. We always camp near a river or on the ocean, this way you can fish for supper, swim, and enjoy the serenity and sounds of the calling oceans tides.

Give everyone a job to do and make name tags for them so everyone knows their jobs such as: Potlings – the cook, possums – dish washers, Undines – water collectors, brownies – campsite cleaners, Salamanders – fire attendees, elves – wood collectors, Gnomes – child minders, Faeries – the entertainment, and then you have the hunters.

Put up a roster so everyone knows their duties and times, as this help to make the work load a lot easier and less exhausting and gives everyone time to enjoy themselves. This is a great way to also bond as friends and family, you then feel the power of a tribe that comes together as a Clan should.

Candle Making

Is a perfect way to having the best candles for your Circle and to make for each other as gifts, or for special occasions? There are so many ways of making your candles personal, you can add dyes, crystals, oils, flowers, even photos on the outside of the candle.

Your Etheric Quarter Candles which are placed at your Quarters should be pure and true so make them with beeswax and place some hardener in them. This way they do not burn down to quickly, as this then becomes too costly.

(WARNING) Most cheap candles from Asia are of paraffin and are basically plastic, so when they burn they give off toxic fumes, so be weary. That is why it is great to make your own, because you know that they are natural, and you are ware of exactly what goes inside them.

Firstly, in making outdoor Quarter candles get yourself some containers or jars to put the wax candles in, this keeps them safe from the interference of the wind. You can then also hand paint the jars to fit in with the matching Quarter, in doing this your candles can just be simple on the inside and you maintain the outer container for future use, when the candle burns down.

It is best to keep the Quarter candles as natural as possible but if you are outdoors, then add some Citronella, Lemon Myrtle and Teatree oils to the mix as this will keep away the bities.

If you wish to decorate the outer layer of the candles as gifts then have a pot of heated and melted way (Clear or the colour of the candle) and add your favourite essential fragrant oil, when you have the base of the candle, then dip it in the pot of wax and then add to the outer side photos, flowers, shells, jewellery, whatever your heart desires.

It is also easy to make drip or plunge candles, all you need is a large pot of melted wax of the right candle, scent etc that you desire, cut your candle wicks so that they are double the length that you require with a couple of extra inches added. Then fold the wick in half as to make two candles and then gradually keep dipping them into the wax and let them dry a bit by placing a rod or stick across the top of the pot that you can hang your folded candle over it, then continue to keep dipping until you get the size and thickness you want with a flat end at the bottom and a taper end at the top.

This makes perfect candles for candle holders and for gifts especially if they have essential oils added to them for healing, love, and or prosperity etc.

Canoeing or Kayaking with the Undines

Pagan canoeing or Kayaking are about connecting with the Undines, and all the creatures that dwell within the Water Element. Remember that you are the visitor floating across their world, and moving with their Magickal flow of life.

If you are lucky to own your own canoes or kayaks, maybe you can paint elemental symbols on them or pictures of welcome for the Undines. The Undines love music so singing to them does attract them to you, well depending on the type of music you are into. Sing songs of water, the ocean, the tides, love, the moon, rain, and gentle breezes.

If it is safe then swim with the Undines and know the power of the water element, and how it dances in the veins of every life on our planet, and here it not only dance within us, but outside us, above us and below us. It is a sacred element, and can grant some special powers. So, ask, but be gentle with your asking.

As you move in the flow of life, ask them for a blessing and in return give your blessing to them. If you can make a special offering such as a crystal, then bless the stone and gift it to the water element.

If you are camping, when you return, and your camp is ready for your camp feast, then speak of the Magick and power of the mighty River Goddesses and Ocean Goddesses and how they are the power of the tides of life and death.

Casting and Creating Your Own Runes

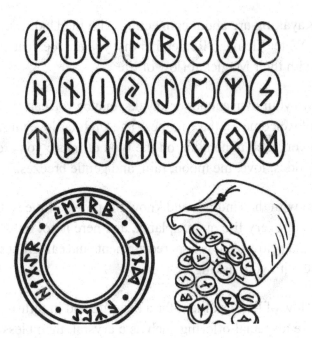

It is quite beautiful to have your own set of Runes, they are great to have and can be an important aspect of the divination process of you as a Wicce. Runes are one of the oldest Celtic methods of divination that we use. They are traditionally made of Birch or Willow, so if you can find some branches about as round as a 10c piece then all you have to do is cut them into sections and then sand them smooth, (I actually like the look of the bark on the outside, it gives them that rustic look.

Then if you are good with a magnifying glass you can etch using the sun and burn the symbols into the wood, or etch with a sharp knife or Boline, or even paint the symbols on them.

If you are good with clay you can make some clay ones and etch into the clay whilst they are still soft before they harden up. You may also like small river flat stones to use as your

Runestones. It is a personal choice but when anything is made by your own hands, it is charged with a certain amount of your Magick, which connects you to them.

The timber ones do look the best, but they are the hardest to do, and take a lot longer, with deep determination the result is magnificent.

Again, it is about personal preference!

Cast and Create Wicce Stones

To create your own Witch Stones is an exciting adventure as all you need to do is know a little about your crystals and their meanings and healing qualities.

Collect yourself 21 assorted crystals that are no bigger than a 20c piece and make sure they all are different. Research their meanings and place all the information into a small booklet that explains what each crystal means.

Then make yourself a drawstring pouch to carry them in and a felt or place mat of some sort to do your Witch Spread.

There are several ways of throwing the Stones, the first is by choosing just one stone for one question. The second is choosing two stones for your question, of what is being done, and the outcome. And thirdly choose blindly three crystals from the pouch not looking at what they are and place in order 1 the question, 2-the action required, 3- the outcome.

It is great to use at Circle meetings by passing around the Witches Pouch of Crystals and each drawing a stone from the bag when asking a question.

Wheel of the Sabbats

Creating a Seasonal Wheel is a beautiful aspect of Wicca as the result is quite Magickal and beautiful. If you are lucky to have an old wooden cart wheel, if not they are easy to make but just take a bit of effort.

1. Make a god for the centre of the wheel by making a large circular disc that has 8 holes bored into the sides of it for the spokes of the wheel.
2. Find and make 8 small circular pieces to be used as the spokes of the wheel, which are all the same size.
3. Acquire some layered pressed plywood and make it the length of the outer measurement of the wheel and as thick as you need. Place the timber into a bath and soak to make pliable, when ready take it out of the back and slowly and gently bend to wrap around the outer wheel, then tie it down to dry and hold its place.
4. The Process is place the spokes into the hug with wood glue or natural resin, wrap the ply wood and then tie off, then dry. After all this has been done, then seal it all with either beeswax or varnish, made from heated resin in hot water, which is the natural way to do it.

The 8 spokes represent the 8 directions, festivals, Paths of Enlightenment, Tools of the Witch and the symbol of the Sun the Hexagram, combining the triangle of light and triangle of dark.

Now choose 8 different members to create seasonal decorations for each of the spokes, so each member becomes that festival. Each then decorates their spoke of the wheel in their chosen design. This wheel is then displayed in front of the Altar at the different Festivals with the spoke of the present festival at the top. This is a yearly cycle of birth, life, death, and rebirth.

Caving Adventure

This can be an amazing adventure for not only the entire Coven, but for all their families as well. We talk about getting to know Mother Earth, well what better way is there than climbing into her very womb of the Earth, and being deep within her bountiful Magick.

The darkness and the silence or noises that are so removed from above ground. Caves can be so meditative and trance-like states can emerge from just being in this underground paradise.

When being in the depth of the cave the best way to enjoy it is through SILENCE as in that stillness, in that silence all forms of messages and truths can be heard and discovered. Time to search for the inner stars of the Cave, see if there are any forms of life, and learn about the formations that are within this Magickal realm.

There are so many places with caves that have guided tours. Where we are presently living on the Central Coast of Queensland, they have orchestral nights with a full orchestra playing inside the cave, this becomes so surreal.

In the past in a place called Yanchep in Western Australia we used to perform certain rituals and ceremonies inside our cave in Yanchep. There are not many caves that are free to use for ceremonies now as they have all been gated up, but if you ask for permission it may being granted.

Choosing Craft or Wiccan Names

When we get involved in Wicca and Wiccecraft, at various stages of our training we select names that are suitable for us, and become the archetype of our Higher Being. It is not just to select a name because of their importance, but it must be significant in the advancement of your own spiritual progression.

When you are Wiccaned/Crafted or Baptised, you would select your own birth name, this is to empower your true vibrations. But you add a name that is Earth based such as a crystal, herb, plant, tree, or animal. So, my name is Tamara, and you can be Wiccaned with the name of Tamara Rose, or Tamara Emerald.

When you are Initiated your name becomes your ultra-ego, the Wicce you must awaken or become, so choose a name that is symbolic of where you are, and where you are going. My Craft name is Avena, which is the Latin (small grain of wheat), it is about me growing from a seed, and being able to flourish and feed the masses. One seed can create millions of seeds and eventually many crops for the betterment of feeding lives. It is also about where I am starting from to where I am wanting to eventually reach on my spiritual ascension.

When you are Ordained into the Priesthood, your name becomes your empowered name, but is only shared with the Inner Circle, this keeps it Magickal and sacred, and used in sacred rituals and ceremonies.

Again, when you are elevated to a higher level such as High Priesthood, this becomes your highest vibratory name as an advanced spiritual human being, on the path to Enlightenment and after death ascension to becoming one of the Shining Ones.

Create Goddess/God Theme Party

As an educational and enjoyable tool, have everyone come to the party as a chosen or selective Goddess from a certain demographic realm, such as Celtic, Nordic, Egyptian, Roman, Greek, South America, Australia, Polynesia/Oceania etc.

Have a different theme and place a heap of Goddesses from the one pantheon into the cauldron where everyone picks one out, these people then must research all about that Goddess and then on the night of the event, teach everyone else (with small booklets on your research) share all your information. This helps everyone grow as a teacher, and also adds to their confidence with public speaking.

You can even all make it fancy dress, and dress and be I the role for the whole evening.

Create Clay Altar Sculpture

Many people feel that they do not have a creative bone in their body, but when they are placed in a situation it is amazing to see how much creativity can flow. Especially when others can give them some encouragement, and usually that is all it takes.

In Wicca we should all have either our own Shrines of dedication in our homes, or even have Magick Circles indoors or outdoors. This Shrine must have a Statue of your representation of your Goddess that represents all that you feel, think and are drawn towards.

Many of us are drawn to certain deities either in the traditional lands to where we live, or to the Celts, Egyptians etc. Whatever Goddess chooses you, go by that inner feeling, and research all that you can, as you must know everything about your Goddess. This way if you are asked questions about her or her tradition, you know for sure, and do not adlib anything.

When your Coven are ready to each make their Goddess Statues for the Altar, make sure you have enough clay (sometimes you can get bulk from a wholesaler) and on the selected day, each person brings everything they need to decorate their statue's.

If you have seen pictures of statues that you like, then bring that picture to copy as your own statue. If you wish to add crystals, seeds, grain, flowers, leaves, tree pods, feathers, beads or even fur from animals, claws, teeth etc. to be placed into the statue whilst it is wet then do this. If you cannot finish your work in one sitting then bring a towel and soak it in water to make it wet and moist, this way your statue will not dry out.

When you have finished your beautiful statue then it needs to be charged and consecrated by the Coven to make her come to life and act as an official symbol of the Great Mother.

Computer Fun Night/Web Design

Nearly every human is lucky to have a computer of some form, whether a desk top PC, laptop, or the like, even our mobile phones are mini computers.

There is usually someone within your Circle that has the skills to educate others about using the computer. As for me my computer is used as a typewriter or word processor and my social media skills are non-existent, but I try, but without someone to help us we become left behind in the dark age, as the age of computers is here to stay.

This night could be about just checking out certain websites for information, having contact with other sources of information, even playing games of Wiccan or Pagan content.

The computer night could also be about creating a Coven website, where everyone within the Circle can have a little input.

You can also put your Covens Book of Shadows on there, or onto CD's for easier access for many. You can download so many things of great value now from the computer, but remember most forms of knowledge out there are maybe 20% correct, 40% confusing and or misleading and 40% absolute rubbish full of lies and deceit.

You can download astrological horoscopes and how to guides that can support your Covens activities. It is and can be if used correctly one of your greatest education tools, just remember in every garden there are weeds that need to be removed!

Confronting Darth Vader

Every Wiccan is aware that we go through Light and Dark cycles, but most of the time we just push them aside and get on with our lives only to find their ugly head emerging again in the future. This is because we truly have not dealt with our Dark Side. We each do not like facing up to the reality of our dark side, but face it we must, that is if we want to ever move forward into the Light.

We do not have to try and destroy our past, just acknowledge it and its course of events, and be healed or heal others through your actions. We must confront our dark side with courage of conviction, and honestly as well.

If you find it hard talking about your negative issues publicly then try to find someone to speak to. Or instead have a Darth Vader Night and discuss; Does evil really exist? What is Darkness? What is evil? What changes or motivates people through Light and Dark? What makes us good or evil? How do we truly feel about ignorance, anger, evil, how do we react to this sort of person? Should we be tolerant and accepting? How do we cope with the differences from growing up in a Judaeo-Christian background or society? How do we feel at the way we are treated as Witches? Are we really evil or is it a sin to associate with us?

There is a lot of healing to be done, but we must start the healing process with ourselves, especially in areas of forgiveness, and tolerance and acceptance. Remember we are not alone in this, as every human being has these issues of meeting with Darth Vader daily. Remember to feel "The Force".

Corn Dolly's

The art of making real traditional Corn Dolly's is exceptional, and it is an art of dedication and much creating and know how.

My first experience with professionals of Traditional Corn Dolly making was at a festival that I attended in South Australia, where a family of heritage traditionally made these Corn Dolly's for generations, there they are a Pagan festival and displaying all their creations, many of which were for sale, some were not.

The funny thing was that they were Christians, who made these for the Pagan community, and when I asked them how they can this with a clear conscience, they replied we do it for the money.

Corn Dolly's have traditionally been made for thousands of years, and are used for either healing, fertility, festivals, celebrations, and for any reasons that your heart desires.

Corn Dolly's are made by using green grasses, wheat shafts, barley, oats, corn etc. whilst they are green and fresh and then weave them into their desired design. Add coloured ribbons to represent what you are wanting, also add herbs, flowers and anything else that is appropriate. Make some with magnets on to stick them on your fridges and fridge magnets. They make beautiful gifts and are great decorations for the Yule Tree.

Costume and International Cuisine Night

This is an exciting way to have fun and fill the bellies with traditional and international food. You can have a theme party of Mexican, Italian, Chinese, Polynesian, German, Greek, Native, Maori, Vegetarian, Vegan, etc. Or you could just have a mix and match, where everyone dresses according to the food that they have brought for the feast.

We all love food and we love experimenting with food, many of us have not tried everything so by having these special nights of fun and feast we get to try an assortment to test our taste buds.

You could even have people bring a dish from their heritage, and then we all have to guess what their heritage was or is, unless it is obvious. You can also add to this where instead of International Cuisine, you could have Food of the Rainbow, with each person bringing a different colour dish, from black, brown, red, orange, yellow, green, blue, and purple. Or have every dish the same colour just by adding a little food colouring.

Whatever your theme please remember to keep it fine dining, so all can sit at a large dining table and be eloquent.

Your event should be voted by all and given all plenty of time to get their costume and or food prepared. It is asocial night and one of food tasting. So, enjoy!

Coven Banner

Creating a Coven Banner that represents your Coven, is a show of pride. It shows your seriousness and genuine feelings towards your Craft. All you need is a good piece of white canvas that is easy to paint on. Cut it and hem it to the desired shape and size that you want.

With our Coven Banner we have a coven member Azarion who was great with wood work and made a beautiful wood Banner holder that had our Coven Seal upon the top of it, and Coven Banner sat fixed just below the symbol, we had a pair of these.

It was always exciting to go to open festivals and see the display of Banners from different Covens, it showed how the Craft movement was growing and changing for the better.

When you have your banner done to the size and measurement and style, then it is time to get your creative artist member to do the artwork and make it a Banner to die for.

Your banner can be squared, oblong, circular, triangular, or a mix of two or more shapes, it is what is best for display and in presenting your Coven Logo or flare. You can always help other covens with their Banners as well.

Coven Book of Shadows

If you do not luckily come from a Traditional Coven where the Book of Shadows has been handed down and copied by each new Initiated Wicce, then it makes it harder to get your BoS. But sometime creating and writing your own BoS makes it more exciting.

In my Covens I find that having our Traditional BoS is a great start for every new member, but it is also beneficial for each member to have their own BoS, which is a collection of every great piece of writing that you have come across or copied from books, even when you have attended open rituals, many covens gift you a copy of the festival or ritual, which can be added into your Bos. If you have someone in your Coven who is great at Calligraphy, or excellent writing skills maybe you could get them to write it for you, even getting an artist to do pictures throughout the BoS.

In my second book of Complete Teachings of Wicca-Book Two-The Wicca, it gives examples of writing out your own BoS, and what is needed within your Magickal pages. Just remember that your BoS is also a form of a diary of events. So, make sure that every Full Moon, Ritual and Festival has the date on it, this shows how your rituals change and grow, as well as you.

At the back of your BoS make sure you have a page for all the Wiccaning's, Initiations, Hand-fasting's Funerals etc. that you have done. Adding the dates, times, and names, or new Craft names. Also, be aware that you can always add to your BoS, or as I do, rewrite it and refurbish it with new modern Magick called technology.

Coven Calendar

This makes the running of your Coven so much easier, having a full programme that is rich and diverse, shows the organisational skills of your Circle. Having the list of the full years events give everyone ample time to change other dates and notify people that they are busy that night, unless it is a very important non-craft event. Such as wedding, funeral, etc.

Having a simple calendar is all you need but if you desire something elaborate and special then bring everyone together and add their personal flare to the Circle Diary or Calendar. It is so simple but can add so many components to make it personal such as artwork, astrological signs and dates, Moon phases, dates for Festivals and other important events, coven birthdays and rebirthdays (days of their Initiations), just add what you would like to see.

My Coven Goddess Diaries are full of information including days of the Goddess and God, famous Elders of Wicca birthdates and deaths. Your design can be as elaborate as you desire, if it is done in a professional manner, they can be bound and sold at your local new Age or Wiccans stores, and at the local markets, this will cover costs and if lucky add some money to your Coven funds.

Our Church and Coven diaries cost about $9 to make, and we sell to our members for $15, and the same price to bookstores, and we sell them for $20 at festivals and the markets, this makes a good profit for next year's venture.

Coven Herb Garden

Having a Coven Herb garden is so nice to have due to always having your Magickal herbs freshly available, and also your Medicinal Herbs at the ready as well. We use to at each New Moon plant a new herb in the garden, usually around the perimeter of the Magick Circle. This way they absorb the energies from the circle which is beneficial.

If you have a different member bring an herb each New Moon, then eventually you will have large enough herb garden for all your members to enjoy. If the Covenstead garden is not big enough then maybe one of the Coveners may let you use their garden for the Coven. If they do this see if they can also have a bee hive as this then makes the honey medicinal honey and very valuable as a health source.

Being a professional herbalist myself, I love having my herb gardens, well my herb farm really. As I am addicted to the country, and starve in suburbia.

As you ceremonially plant each herb get the person who brings it along to give a talk about its name, properties, culinary, medicinal and Magickal benefits etc.

When the herbs are mature enough to tithe from it, remember to only take between 10-20% of the plant each time, as this will make the plant fill out and be fuller in the coming seasons, and a better herb, with a greater yield. Which means that there is more to share with your Coven members, as it should be doled out evenly for all members.

Coven Networking

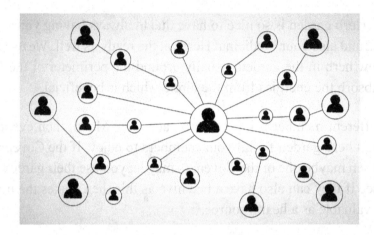

There is an ancient saying; "Ye may not be a Witch alone!" Which is so true, the more the merrier? Even if you are a solitary and never belonged to a coven, it is great to mix and mingle. Sharing of ways and having invitations to other covens to join in with your fellowship is an important aspect of Wicca and its beneficial growth.

We used to always at the Lesser Festivals invite other covens to come and join in with our festivities. This was great for everyone to meet and greet other craft people in our larger community. It was also being available and sharing of energies and differences. As each coven usually works a little different even the basis is usually the same. The one thing about my circles is that they were never the same, they varied so much from ritual to ritual, this made them newer and fresher.

The joining of other covens can also have its drawbacks but genuinely it is on benefit to help our faith grow. By inviting others to your Circle, means that they could reciprocate, and you could get invites to their circle.

You could then do jointly little newsletters or share in Coven Calendars and Diaries, or even sell them your diaries, which helps get them out there.

Coven Sanctuary

If you are a suburban or city Coven, then the chance to purchase or acquire some land in the country is a great asset. If you do not have enough funds for this, then maybe a member of your Circle has some rural land that they are willing to allow the Coven to use as there Covenstead.

The idea of having some land away from prying eyes, and with the freedom to have your ceremonies out in the open is the most exhilarating time you will ever have as a Wicce, as there is nothing more beautiful than being in the country with a God lit fire, and a sky full of stars and listening to the sounds of Nature.

If you have the chance as a Coven to purchase some land as a legal sanctuary, then do it, as it is needed in our times to have such a place for all to attend and gather. You can add some cabins, or have a tent site for large festivals for those wishing to stay the night, to start with porta loos are great. Eventually with enough help and funds you could build a full Pagan and Wiccan retreat for all attend and then host great festivals, this way the funds are going into your coffers rather than outsiders and building their financial base.

Make sure that if this is for Wicca that it is legally protected by wills or legal documents so that no one can just come in and bulldoze the place for more urban homes. This could equally be owned by all Coven members, and if some wish to leave that they can sell their part to other members. It is also a great investment where you may start with 5 acres, and then sell that to acquire 100 acres or more.

Coven Scrapbook

This your Magickal Diary, where you could keep a permanent record of all your most important and memorable events and activities. We have a Scribe who oversees this endeavour.

When you have special events take notice of them, record them, photograph them and keep record of attendance. Sometimes we forget so much that has eventuated in our lives, that just browsing through a scrapbook brings back the memories, that fill our hearts. Even photographing some excellent dishes

We started having video filming throughout our ceremonies so as to see all that goes on, and capture certain things we don't see. We never take photos during rituals but afterwards it is all on. The more the better.

Capturing everyone in ceremonial regalia, is quite alluring and knowing that we were all happy there on that special night. When your coven goes on excursions, trips, visiting sacred sites or other covens, but always ask first if someone minds their photo being taken, as some people do not wish public notoriety.

Archives are the food for fond memories, and as you get older they are usually all you must remind you of an amazing and exciting past. Even place certain patterns or ways of making the tools in these pages, such as designs etc.

Covenstead Spring Cleaning

This is a very important aspect of Coven work. Honour your Covenstead and your High Priest or High Priestesses home, always offer to help around the place, not just on the night. But on different occasion the members should get together to just come around and do some extra bit of housework to help at the Covenstead.

Many Wiccans feel that the appropriate time for cleaning is Spring, I feel it is when you can all get the time together to offer a helping hand. Usually it is good to have half the people indoors and the other half outdoors, remembering many hands make light work.

This is giving back to the homeowner, and helping them out, as I found that in my past of running large groups, that I was offering little to no assistance in the way of caring for my properties. Even when I had my home being run down by hundreds or people using it, not many people offered to help.

There are so many points about spring cleaning to remember that many property owners forget such as cleaning the eaves, window washing, trimming gardens plants and trees, maintaining reticulation to keep the place green and alive. Weeding is the biggest time user, and even the dusting or washing of walls is needed.

Whatever assistance you can offer in a Covenstead Spring Clean is always a welcome gesture of your feelings toward the host and hostess.

Coven Songbook

We have found that to us the importance of music and songs in our Circles is immense, in fact I cannot remember ever having a circle without music, dancing or singing, as it is part of our culture.

As we have had professional Bards and Musicians in our Circle, it is always a dream to attend these festivities. Our High Priest Lord Ariston has always been an asset to our Circle, not only because of his musical abilities but due to his being a very spiritually trained man. Especially in the fields of Chakra Toning, Meditation, Crystal healing and much more.

With the amount of beautiful songs in the craft it is a great idea to have your Coven songbook with all your favourite psalms, songs and ditties to get the spirit pumping.

You can make this as elaborate as you desire as well, by even having the musical scale and notes for all who can read music, to follow along and play our songs. Make it a professional songbook, and then sell it to other craft people or to your local book stores, even at festivals.

Coven Volunteering

Arranging to have your Coven volunteer at different places helps to get our credibility out there, and to also meet and help where help is needed. You do not need to go as a full group, but many may just offer their services at Retirement Homes for the elderly, animal retreats, parks, charitable events, animal rescues and shelters. There are so many places in need of support and help, that they never get, especially as the government have reduced a lot of their charitable donations, it is now up to us the community to take over and do the work. We take so much we must remember to give back.

My Coven offer in many charitable volunteering manners, especially helping when the Dalai Lama comes to town, we offer as a full coven the services in security and fund collections, and assist in management. As I am a lover of Buddhism, and have personally met with His Holiness several times I feel it is my duty to assist this great man and his causes.

We also have several that often help at old people's homes and with animal rescue shelters. Also offering the time to assist a fellow member who need odd jobs done around their house as they have not been able to due to ill health or lack of support and funds. We must help wherever help is needed, this is the true aspect of being a Wiccan. "Give and ye shall receive".

Council of All Beings

We are in a time when it is sad to say that man has been the assault on Nature and are acting like parasites, drawing and taking from everything and every creature. The animal kingdom does not have a voice and cannot speak for themselves, well they do try, but we don't listen, because through ignorance we are deaf to anything that is beyond our scope of reality.

Create a Coven Committee of spokespersons where each Coven member should either choose or be selected to act as a spokesperson for a set species of animals, always start with endangered species. Start with our little brothers and sisters that are in our local vicinity, and then gradually expand the distance, to the whole town, then the city, the state and then the country, and with enough people participating you can speak on behalf of all creatures of the world, start the vibration and it will happen, look at what Greenpeace and Sea Shepherd have achieved.

With this mighty council you can discuss and maybe publish your views on the environmental impact that their devastation is having on the world. Also speak of what we as a species the human are having on not only their livelihood but eventually ours, and then the planet.

Each council member must properly and sensibly research all they can about their species of animal, (Truths only not theories) and research about their habitats, their food supply, their forestry, be informative as you learn about this you can share and teach others, even do talks at schools and help them to create a Council of All Beings as well, it can then spread across all schools and with love and positivity change the world as it is and save a species before it is too late to save anything.

Even do Magick and ceremonies assisting in saving this species, collect donations for Wildlife Preservation Society's.

Create an Astral Healing Temple

Many are not aware but if you create your Magick Temple on the Astral first before physically creating one, that it can travel with you wherever you go. As an Astral Temple is a place that can be used for all things, especially as a healing Temple.

A friend of mine Lady Elizabeth has her Astral Temple and she has created it as a hospital, so that her patients can be admitted like a normal hospital, then hourly or daily cared for as if they were physically there. She also does Psychic surgeries on them and even gives full blood transfusions, and transplants.

She is a master surgeon of the Astral and Magickal realms. I know of many that have been in her Astral Hospital and they were completely affected and healed by this grand lady's abilities, and her ability to connect with the person psychically.

Also, is good that you are aware that to truly heal someone, they must be informed first, as we should never do Magick on anyone without their awareness and approval. This way they can be healed on every level, starting mentally, astrally, psychically, physically and thus spiritually.

I feel that it is important to say that your Astral healing Temple should not be abused for normal matters of healing than time will mend in due course, as this is a waste of the powers and energies of your Magick Space. So maybe do a Tarot spread first and ask the question "should I heal this person, and if so how should I go about it and to what degree?"

Create a Bush Magick Circle

It is great if you are lucky to have an outdoor Circle, better to have rural outdoor Circle, but better still is to find a space in the middle of the bush or forest, where humans dare not go, and with the assistance of your Coven members create a beautiful and natural Magick Circle.

Having a bush Circle means that you are away from neighbours and free to do as you like, it means also that you are truly with Nature and all it has to offer. The excellent thing is that there are no street lights and the night-sky is so lit up it is beyond beautiful.

In making and preparing your Bush Magick Circle, all you need is the Coveners and them ready to get their hands dirty and the tools to clean and prepare the space, such as rakes, shovels, chainsaw, even a wheelbarrow can be handy. Then it is time to split the crew up into set jobs.

Some to find some rocks for the perimeter of the Circle, some for wood hunting for the Bale Fire, if you are lucky to have a couple of big trees down they can be used to make seats, or find a stump that would make an excellent Altar. Try to find the space that is close to where you park your cars, and a place that is safe.

Start by clearing the Circle space, then with the rocks make the perimeter, and dig a shallow hole in the middle for the fire. Place your stump Altar in the North, now your Magick Circle is ready to be Banished, Consecrated and Cast for your rituals.

Creative Night with the Goddess

This the night we invoke the Muses to assist us in our creative flare. You might not think you are creative but believe you me, we are all creative, and once we let our creative juices flow, there is no stopping it.

Whether we love painting, arts and crafts, sculpting, ceramics, floristry, poetry, music, singing, even garden designs. It does not matter as we are creative in our own way, and if we invoke the Goddess our creativity will be incredible. As people who feel they have no creative talent are amazed at just how much creativity and artistry they really have.

If you wish, before you start sit in a circle and hold hands and call the Muses to gift to you the ability which is truly unique and your own. If you have musicians let their flare be in the background to stimulate the senses of all members who are present. Even write a Magickal piece of music or song that is about The Goddess and Creativity.

After everyone has done their beautiful form of creativity put them on display and create a Gallery of Art scene. This way everyone can come and check out all the master pieces and maybe review who the winner is, you can have several categories such as advanced artist, home artist and artist in training. You could have small trophies of gifts or certificates for each category.

Be warned! Once the creative juices start to flow there will be no stopping you!

Create a Sacred Mound

In Creating a Sacred Mound in honour of the Earth Mother, you need to first have a ceremony or divination to ask if the Earth spirits of the area will permit or even want a Sacred Mound. In Aboriginal custom you always honour the land first, then the spirits of the land and then the ancestors of the traditional people.

In honouring these we are also asking for permission to use their land that is on loan to us. So, if you have a rental property it is hard to build an elaborate mound, so maybe just build a Shrine instead. But if you are lucky enough to have your own suburban land or better still a rural farm property. Then you can create an elaborate Mound to represent the belly of the Mother Earth.

Start by divining the perfect spot, and then ask the spirits of the land, and then it is time to mark out the size that you want the Mount. Place stakes and string to mark out the exact shape and size of the Mound. If it is in the shape of a female body then place her head to the North, the realm of the Goddess and God.

The hard work now comes will filling and making the mound out of whatever you find, and many wheel barrows of soil and rock, you may even want to wet the surface and plant lawn seed to create a beautiful green lush Mound that lives and breathes.

Crystal Healing

Crystals we all seem to know a little about, but then there are those who take it to the next level. In my Coven we have two people who are empowered by learning as much as they can about crystals. Ariston is a healer and uses his crystals for healing, and to open portals in different dimensions. He also uses them for ritual as Magick Wands and for directing energy.

The other is Adam, who is a professional author and teacher of crystals and their many uses. He teaches and does workshops to help people understand the powers of crystals and their myriad uses. Even in Crystal Essences, he is probably one of Australia's most qualified in his field.

I myself use to always joke to them about their many rocks that they had lying around, joking to see if I could get a bite from them. I always pleaded ignorance acted dumb about crystals and in comparison, to them I was.

Crystals are also used in Chakra Clearing and Balancing, and Ariston has a powerful phallic shaped crystal that is quite large that we use as our coven Wand to invoke the Goddess and God at Full Moons and Festivals. Crystals are exciting but remember, we take them from the Earth, so we need to give back, everything that comes from the Mother must eventually be returned to the Mother, it is the law of Nature.

Crystal Gazing and Clairvoyance

Clairvoyance = CLEAR SIGHT, the development of the intuition to a level of practical usage. On the Kabbalistic Tree of Life, it is the ability to perceive Hod from Netzach, and Netzach from Hod, to see them as action and reaction respectively.

The use of clairvoyant tools such as the crystal ball will aid in the development of the intuition. The crystal is a focus point for you to use your imagination in a positive visual way by a concentrated effort of Yesod's artistic energies.

Once you have acquired a crystal ball it is necessary to fee it from any auric influences that may be attached to it (because of previous ownership or handling etc.) this is achieved by the LBRP performed in a salt and water Magick Circle, followed immediately by covering the crystal with black silk, which will keep it protected until you begin to work with it yourself.

The crystal ball is used on a special Scrying Table, which is ideally constructed of dark wood with writings of gold, or on a specially made Scrying Cloth, the table when completed should also be covered with a silk cloth (to contain no aura but your own). A small holder for the crystal ball is required, this too should be your own construction, painted matt black and kept covered with black silk.

It is necessary for the preparation of this Magickal equipment to take place during the New Moon up to the Full Moon. This is most important to your success, as the Moons magnetic and perspective aura benefits the crystal immensely. Further to your success, all crystal gazing preferably should be done in a controlled environment. This is best achieved by the construction of a salt and water Magick Circle, in which you have done a full LBRP and invocation ritual. The circle should be set in a clean, darkened room where you will be undisturbed. Take care that it is free from any objects that may reflect in the crystal, and thus disturb your attention. The room should not be dark, but rather shadowed with dull unmoving light, somewhat like a Moonlight room. It is necessary to time you're sitting, so set a clock where, through the face is visible, and the ticking inaudible.

Before commencing your crystal work, attention to self-preparation is of prime importance. Fasting for at least four hours before your ritual is most beneficial, in contributing to a relaxed state of body and mind, enabling easy energy production. Before you start meditating on full relaxation followed by the Middle Pillar Ritual. After this you may go about casting your Magick Circle.

The Art of Crystal Gazing may be classified as follows:

1. Images of your thoughts, personal opinion.
2. Images of ideas consciously acquired from other by telepathy etc.
3. Images, pictures bringing information as to something past, present or future, which the gazer has no way of knowing.
4. The ability to see accurately the qualities, quantities and distribution of the Elements of any given 'field'. (Under this 4th heading comes true crystal vision.

Do not be disappointed if when and even after you have completed the preliminary exercises set forth here, you do not apparently perceive an answer to what you are seeking after the first or even following attempts. On the other hand, if you have a GIFTED POTENTIAL to be a Seer, you may be beginning perceiving on your very first sitting, you are advised to disregard it, as continuous success will only come as a growth development and these exercises will secure it.

Practise and sincerity will eventually develop an automatic ability to obtain results in the exploration of any given field. Doing Oracles for people is a good start, allowing immediate reference points, depending of course on what they wish to enquire. When doing this the person should keep silent and remain seated at a distance opposite you, all questions asked should be in a low and low tone.

Although the Moon is in harmony with the crystal, the days and times you do your work will depend on the nature of your enquiry. As you develop your work will lead you to a kind of Astral Workshop. This will be your own creation and an art form of the Four Quarters, in action allowing you to see and use it in your everyday life.

Coven Role Selection

When starting a Coven for the first time you will always have a leader which is usually the most knowledgeable and ranked of either High Priest or High Priestess. But as your Circle grows it is important to delegate responsibilities to each new member and make them through ceremony, the chosen in the field, selected and voted for by the Coven community.

- High Priestess – is the first and most important to have as the Clan Mother and representative of the Goddess. The HPs runs all the Lunar events such as New Moons and Full Moons.
- High Priest – is the consort of the HPs and is the Clan Father and representative of the Horned God and is responsible for all the Festivals and the exterior running of the Coven.
- Maiden – The assistance and lady in waiting to the HPs to act when needed as the HPs. She also makes sure that everyone is properly prepared and readied for each gathering, and that all the tools and regalia are ready and clean as well.
- Man, in Black – The Principal Ritualist under the HP. He is what we term as the "Coven Cop", as he deals with all matters of discipline, and keeps order within the Coven Community.
- Warden of the East (Male) – They are the keeper deal with every aspect of the Air Element, its direction and tools, they summon and call forth and banish their realm, they are the Keeper of the Gate of the East.
- Warden of the South (Male) – as above but they are in control of the South and the Element of Fire and all its tools etc.
- Warden of the West (Female) – same as Air but with the Water Element and all its realms and tools.
- Warden of the North – (Female) -same as Air but with the Earth Element and its realm and all its tools.
- Wiccans – are usually guests who are respected as Wiccans, but have not been Wiccaned, Crafted or Initiated.

- Wiccelings – Children who have been Wiccaned and accepted into the Coven.
- Bunnies - They are adults who have been Wiccaned and or Crafted to enter the Outer Court of the Temple, their job is to keep all the Altar Tools and Magickal of the Coven clean prior to Circle. They also act as servers on the night, as a sign of humility, (but we usually all dig in).
- Wicces – They are Initiates who have undergone full Outer Court training for over a year before being accepted and Initiated into the Coven as Wicces. They are then taught the lesser uses and how to cast and perform the Magick Circle, and they copy out the Coven Book of Shadows.
- Priesthood – These are Wicces have been Wicces for a minimum of a year and who wish to dedicate their life to the pursuit of the Goddess and in becoming a Priest or Priestess they become also the teachers, the healers, the Celebrants and professionals of the Coven.
- High Priesthood – These are Priests and Priestesses who have trained for a further 1-2 years in the priesthood and who wish to hive off and form their own sister Coven.
- Elders – These are the respected High Priesthood who are either run their own coven or who have retired from such a responsibility and are now just respected Elders of the community as Crones, Sages and Official Elders.
- Wicce Queen – This is a High Priestess who has had several High Priests or High Priestesses hive off and form their own coven. A Wicce Queen is the titular head of all her Covens, and is called this title when having more than 5 covens or more.
- Magi – This is the High Priest as with the same as above, but they are now into the mode of being a Magician, and work on a higher level.

These are all the stages for those who wish to tread this ancient path and through blood, sweat and tears strive through all these ordains elevations to reach the pinnacle and eventually also at the end of their journey become one of the Shining Ones.

Dancing your Power Animal

Dancing your Power Animal is exciting as it is recommended. We should all be in touch with our Power Animal and this can be done by going through a Trance state ritual and calling to the spirit of your brother or sister animal.

I believe that we should only call the animal spirit of the land we live on. In the Book by Michael Harner called "Way of the Shaman", he explains this ceremony. In Australia we have many kindred animals that we as Australians should connect with, as in the US, UK, Europe, Polynesia, Africa, Asia etc.

There is no point calling the spirit of a Brown Bear, when you have never seen one or been near one, or it is not even an animal of the land you live on. So, in a Council of All Beings what animal is calling out to you, and what animal can you speak on behalf of and more importantly what has their spirit and energy got in comparison to you.

To find your true Power Animal it needs to be done individually, as it is personal and empowering. It is also to visit your animal in the wild either physically or through dreamwork. When you are ready find a drummer, who can assist you into finding your Power Animal, and let their spirit move you, not your spirit.

The longer you are in dance mode as the animal the better as the joining of two spirits can come together releasing a spiritual bond, and a power flow of energy. You must eventually feel as they feel, think as they think, hunt as they hunt, eat as they eat, and make love as they make love. It is a joining of two to become one. Remember that your Power Animal is Kin and not a servant to do your bidding.

Dealing with Death

For so many people it is very hard to deal with Death, especially when it is someone very close such as a loved one and a family member. Many say oh don't worry it gets easier, yes after a lot of time it does get easier, but you never ever forget, and even the pain of the memory can sometimes bring back tears and a feeling of being alone.

But dealing with Death is about understanding its purpose in the Big Picture, what do you believe happens after death, is there a Heaven or a Summerland, where we will be reunited with those who have passed. There is another thing to remember, that we as Wiccans believe in reincarnation, so can you remember your past lives and their deaths, can you associate or connect with them by their association with your previous life. How did you die in other lives? How would you like to die in this life? How would you not like to die?

Have you made up your will, for your family and friends, and more importantly as a Wiccan have you made a separate Spiritual Will, so that all your tools and regalia are looked after according to your wishes, especially as some family members may think of them as junk and just throw them out not realising their religious significance to you, your life and your next life. In this life what do you want done after your death? What kind of a funeral are you wanting? Are there any specifications that you MUST have to help in carrying your soul body across into the next realm and the next incarnation? Do you want a Wakes?

I myself just wish to be buried on my home farm and an Oak sapling to be placed on top of me so it grows and absorbs my body as its food for a great spiritual and Magickal life ahead. Then others can use my branches for Wands and the like. "Blessed Be and have a part of Me!"

Diana's Bow Tournament

Diana's Bow Tournament is a great way to connect the Huntress of the Moon, Diana. The time for doing this is just after the New Moon, when her Crescent Bow is high in the sky, get as many of your members together, and book an Archery Club for your grand Tournament. They will teach the novices, but if you have members who are Archers and have their own bow and arrows then you can do this on your own land or in a park somewhere, if it be safe.

If you have a skilled archer then get them to explain in full the safety issues and how and what and what not to do, it is always great to have instruction from a pro.

When all have been instructed with safety, then let the Tournament begin! You can set up three different courses one for skilled, one for those not so skilled, and for novices. As for targets these are easily purchased from archery stores and gun stores. We use a large bale of hay and then place targets on them. But you could also use hula hoops, balloons, swinging pendulums or even types, scarecrows, staves, cardboard shapes, even pieces of metal for different sounds. We sometimes set out a series of about 12-15 different size bells and swing them from a tree, give each bell a specific point, the larger bells smaller points and the smaller bells big points.

Invoke the archer legends such as William Tell, Robin Hood, Cupid, Apollo, Apollo, Diana, Rhiannon, Artemis and Astarte.

It can be a very fun day, include the children as well and make it into a picnic, you could have all the women dressed as huntresses and the men as hunters, prizes for best costume, and for best skills, even prizes for no skill.

Discover your local Trees and Bushes

As Wiccans we all love our bush walks, but how many of us know what we are looking at or passing, do we know their names and their importance, what do they offer us as medicines or the like. There are thousands of trees in some species but they each have a different name and medicinal purpose if any, or maybe they are good for making essential oils, or bush tucker.

But we need to know their names, as we hate it when people do not address us correctly with our real names. Each name is the energy source of the tree or plant. The sacred Devas the spirits of the Tree can speak to you if you listen with sincerity.

When you go for your bush walk to meet and greet new brothers and sisters, do not forget to take gifts for them such as crystals or even compost and fertiliser for their good health.

When you pass a tree that is sick or contaminated, stop and give it a blessing, but firstly ask of its name. Take a leaf and research the species if you are not aware of what it is. Leaf your healing gift and continue. You may be lucky enough to come across a tree or bush that outshines the rest and has beautiful flowers smiling at the world. Take a moment to adore it in silence and talk to the plant, introduce yourself and exchange names and energies.

Leave as a family member and let them know that you will hopefully return, take your bidding and part for the time being.

Dream Circle

The study of dreams is not a field that I have focused on, but I have little knowledge. A good friend of mine is a great interpreter of dreams and their meanings, as she has studied this field for over 20 years.

To have a Dream Circle and share information about Dreamcraft, you need more in-depth parapsychological reading and training especially from the works of Dr. Carl Yung titled "Jungian-Senoia Dream Workbook".

Disregard the Gypsy Dream books as they are very false and misleading, they were created just as a money-maker, when the New Age started to the shake the apple tree, and everyone was getting into the new movement of Magickal spirituality.

It has always been a good trial for every Wicce to have a Dream Journal by their bed, as all dreams should be recorded as soon as possible as our conscious mind seems to let them fly away and we forget very quickly. Many of our dreams are relevant to what has happened, is happening or will happen in our lives. Psychologists sometimes see dream as a deep seated unconscious scene created by the stress or high emotion that is in our life at that present.

Practice intense lucid creaming, and if qualified use some hypnotherapy to help guide your dreams, even to assist in remembering your dreams more vividly. As a good Dream Tea mix before going to sleep usually about an hour before is 1 part Chamomile, 2 parts Mugwort and 1 part Skullcap. It really helps with some delectable and colourful dreams. Do it as a Coven and sleep as the spokes of the wheel within your Magick Circle and share your dreams.

Dreamcatchers

The making of dreamcatchers is a beautiful experience and with a whole coven's different forms of creativity you can come up with some rather beautiful and exciting creations. Remember that the essence of Dreamcatchers is to catch your nightmares and to let your good dreams come through.

Their power source is of Mother Earth and all the species of Elemental Beings on the Earth. Involve the gifts from the Earth and its animal kingdoms, such as the "Winged Ones"- birds, insects, Sylphides, include feathers, sticks, leaves, etc. "The Crawling Ones"- such as reptiles, salamanders, snakes, claws, skins, fire stones, etc. The "Swimming Ones"- fish, dolphins and whales, even gifts of the sea such as coral, shells etc. The "Standing Ones"- the trees, bushes, plants, herbs, flowers, and the Gnomes, include crystals, rocks, nuts etc.

Then collect some rolls of gut sinew (or you can get the imitation one now that is much stronger and with no life to kill in getting it). You will need, sticks, twine, saplings branches, leaves, feathers, crystals, arrow heads (if you want), even some herbs that dry well can be added as a Healing Dreamcatcher.

Your Dreamcatcher can be any dimension that you desire, you can even make a Coven Dreamcatcher the size of your Magick Circle if you desire, (but where to hang it?) Enjoy the weaving and designing of your Dreamcatcher, we also find it great if you are doing it with a partner, and then help them to make theirs.

Drumming Circle

A Drumming Circle of Medicine Circle is a great way to get people to come together for the Higher Purpose of Healing those within their community and without. When you have several Drummers each with their own drums it makes it a very Magickal Healing night. There are so many methods to creating a drumming circle but firstly everyone must be One with the Drum, for Drum is your friend, drum is your Magick, Drum is the Heart of yourself and the Living Mother Earth.

When you hold the Drum correctly it represents the voice of the Magick Circle and the four directions and Elements of Air at the top of the drum, Water at the right of the drum, Earth at the base of the drum, and Fire at the left of the drum. Each Element resonates to a specific beat of the drum.

- Air One paused beat.
- Fire Two open beats.
- Water Three beats with the first being a strong beat and the following two being lighter.
- Earth being the Warrior beat of Four beats.
- Spirit the centre of the drum which is a continuous beat.

You can either follow these or create your own spirit rhythm, and each can beat their own Element which makes a musical healing sound of power.

Dumb Supper

A Dumb Supper is traditionally used at Samhain (Halloween), it is a Banquet table set up with a 10% proportional tithing of the bounty of your feast. This is set aside for your Ancestors, and the Shining Ones who you will be invoking and calling upon to join with your festivities.

It is good to keep the colours of the table with a mix of oranges, reds, purples, and blacks. Add some large candelabras to make it extravagant, and add either side of the table a couple of Jack-O-Lanterns, with candles in them.

When you perform the Ceremony of Samhain, and all having whispered their losses and sent their messages to their ancestors, and those who have recently passed, we then invoke the Shining Ones, the Great Teachers and Elders of our Traditions. We open our hearts and souls to them that they can teach us of patience, virtue, tolerance, acceptance, understanding, loyalty, and of the Magick of the past.

We ask to share their ancient wisdom and reveal certain truths to us, that we can continue in their footsteps, and bring their knowledge back through the Shadows of time and space, and awakening our very beings with the light and truth.

When all the hard work is over, and we have spoken and chatted awhile it is time to dance and sing and invite them to join in to our festivities, this is followed by the Great Feast inviting them to sit at the special table in honour of their presence.

At the end of the night we do not dismiss them but ask them that in their own time, before the rising sun that they return from whence they came.

Earth Walk

Earth Walking or Walkabout as the Australian Aboriginals call it, have been done for tens of thousands of years by not only the Aboriginals, but also the Native American Indians and the Japanese as a walk of silence, listening and learning, by just being a part of Mother Nature.

It is in the stride of your step that determines what lessons are to be learnt, the stronger the stride the more of the warrior is needed, the gentler and softer the stride the more meditative and forms of relaxation are needed.

The pace of your step can be in rhythm with your heartbeat and together they can create a form of trance state, that enables you to go a little deeper, and search further within, than is wanted but needed. Whilst on this journey do not commence with an idea in mind of what you want, but let the breezes of Nature spirits speak to you, and guide your footsteps to where your lessons are to be learnt.

This is better always done as individuals alone with just Nature as your guide and protector and teacher, but if you desire to do it at a lesser level with your Coven members, then this can also be done, maybe meet at a special place, and then each branch off in separate directions alone, and then at a designated hour or time usually between 2-3 hours, longer if you are more advanced, come back together to share your experiences.

Remember to pause at special places if Natures asks you to stop and learn, even sitting and meditating is the best way to enter the Silence and listen, you could even have your drum as a tool to guide you.

Remember Mother Nature is our greatest teacher, but mortals learn but slow!

Earth Healing

Even though we usually spend most of our energies on the night of the Full Moon, and gift it to Mother Earth as a healing gift, we should never just do this only at Full Moons. We need to make excursions into certain parts of our area that we know needs healing or protecting.

Near my home is a Magickal Aboriginal site which are wetlands, one of the only few that are left due to major highways destroying at 8 other wetlands for their bitumen poison, and when they do this certain species of animals have to be moved on and find new homes. Like our Black Cockatoo which have specific nesting grounds near these wetlands, and they too get destroyed so the Black Cockatoo has to research and find another place for their existence and the existence of their young. They only mate once every two years and usually only have 1-2 eggs.

We may have areas that have been poisoned by passing roads and the poisonous fumes from cars, there are so many places that we could venture to and assist just with a small amount of our energy to give back to the Earth. You can make this a special day by taking your children and teaching them about loving Nature and healing the trees, remember that in their innocence is the Power of the Goddess and God.

Maybe go to a Koala habitat where trees have been removed or are dying, their very food source, and send the trees your healing powers, and don't forget the animals, many of them are getting sick, so send them your love and healing energy to make all well.

Everywhere and everything on this planet needs healing, always start the healing process with yourself first, and then when you are full of power and energy, gift your healing power to all.

Educating Locals

I have always heard the phrase if you want peace then you must fight for peace, and if you want acceptance then you need to fight for that too. I believe that eventual peace and acceptance comes from within, not from frustration or anger, but from tolerance and educating the ignorant.

When I created and Founded the Church of Wicca in Australia, as Australia's first legal neo Pagan Church, that was just the beginning process. The hard work was now to come, so I sent our Media release forms to all newspapers, magazine companies and to the local councils and police departments. This let them know before the gossip and anti-establishment started commencing with their holier than thou attitude of evil versus good.

Education comes in all forms, but if we let egotists who lack in the knowledge and skills of communication, they can do more harm as self-appointed whacko's than genuine Priests and Priestesses of the Old religion.

I made myself available with my Priesthood to be approachable with more questions and to let them know the basics and the truth of who and what we are by removing all the fantasy side of Wiccecraft. I was approached quite a lot by radio stations and did several TV shows as well. We emphasized the fact that we are different to most in our beliefs but that does not make us crazies.

In opening letting them know that we are in their zone or area, they can be educated that we are normal tax paying citizens and business owners, who just have a different view of religion. The offering of being available for any and all occult matters and questions pertaining to the occult and Wiccecraft will eventually create a repour with them society and legal groups around us, and slowly watch the shadows of darkness fade from people's sights. Magick is afoot, and the Goddess is alive!

Elders Day

Elders Day is on the 23rd November, this is a special day where we honour and show respect for our Elders, the Archetypes – the Crones, Sages, Magi and Wicce Queen if we are lucky to have one.

As we get older we live our lives by our memories, and our Elders love their storytelling, so always ask them to tell us of some stories of old, something of their past, especially in their eyes how much the world has changed. Do they feel the changes are for the good or the bad?

But it is a day of listening to them and honouring them with love and respect, by giving them a very special day to remember. The sad thing about our present generation is that we have less and less time with the elderly, we place them away from our view so as to not have to put up with them. But they are us in the future, if we cannot share and give a little of our time to show them how special they are for giving us the world as we have it today due to their hard work and efforts, then we are the ones who are losing out, not them.

I was lucky to have lived with both my grandmothers, and loved every minute of it, as they were great teachers, but both very different in their ways and views. We need to consider how it feels to be getting older, and how they feel getting closer to the Shadows of death with nothing to be offered in their lives but the waiting of the Crones footsteps as she approaches to take them away. Many of the elderly have stopped living because we have stopped caring.

We need to confront our own fears about age and death, and being powerless and fragile, of not being able to care for ourselves properly, and of being utterly and alone, knowing that we have family, but they are TOO busy to visit or share a little time, how sad we have become as humans. So, get off your arses and help the elderly with; love and light and honour and thanks!

They all have stories to tell, they just need someone to listen. So, take some pens and paper and write their stories as I did for my grandmother. Maybe even if you have recorder record their life story, this shows them your interest, and they love to tell their stories, some may be a bit shy at first, but once they start talking, they will go on and on.

Ask to see some photographs of special events or occasions in their life, of when they got married, their parents, children, grandchildren, and great grandchildren. This may be the last chance they have to share their story, and to help them remember the greatest lives in their life.

You may be their only visitor, as they may not have any family members alive, and when we all get to a certain age, we have little friends as they too have probably passed on to the Summerland.

It takes but little effort and time and energy to sit and raise the spirits of an old soul with an equally beautiful truth, Theirs!

Elemental Day

Elemental day or Night is about focusing and connecting to one Elemental and making a full evening or ritual about that Elemental, start from the east and focus on Sylphides of the Air Element, the Faeries, winged ones, shining ones, birds and insects. Then on the Salamanders of the South of the Element of Fire. The Salamanders, lizards, goannas, snakes, serpents, dragons, crawling ones.

Then focus on the West and the Element of Water, the Elementals of Water are Undines, mermaids, the swimming ones, creatures of the sea. Another evening focus on the Element of the North which is Earth, the standing ones, such as the trees, bushes, plants, herbs, flowers, and the Gnomes.

If finish all these and wish to continue at a deeper level then also focus on the Tools of these realms, each time you get together you can elevate your focus with slowly going deeper and higher in learning of everything of these realms within the Elements.

In order they are:
Elements – earth, air, fire and Water, and the centre spirit.
Magick – physical, mental, astral, psychic and spiritual.
Elementals – Gnomes, Sylphides, Salamanders, Undines, and the Shining Ones.
Tools – Pentacle, salt, crystals; Wands, Thurible, Incense, feathers; Athame, Sword, Fire, Candles; Chalice, Cauldron, Water, caves, etc.
Lords and ladies – Euras, Notas, Zephyrus, Boreas.
Archangels – Uriel, Raphael, Michael, Gabriel.

There are so many other things to focus on with each direction, but this will take you years of fun and research to get to the end of where this path takes you.

Eleusinian Mysteries

The Eleusinian Mysteries were sacred and ancient rituals of Initiation that were held annually in Spring for the religion of Demeter and Persephone which was based at Eleusis in ancient Greece. They were and still are the most popular and famous of all ancient and secretive rites from ancient Greece. But they were also based from the ancient Agrarian cult of the Mycenean period.

They were representative of the abduction of the Goddess Persephone from Her mother Demeter by the Lord of the Underworld, Hades, this was done in three cyclic phases; the descent – representing the loss, the searching and the ascent back to the Earthly realm in Spring.

When she was taken the world was sad and winter was formed, that brought coldness and chaos, then the world was in darkness and life became stagnant, and the birds stopped singing. But eventually one who loved Her so much went down into the Underworld to ask for her freedom. An agreement was eventually met, where she would remain in the underworld for the half of the year (the winter months) and she could return to the Earth for the remaining half of the year for the summer months. This Mystery is shown in the aspects of Initiation as it is in life, with birth, life, challenge, fertility, initiation, death and then rebirth. We should always be challenged at what we do, and it is always good for the coven to remember this by re-enacting this Mystery at least once a year, usually at Spring.

Elphane Chess

Is a silly game but can be quite creative, all members bring along leaves, seeds, flowers, pods, pine cones, shells, feathers, and any other object that can be added to this Creation wheel of Elphane.

It starts by one person placing an object down on the ground and the next can either place their object next to the last one, or move it to where they feel it looks better. With each member turns a pattern starts to emerge, and creates an energy spiral of natural objects that link and can reveal a story.

Watch as it forms, changes and grows into your pattern, the pattern of the Circle and all within. Let it reveal its truth and its ancient etchings can reveal themselves. Then it is time to sit back and look at this Magickal creation, discuss it, and be in awe of its formation. I have in the past made these but on a large board and placed glue and tar on them, so each item becomes glued to form an artistic impression of the Circles Natural energy pattern.

See what patterns speak to you, maybe it will reveal a lesson that can see in its design. When all agree of the beauty of the design then it is sealed and glued in its original shape and with all the objects stuck to it, to form a pattern that you may wish to keep, or you may just leave in the circle for Nature to do as she wills with it.

It depends on whether you made is a gift to the Circle, as a lesson for all, or to create and energy art piece of the Circles members.

Environmental Learning

SAVE THE EARTH FROM POLLUTION

The one good thing about Wiccans and Pagans is that they are Environmentalists to varying degrees, or at least they should be. It is important to know the environmental impact on the land near your home.

A lot of people take it for granted living in an area and think it is all safe, and clean, but many estates could be on landfills, or areas where there have been contaminated items dumped, or even a market garden that used tons of pesticides and poisons for their crops. The children seem to be more aware through school teachings about the environment and what and how to be more aware and to do your bit just in your home. It starts from home, and then through education gradually grows to our neighbours and friends.

Think of the health of not only yourselves but all the Nature creatures around you. Try not to use pesticides in your gardens and around and in your homes as they are toxic and have very negative effects on your health and your children's health, even your pets are included, and death can occur with mixing too many products with other products, as there could be a chemical reaction that is toxic and poisonous.

Share your knowledge with neighbours, and educate businesses, shops and restaurants in your area that it is smarter, healthier and cheaper by using natural products. You can actually get professionals out to check the soil of your land for any pollutants or toxins, you can check your paint in on your homes for lead, does your home have asbestos, bats carry certain diseases that can kill humans and animals, just know your neighbourhood and treat it Naturally!

Eostre Egg Friends

On the eve before The Spring Equinox, get your family together and boil some eggs in some coloured dyes. Then have on the ready different art pens, crayons, pencils, paints, glitter, small leaves, flowers, talismans, objects of beauty, shells, feathers, etc. and some glue to stick these on the outer surface of the Eostre Eggs. Each person should decorate theirs according to what they are feeling, but the Eostre Egg should represent their own personal characters. (Everyone makes a egg even the children and the elders).

Then on attendance at the Rites of Spring Festival, the Elder collects all the eggs and then takes them all outside into the gardens preferably around the Magick Circle and hides them, some in obvious places for the children and others in not so obvious places. When they are all hidden, everyone is led by the bards playing their instruments and searching for the hidden Eostre Eggs, (the children are helped first), we hide the children's eggs all in one specific area and mark it with ribbons or balloons, so it is easy for them. It also keeps the adults away from this area.

We all then search for the eggs (if you find your own put it back), when you find an egg, then it is time to search for who's egg it is, when you find out who they are then hug them, introduce yourselves, as you are now egg-friends for the next year. Here you will stay in touch and try to get to know each other as likeminded kin.

It they have not found their egg then you can help them to find one, as soon as they have found their egg then they hunt for the creator as well and run to the centre of the circle and sit in a daisy chain behind the first person to find their egg, and the massage chain begins and continues until everyone has found an egg and has a new egg-friend.

Exploring the I-Ching

The I Ching (pronounced ee-ching) is a collective of commentaries and interpretation PATTERNS OF EXISTENCE, each pattern being symbolised by a hexagram. A hexagram is made up of six lines, each line being broken __ __ or unbroken _____, the different combinations making up sixty-four hexagrams. Sixty-four may not appear to give many alternatives of change and growth, but let us have a look at the reason for this seemingly arbitrary number. First, let us take the Chinese symbol of reality, the t'ai chi t'u. It is the equivalent of the Kabbalistic Tree of Life.

In a modifying form, this is symbolising polarity, the first step after Unity (Infinity). Begins with growth towards physical reality.

Polarity is so important because it gives a possibility of action, for example; a flat battery is a unified thing, there is no difference between the poles, and thus no energy or life. But a live battery, which is divided into positive and negative poles, causes a flow between the poles, creating energy, activity, power and CHANGE.

But again, for each pole of the t'ai chi t'u to have power, it itself must have polarity. If we symbolise white as ___, and black as _ _, then the first symbol is __. That is four alternative actions, or different paths for reality to take. Then of course, the third symbol. (a little research into these signs is beneficial as it is not an area that I know much about).

These are the eight TRIGRAMs that in combination make up the sixty-four hexagrams. The next three steps are obvious:(again some research into the symbolism here))

With the last symbol we seem to have a pillar of ever-refining subtitles, each layer going back to Infinity, with an infinite number of possible combinations of black and white. Sixty-Four I quite a manageable number, while still varied and subtle, and the combinations of Change are not restricted to just single hexagrams.

Often the hexagram changes or is combined with another, which gives 4,032 possible descriptions of a particular state of affairs. More will be explained about practical working later. I use the word 'pillar' above to describe the intricate combinations built up into the t'ai chi t'u. let us see how this pillar can correspond to the Western concept of the Middle Pillar of the Kabbalistic Tree of Life. The level of complexity of the Chinese Tree that corresponds to the Sephirotic Tree is the level at which TRIGRAMS are formed.

There are eight trigrams, plus the basic symbols __ and _ (__ is not the same as =, because __ is white to infinity, whereas = is white only for three levels.

I will deal with the two possible ways of comparing the Trees. There are probably other ways, as Magickal symbolism is flexible (as it should be), but these appear to be the major attributions. If we take the point that is white of the white of the white etc to infinity, and the black of the black of the black etc to infinity, which are ultimate extremes, then they could be regarded as respectively Kether and Malkuth, the two extremes of reality.

Chokmah and Binah would be more limited levels = and = =, the 'parents' of the Positive and Negative Pillars. This is one way of comparing symbolisms. The other way is where we have Kether represented with the dot _ _ a unity, which is the t'ai chi t'u BEFORE it divides into Duality. Here Chokmah and Binah would be _ and _ _, and in this scheme of the Tree, Daat would be considered. Daat is represented as =, and Malkuth is = = (the other six Sephiroth are the same in both systems and will be described later.)

It seems to call Daat-Heaven, which is the title of the trigram = but if we consider it as being the Sephiroth through which we view the Supernal Heavens, and through which they affect us, it is an understandable symbol. This is a version of the Tree as it affects us, as it appears to be an individual looking "up" from Malkuth. It is subjective.

The first version is the Tree objectively, looking from an Infinite viewpoint, balanced in all directions. As for the other Sephiroth of the Tree, let us look at the eight trigrams and their meanings.

The first two are = called the CREATIVE HEAVEN and = = the RECEPTIVE EARTH. We have already dealt with these. (It should be obvious that the receptive could be either Binah or Malkuth. The other six Sephiroth fall into obvious pairs-Chesed and Geburah, Tiphareth and Yesod, Hod and Netzach. The six remaining trigrams also follow this pattern of pairs, they are the GENTLE and the AROUSING, the CLINGING and the ABYSMSAL, KEEPING STILL and the JOYOUS

- **The Gentle** – is like the title of Chesed-Mercy. The Gentle is called the Eldest Daughter (Chesed is a feminine Sephiroth, even though it is on the masculine pillar). The I Ching says, *"among men it means the grey haired, those with broad foreheads"*, reminding us of the Magickal image of Chesed-the merciful old king.
- **The Arousing** – is Geburah-Thunder, the dragon, decisive and vehement, horses which gallop, the strong. It is the Eldest Son, Geburah being a male Sephiroth on the female pillar.
- **The Clinging** – seems an odd name for Tiphareth, but it is described as 'fire', the Sun, lightning, the sign for dryness. The Middle Daughter. We usually associate Tiphareth with masculine, but in Chinese symbology every extreme contains the potential seed of its opposite, and must, in time, change into it, so it is not unusual for a Middle Pillar Sephiroth to be regarded as in a state of Change, or equilibrium.
- **The Abysmal** – is Yesod, water, ditches, melancholy, the Moon. It is the Youngest Son, again the opposite of Western symbolism, which ascribes the Moon as feminine, and again, Yesod is a Sephiroth that is in a state of balance, a point of change between the Pillars.
- **Keeping Still** – is Hod-the Mountain, eunuchs and watchmen, the fingers, the dog, black billed birds. Eunuchs are a-sexual, as are Hermaphrodites, the Magickal symbol of Hod. The Watchman of Hod is Anubis, guarding the doors of the subconscious mind, and the dog is his symbol. Thoth is a black-billed bird, and fingers and their activity have the capacity to act upon the World, like the intellect of Thoth.
- **The Joyous** – can only be Netzach, the lake, the Youngest Daughter, a Wicce, it is mouth and tongue, the concubine, the beautiful naked woman, a symbol of Netzach.

(The quotes are from the Richard Withelm translation of the I Ching, with an introduction by Carl Jung, which if you are going to get a copy, is the very best version available).

There are many other symbols used by the Chinese for the trigrams, most of which are in accord with Western symbolism, but I have used only the most familiar. Here are the two versions of the Tree, described above, in the Kabbalistic and Chinese forms.

Figure 1 is my own concept, figure 2 was pictured in Aleister Crowley's "The Book of Thoth" (slightly modified-Crowley revered the symbols of Chesed and Netzach, [referring the Gentle to mean Netzach, and the Joyous to be Chesed. This illustrates the flexibility of the symbolism, it is appropriate in either position, but still meaningful however used).

The I Ching does not tell the future, rather it gives an idea of the Forces of Change that are in Power in a situation and gives ADVICE on the best way pf handling and transforming these FORCES into a constructive pattern. (It has many other abilities of course, but this is most frequently consulted function).

The concepts follow the idea: "AS ABOVE, SO BELOW" as the Chinese consider that the forces that mould daily life are the forces that guide the changing of seasons. Nature, the weather, or just the day. This rhythm that every living thing follows (and everything from rocks to clouds, is living), is the same rhythm that the hexagrams follow.

For example, given a hexagram that is considered 'dark' such as number 2 which changes to no. 24 with the introduction of the 'light' line, it is inevitable, in Chinese thought that the light line will rise up and banish the darkness-No. 24 is titled RETURN (the Turning Point), the time of darkness is past. The winter Solstice brings the victory of Light, just as the Sun's power grows from the darkest time of the year. There is another Illustration of the paradox that was discussed with trigrams "The Clinging" and the "Abysmal".

The tools are an I Ching and 100 sticks. Most books suggest only 50 yarrow sticks, but a Wicce needs twice that number. Yarrow readily available and grown in Australia from Herbalists and many growers, but if not readily available then Bamboo is a good substitute. Take a new clean blade, cleanse it and do the LBRP over it, then ask the permission of the trees if you can cut them. (they will reply to your question). Ask that all Devas and Elementals leave these trees and this space prior to your cutting and then with singing cut your 100 fine sticks (1/4 inch or less in thickness and between 6-16 inches long).

First, I will describe the meaning of the traditional way of using the 50 rune sticks, and then explain what you need the others for. Take 50 sticks and put one aside. Divide the 49 sticks left randomly into 2 piles. Pile A on the left, and pile B on the right. Take one stick from pile B and put it between the little finger and the ring finger of the left hand.

Then take pile A, and holding it in the left hand, take from it group of four sticks, until there are four or less sticks remaining. This remainder goes between the ring finger and the middle finger of the left hand. Then holding pile B in the left hand, count off the pile in fours also, putting the remainder, four or less between the middle and the index fingers, the sticks will add up to either 9 or 5 for later explained purposes, write down the number as either 8, in the case of 9, and 4 in the case of 5, occurring.

Gather up all the sticks that were discarded in fours, again divide the pile into two, and repeat the process. This time you will be left with either 8 or 4 sticks. Put these aside, record the number left, repeat the process once more, again getting 8 or 4 sticks. These are the combinations that you can get and their many meanings, just look them up in any good I Ching book, even go online for a quick review.

This may be confusing so here is my method. Start off with the 100 sticks, and have two silk bags readily cleansed and Consecrated, a black and a white one, and a grey bag for temporary use (Until you have finished 50 readings). Divide the 100 sticks randomly into two piles of 50 each. Put 50 in a grey bag and use the other 50 for a reading, as explained above. The single stick discarded at the start of the reading goes into the black bag. When you have finished, take one stick from the grey bag and add it to the 49 sticks you just used. Keep these 50 sticks in the white bag.

Now you have a positive and a negative group of sticks. Keep the black-negative pile until you need it, you won't use it very often, but its very existence makes sure that the white pile remains active and positive.

Use the white pile for your readings, as you will find after a while that the stick is discarded at the beginning of each reading will always be the same stick. (remember that now it goes back into the white bag, tom stay with the white pile, now that the sticks are polarised).

The stick represents you, as a factor involved in the change and rhythm of the Universe, you can mark it for yourself or your Magickal name, once you have found this specific stick. The black pile is used for more advanced Magickal techniques, when you are working with the Elements for instance. For most work you will only need the white pile.

Anyway, there is much more about the I Ching that I have not touched upon. This will give you one introduction to concepts and techniques of using it, the rest you can have the joy of discovering for yourself. It is a very beautiful and very powerful way of learning about the rhythms of change, the way these rhythms affect you, and hoe you can use and grow with them to infinity.

Eros/Eras Betrothal Festival

This is something that is quite beautiful for couples, or maybe even couples to be. In fact, this date is my anniversary for me and my husband.

It is easy to buy Valentines decorations around and before February 14th, which is actually called traditionally "Betrothal Day" before it was adopted and stolen by Christians and changed to St. Valentine's Day.

So buy heaps of hearts, and red and white decorations, deck the halls and the home with roses, lights, hearts and balloons with loads of streamers, and make sure the spa (Cauldron) is brewing.

Maybe make so it is also a romantic evening with small tables set up throughout the garden, each be set for two. That way on Betrothal Day all can be in their romantic pairing as well as share the eventing with others in love.

Get each couple to bring a different course, and the men to bring the wine. Play in the background love songs and mood music. Have a platter of grapes to peel for your loved ones, and maybe even wear some sexy costumes.

Essential Oils

If you are lucky enough to have an Aromatherapist in your Circle then they are the perfect ones to give a talk, and show and explain the varied uses for different Essential Oils, even fragrant oils have their benefits. As an herbalist I am aware of the many benefits that essential oils bring, as they are all extracts from herbs and plants and trees.

But I am not an aromatherapist, even though my training has touched on this field, but I am far from proficient, but as I said if you have someone to share their wisdom with the Coven, then that is very advantageous. The showing and smelling, of essential oils can be so informative. Earning the skills of smell and the many uses of aromatherapy is so beneficial.

If you are lucky you can actually make your own blend as a personal scent for your normal life instead of wearing toxic perfumes. I usually get those in my Circles to mix and make a special blend for their Initiatory Anointing Oil. This way they have it personalised, and it becomes more Magickal, as I believe everything that is hand made for your Magick is far more superior than something that someone else has made for you.

Face and Body Painting

Face and body painting is an exciting past-time, even our ancient forefathers and mothers donned their faces with Woad for several reasons, whether it was for war, prayer, ritual, weddings, Magick etc. Man has always loved the ability to change their appearance through wearing face paint.

Shamans paint their faces to represent the item or animal that they are working for or with, they also dress in like manner to attract their prey as in hunting. This amazing idea has been passed down through millennia from caveman to the Egyptians and the Atlanteans who loved adorning their faces with makeup, down through our present society where women adorn their faces to make them more appealing and attractive.

But the face painting I am talking about is symbolic of our Magick, the decorating with symbols and signs of Nature and beauty, this helps us like the Greenman and Greenwoman to become one step closer to Nature.

Children also love to paint their faces, so if you have that creative Wicce in your circle, then get her to teach everyone how to face-paint and create animals, insects, birds, flowers, herbs, shells, faeries, elves, make the faces as the Elementals and the Magickal beings of the hidden world.

If you have someone good at Henna, then offer to paint everyone's hands and faces (if they wish as henna can last for several weeks so be careful). I have had henna paintings done in Perth, India and Egypt and adore the artistic work that is involved, so be free with your creative thinking and see what you can come up with, and remember to take photos for your albums of Brag.

Fantasy Role Play

Fantasy role playing can be fun, if you do not take it seriously, remember it is not role playing for partners but for family and friends. There are so many roleplaying games out there now starting with Dungeons and Dragons and a million others. But the role playing am talking about is in you coming as and acting your role all night as an elf, imp, faery, salamander, gnome, undine, Sylphides, mage, hero, troll, orc, devil, centaur, Pan, satyr, psychic, gypsy, healer, doctor, mutant, or even as a fellow coven member.

You can play full games in regalia or with story-telling, or as the aboriginals do, dance your fantasy or animal. You can swap jokes, talk about mind boggling challenges where you have failed.

As you are a fantasy creature your imagination can just run wild; "how you saved Thor from a bloody end, and end took you and made love to you all night, but in the end, you had to let him go as it just was not fare to keep a God like all to yourself".

So you are not your real self you can just let go and be wild, remember it is not you, it is fantasy. I find that sometimes events like this help shy or quiet people bring out their concealed and real character.

Farewell to the Sun Ritual

We always seem to have rituals to welcome the Sun, but never the opposite. We need to say farewell to the Sun as a friend and ask it to return for us the next day. It is about the inner depth of acknowledging that you wish to open your eyes the next day and see this marvel again, this ancient symbol that is the source of all life on our planet.

So, create a ritual and honour the Sun, send it on its night journey of slumber and rest, that it along with you shall arise the next morning, alive and alert with the energy to face the new day with strength, courage, positivity, faith, love, warmth and light.

The ancient Aboriginals and the Native Americans always did this, so should we.

So maybe get all your Coveners to write their own small ceremony addressed to the Sun, and then bring them all together to create and form a larger in-depth ritual Saying Goodnight to the Light, knowing that you will greet them again the next day.

Father's Day

Instead of there being a traditional day to honour fathers, you need to make it more open and as a surprise. In my covens all the ladies select a night without telling the menfolk and make it a special night of honouring the masculine in life.

We start with our menfolk, whether they are fathers or not. For only time can tell who the fathers are and will be. But they must be honoured as the masculine forces in our lives, except their solar energies and the gifts that their maleness brings to our Magick Circle.

Even offer them some womanly sensuality (not sexuality) but sensuality, the offering of a massage, or foot rub, facial, mending their clothes if they are single, helping them with food etc.

Then it is time to honour all our fathers, and then our grandfathers, great grandfathers and so on throughout our entire ancestry. Then send out love to all fathers of the world, send them our praises and our love.

Don't stop their honour the fathers in Nature such as the animal kingdom, birds, fish, amphibians, the trees, rocks, crystals, elementals, elements and the list go on.

Try to remember this is about empowerment in giving to the maleness of our world and adoring them for their true inner beings.

Fertility Orchard Blessing

In traditional Wiccecraft when our ladies are pregnant, the womenfolk get together and take them out to the orchards where fruit trees are in blossom. If you are lucky to have an orchard, then that is great if not maybe ask a farmer if you can walk through there fields of blossoming orchards.

If you can make a bower of blossoms, then give to each pregnant maiden and make as a headband. Then let them walk through the fields, espousing their desires for their unborn child, as they too are in blossom waiting for the birth of their fruit, as with the mothers to be.

It is a personal and Magickal moment for the mothers to be, so let them be, let them make their prayers to the spirits of fertility and good health. Let them awaken nature and the elementals around them along with the devas. Ask for their love and energies in assisting you for having an easy birth, and a birth of love and life.

It does not matter what trees are in blossom as they all are part of the fertility of nature, from bud, to blossom to fruit to life to death to rebirth and back to bud again.

Just before you leave the field offer your prayers and energies also to the orchard and its fertility for a ripened fruit and successful harvest and great bounty of life.

Festival Bowers

Many people because of the Judaic religion only seem to focus on the decorating of their homes at Christmas and maybe Easter, but we as Wiccans are lucky to have 8 Festivals in the year where can decorate our homes and fireplace with bowers of the seasonal times.

In doing this we share our Faith with others, even if they are not told they can see with their eyes the beauty it beholds.

- **Yule-Midwinter Solstice 22nd June (SH) December 22nd (NH).** Decorate the home with living plants that are festive and colourful, also a Yule Tree, add decorations to your house to welcome visitors with wishes of joy and of your spiritual path. We set the candles to bring back the sun's warmth, we decorate the home with greenery to bring back the green of nature and its representation of birth and life, even when Nature is sleeping, and we decorate the home with gold to bring back Magick, red to bring back the warmth, green for life.
- **Imbolg-2nd August (SH) February (NH).** This festival is also called the Festival of Lights, it is about releasing the spirits of the Earth and Nature, to bring more light into the world. It is about seeing through the darkness and not destroying it, as we need everything to be in balance. Honour the Dark in the world as we honour the Light. We need to understand both and fear neither. This time we illumine our homes with as many lights and candles (safely) as possible. You can fill your garden with solar lights to bring out the elementals to dance and play. Make some small rafts out of paper and cardboard and place a t/light in them and send them on the waterways for light and love, see them carry away your tears, pain and negativity and illumine the world with more light and positivity.
- **Spring Equinox-21st September (SH) March 21st (NH).** This is the time for seeing the blossoms of Beltane, where we see nature in full life. A bounty of the Spring and all life abounding with new young life. The birds, animal and all of Nature smiling at the world. It is the most colourful time of the year when mother nature shows her myriad of rainbow colours to the world. It is time for the choosing a of a Spring

Queen and Spring King to be elected, and for us to paint and decorate our Eostre eggs to find our spiritual Egg-friends.

- **Beltane-**November Eve (SH) May Eve (NH). Beltane is the Festival of Fertility, where we light the Bale Fires, to bring back through our ancient faith all things back into balance and harmony, light and dark, male and female, goddess and god, night and day, good and evil, life and death, youth and old age, pain and joy. For these are the lessons that we are meant to understand. By bringing them back into balance we start the road to awakening the Magick of this world and all within it. It teaches us to honour the opposite of everything and not fear it just by not understanding it. Decorate your home with flowers and fruit of the season, symbols of the Goddess and God representing fertility and the eternal dance that we must all play.

- **Midsummer Solstice –** 22st December (SH) 22nd June (NH). This time is about family, about sharing the outdoors, and bringing the outdoors inside. It is time to connect with Nature and the power of the Sun and all its masculine energies that it has and its healing powers of warmth and light. Bask in his radiance and share the time with family and friends. We have a Pagans in the Park Picnic, and also set up the Maypole to bring fertility back to the Earth. Here we are happy as our Lord God has returned and been reborn unto this world.

- **Lughnasadh –** 2nd February (SH) 2nd April (NH). This is the harvest Festival where we use the first of the harvest to make as sacrificial offerings to the great Earth Mother and the Horned God of Grain and the fields, he who must die to be reborn. We honour the Earth for the bounty she has gifted us, and we feast and celebrate what the sun has brought. Decorate your homes with fruit, grain, and flowers but mainly all the harvest that we consume, make loaves of bread and share of your bounty with family and friends.

- **Autumn Equinox –** 21st March (SH) 21st September (NH). The Autumn Equinox is about letting go of the past, forgiving ourselves and others, of removing obstacles built on guilt or past pain and anger, it is about forgiveness and learning to say I AM SORRY. What lessons can we be taught through this. Decorate your home with Autumn leaves that have fallen, display them in all their myriad colours and beauty. It is time to start storing food as well for the winter months that lie ahead.

- **Samhain-**(Halloween) – May Eve (SH) November Eve (NH). Time to decorate your home with all the All hallows decorations, carve the pumpkins, to keep death away from your door and to pass on by. Let all know of your true tradition of this Magickal night and its many mysteries. Maybe even carve some friendly pumpkin for a change

First Aid

I have always lived in the country, and always believe in being prepared for the worst. When it comes to one's life and survival we need to always be ready and prepared. It is important for all of us to learn First Aid basics.

With my circle I used to get the ST. John Ambulance people to come out and do a full training course for the circle and educate in what to do in cases of dangerous events. Such as heart attack, snake or spider bite, fall, poisoning, etc.

Because we have large circles of people attending our homes for rituals etc. we must be responsible for our guests, this means being able to help them if danger threatens. The idea of learning skills from Paramedics and learning how to correctly save someone's life, is only the difference between ability and seconds.

So, do yourself a favour, and get the Coven together and discuss this important aspect of survival, as your very life may depend upon it. It does cost money but as a group you can usually get a good price, but what is someone's life really worth, it is only money, right.

Full Moon for Men

It is a known fact that men like doing things without women, and women like doing things without men. This does not change within Wicca or the world of Magick. Full Moons have always been about the Women's Mysteries. But in this day and age of the 21st Century, we know and realise that men too have their feminine within the masculine, they also have the need to connect with the Goddess through their feminine side as well as their masculine side.

We each have a deep need to touch and be touched by the Great Mother, this is why in our Circles once per annum we separate into two Circles and the men have their Full Moon and the women theirs. This is a great way to also share more personal and in-depth thoughts and feelings with your brothers or sisters. As there are many things that men find it hard to say in front of women and vice versa, this is because we feel they just will not understand.

The only reason for this not being aware and understanding the opposite sex is that is how we have always been programmed. That's why it is called Men's and Women's Mysteries. Actually, it should just be Secrets Untold Mysteries.

So it is an excellent way to connect with our kindred sisters and brothers on a much deeper level. It means that within the men's circle, it is the male who invokes and awakens the sleeping Goddess both within and without. It is about having the skillset in understanding the feminine within the masculine and being and becoming one with the Goddess in all her forms, physically, mentally, astrally, psychically and spiritually. In so doing this your awareness of women and their Mysteries will be inevitable. The knowledge changes and you will forever change after this deep Awakening.

So, give it a go and allow yourself to become all that you need to be as the ultimate feminine, which is the Goddess.

Full Moon for Wiccelings

In our Circles we allow the children to also perform their forms of the Full Moon to welcome the Goddess into their Circle. This is where they would invoke the Faery Goddess of Elphane, she is the Goddess of children and of innocent hearts.

The ages of these children may vary from 6-13, and it is the eldest of the children who become the Wiccelings in charge of the Circle, they will act as leaders representing the HPs and the HP. Sometimes when they first start doing their own Full Moon Circles it is good to have an Elder with them to instruct them.

They will have the Altar set as the adults but only with chalice for water, chalice for fruit juice, pentacle with salt upon it, thurible with incense sticks, and their own personal Wands which they have made themselves during a Wicceling Workshop.

They allow the other children to also assist in doing the casting of the Faery Circle for children. They can make up their own words, and this makes it more Magickal, also the Goddess is attracted to laughter especially from children, so let this circle be one of serious FUN.

Full Moon for Women

Women's Full Moon Circles are the same as for the menfolk, but more important as the women Wicces need that deeper in-depth working with the Goddess that cannot be done with men present, it is a deeper insight into women and their bodily changes. This sort of Women's circle is about sensuality and the honouring of each aspect of the Goddess in all the women present. We invoke the Goddess into all the women, not just one. It is about a circle of Goddesses that are needing to suit each individual Wicce within. At the time of the Full Moon each Wicce must have some special needs and special Book that she must convey to the Great mother.

So the High Priestess will create a web of channels that step from the macro universe to herself, and then sending out the webs of connection to each of the Wicces within the circle. Like a spider Web of energy, the HPs then invokes down and through herself and then sends forth into each of the Wicces a different aspect of the Goddess that she believes that they are needing. This is very tiring for the HPs so please make sure that she is well qualified and trained to deal with such a awesome responsibility and charge.

Each Wicce receives the touch of the Goddess without knowing what aspect the HPs was invoking into them, they allow themselves to be fully open receiving and understanding everything that they sense and feel and see. After all has been achieved, the HPs gets everyone to start taking some deep breaths and to start relaxing and thanking the Goddess in their own special way, and then send them on their way.

After the cakes and wine have been shared they each in turn share their experiences.

Get Acquainted Garbage

This is a fun way for the budding archaeological Wicces in your Coven, to have fun in going through your garbage. This is a much lighter side of the Coven activities, where each member prepares a box of their own personal brands of trash, this is for the scrutiny of the Coven Archaeological Survey Expedition of the other members in your Coven.

You may include some old photos of yourself when you were very young, odd food containers, a page from your personal calendar, coasters, cryptic notes from friends or family. And other miscellaneous things that you possess, even jewellery or a piece of old clothing just you will again fit into when you have lost that weight.

Just remember that by your garbage you shall be known ha-ha. What a Magickal and revealing way to reveal the unexpected hidden facets of your inner personality, and your naughty self that the others are not aware of yet.

Gift Exchange

Gift exchange is a wonderful thing, we all love buying gifts and seeing the looks on peoples faces when they receive their prize, but we also love receiving gift as well. The one thing about gift exchange with covens, families and friends, is that it makes it very affordable.

As it has become very expensive if we have to buy all our family members gifts, then our friends, then our work colleagues, and then our Coveners, this all calls for us to take out a second mortgage these days as gifts are very expensive.

So, gift exchange is the best way, as we all choose a price value of the gift $20 - $50 and we set about finding a gift for that total value, I love receiving gifts that have been personally made or researched.

But I feel that we should never intend our gift to go to any one person, but through random choosing. So, as we give a gift, the next person then gives out their gift, we all come with one gift and we all leave with one gift. Sometimes it is always fun to have a joke gift, and to see the face of the person thinking that this is really their gift but instead they end up with something far better than others, this is usually the last person, but can be random as well.

Many times, we get what we need or desire, without the asking.

God Debate

This is about learning about the first Christ, the first Sun God, where they were both described as "The Way", "The Light", The Truth", The Life", "The Son of God", "The Word", "The Messiah" and the "Good Shepherd".

All these terms were used for thousands of ears before Judaism even came into being, so, again we see that they too have adopted or stolen our history and past, and the very wording of our own divine Sun God, as their own. Mithras was usually depicted as seen carrying a lamb on his shoulders, just as we see the same with Jesus but much, much later. Midnight services are found in both religions, but ours first. The Holy Pagan Virgin Mother was also adopted by Christianity and called "The Virgin Mary".

Even in the same way "The sacred Book of Mithraism" was bastardised and became Peter, the foundation of the Christian Church. Come on people at least be original, oh yes you were in making a warrior religion to destroy all opposing religions of the ancient world, and make them all your own.

How sad it must feel, and how insecure they must feel that nothing they believe is genuine nor real, that they are in truth honouring pagan deities, and doing this honouring with our pagan festivals and rituals. When will man learn to start being original.

This should all be about re-education and letting people know the Truth, it is not about attacking Christians but in the true education of their faith as a stolen faith of the ancient Pagan religions of the Earth, before they tried to wipe us all out.

Goddess Within Workshop

Us usually if done properly this is usually a girly sleepover, and takes all weekend. All the ladies bring whatever they wish to decorate and design their Goddess Within statue/bodysuit with them. They all up-front go shares in the plaster wraps that will be used to wrap their bodies and make their Goddesses for their shrines.

You can place whatever you desire on your Goddess Creations, how this is done is that you usually do this on the weekend of a Full Moon, and you would on the Friday night do the Full Moon ceremony and invoke the Goddesses into each of you and awaken the Goddess Within. See what visions or apparitions of the Goddess that you see, and remember this is your Goddess Within, so when it is time to design your Goddess Creations be creative and sure.

The next morning after all have arisen, have a bold breakfast and then get yourselves all prepared to make the body suits. This is done by placing yourself into groups of three. Have a large tub or bucket each of plaster, (do not make it wet or it will never dry and it will slide off) and have heaps of strips of calico or thin cotton fabric to soak in the plaster. Have one of the three ladies lay down skyclad (naked) and get her to rub Vaseline over her body from her upper thighs, genitalia, stomach, breasts and up the neck.

Then after the plaster has been soaked and absorbed into the fabric then start to take off the excess plaster from the strip and lay it across the body, continue adding the strips of plaster fabric and press it all down, carefully over the body getting rid of all joins and lumps, place as many thicknesses as you can usually about 5-10 layers will make it very strong. If you are braver, tie back the hair, Vaseline the face and place some straws in their nose and mouth and then plaster sheet their face as well, so that way they have a full body torso with head as the Goddess Within.

When this is all done, get a fan out and start to fan the plaster figure, to help it dry. Then move onto the next person, and the next following the same steps. When all the ladies have had their bodies created and their moulds are dry and hard which could take 12-24 hours, then you can take them home. This way you get to design them in private and reveal your Goddess Within Creations at a later stage. If you decorate your figure slowly and take your time, more of your creative juices will low. Time and patience makes the best art pieces, especially when we are creating our Goddess Within Sculpture.

Sometimes the reason for decorating at home is that they can become a bit brittle if not done properly. So, the less we move them the better, make sure to place behind the head a large hook or rope to hold your Goddess Within Creation up on the wall in full display.

But if you wish to make a weekend of it and get help or help others who are less creative, then make sure you have plenty of room so as to decorate them carefully, and enough space to leave them if they have to set overnight. Remember you cannot decorate the plaster shells until they are fully dry, as they may break or create cracks that could destroy your sculpture.

When all the sculptures are complete either take photos, or bring them together in a gallery show, and reveal them and tell their stories of who the Goddess is, share this experience and know that you have Awakened the Goddess Within and brought her into reality as a sculpture to adore and always remember.

Goodbye Guilt

We are all aware that we each carry Guilt within us to varying degrees and we arc aware just how destructive it has been or can be. It is great for the new religions of the world that use guilt and fear to control their large numbers of followers. But we are not sheep, and should not be told what to do by anyone, we each possess the ability to know right and wrong, good and bad, and it is our choice which side we lean on.

We do not have to rely of puritanical systems of belief telling that we are damned from birth, and that we owe allegiance to them as they are the only way to get to paradise. Wiccans are not so insecure and do not need to play these games of insecurity, it can only help us to release our Guilt and act from more positive affirmations and positive motivations of love, tolerance, understanding, kindness and trust which bring absolute acceptance and that special Oneness that we are all needing and searching for.

It is very healing to have someone that you can openly discuss your feelings and your Guilt, as it must be discussed to be free and released from your Aura. Devise Magickal strategies on how is best to release your feelings of Guilt. Sometimes confronting the situation or person front on can be absolutely healing and invigorating. For women it can be ancient method of release as in giving birth, but in this ritual, you sit in a push up position looking down at a mirror and when you are ready to release, then push with all your might until you feel as if you have released all the pressure called Guilt and have it expelled and banished from your life and aura.

Whatever method you use make sure that you let go with a big sigh afterwards, and let it go and sink deep into the Earth to be absorbed and changed into a beautiful energy of love.

Greeting Cards

I love making and designing Wiccan and Pagan Greeting Cards, I use some of my artwork as the front of the cards, with my captions or poetry that I write for the inside. Whoever is the most gifted artists in your circle get them together to design the cover for the cards, and get together your poets and song writers and get them to write the inner messages of the cards.

I have a series of Pagan/Wiccan Greeting Cards by the Witch of Oz, they are titled;

Happy Solstice!
Get Well Spell
Happy Betrothal Day!
Happy Rebirthday!
Thankyou from the Angels!
Happy Earth Day!
Happy Air Day!
Happy Fire Day!
Happy Water Day!
Happy Birthing Day!
Welcome into this World!
Happy Mother's Day!
Happy Father's Day!
Happy Elders Day!
Hand-Fasting Blessings!
Wiccaning Blessings!
Initiation Blessings and Congratulations!
Congrats of your New Home!
Maiden to Mother-Congratulations!
Lad to Father-Congratulations!
Safe Trip!

Greeting the Rising Sun

This is great when you combine it with a camping trip, get all the Coveners together to enjoy the weekend, even by bringing their families as well if you wish, but sometimes it is better depending on the ritual that is to be performed in just having coven members. Make sure that everyone turns in early so that we can all get up an hour before sunrise, do not eat anything but maybe just have a cup of tea or a coffee, that is all.

Prepare yourself and all to silently assemble dressed comfortably and then scatter into the forest or at the beachfront. When first sitting ask the Goddess of the Dawn, Aurora for strength and guidance.

As the Dawn approaches all and all are settled and silent, just waiting for the Magick of a new day, as the sun kisses the sky as in a birthing and a burst of magnificent light. Just in your own silence greet the morning sun, adore and praise the Light and warmth that it brings. If you have drummers you can drum the welcome of the Sun, or just silently meditate, or even if you have a yoga instructor who can take you through some Yogic Asanas called Surya Namaskar (Saluting the Sun", or you may wish to do some Tai Chi, or even some chanting and singing. But make sure it is all about the Sun. When the full Sun Disc has passed the horizon, stand with arms outstretched and offer your prayers of thanks to the Gods and Goddesses of the Sun: Bast, Ra, Arinna, Amaterasu, Akewa, Etain, Omikami, Ushas, Spider Grandmother, Apollo, Helios, Mithra, Horus, Lugh, and many more. After a few more moments of silence and deep contemplation, all hug and share their Light, and then return to the campsite and prepare your hearty bush breakfast.

Gyromancy

One of the ancient methods of divination is called Gyromancy, this is the divination of the Wicces, and is performed with a Magick Circle, for this you can either lay out your 21 Major Arcana of the Tarot Cards, and or lay out the alphabet around the perimeter of the Circle.

Then it is time to walk around the circle in a Deosil manner until to get dizzy and make a slight trip, then that is the first card or letter, place in the inner circle, then tart off again and repeat the process several times, until you feel you have enough cards or letters that can give you some message.

After a while hopefully a message, using letters is the basic way, but if more advanced use the Tarot Cards as their messages will be deeper and more enlightening, if the spirits allow it.

There are so many unusual occult forms of divination that many never hear about such as Cromniomancy-this is the finding of signs in onions sprouts. Ceroscopy- can be fun, you pour melted wax into cold water and read the shapes given by the Elementals. Margaritomancy – place pearls under an inverted pot and they will bounce upwards if a guilty person approach. Alectryomancy-recite the alphabet until you hear an external sound then stop with that letter, then try again. It may make a name or something in need.

Halloween Education

This is a weird one as America has made Halloween as a bit of a party horror theme for children. But it is an ancient ritual for adults and not the children. It is about educating and re-educating the public.

When I was in the media lime-light radio stations were always calling me at these times and asking questions for the audience. It helped not only us by being in the limelight as knowledgeable people, but in educating the media and their audience. They contacted me for nearly every other event as well such as Easter, Christmas, Full Moons, Equinoxes and Solstices, and many more, sometimes just to fill in a gap on their show.

It is about researching this topic fully, and being fully knowledgeable in the area of knowing the field fully that you are speaking about, and also with confidence being able to communicate it to the public especially it is a large forum or audience, be sure that someone will throw something at you to try and stump you.

I have been there when lecturing at the Queensland University on Witchcraft when asked a question that I did not exactly know the answer, and I just turned the question back onto the student, and asked what they know about the subject that they were asking. They in fact gave me the answer, and taught me a little more without ever realising it. That is called Wicce ingenuity!

Hand Painting Elemental Capes

For our Coven we have Wardens, who are the Gatekeepers of the Quarters. They deal with everything in their Quarter, the tools, the candles, the Invocations and Banishing's, as well as the presentation to the Lords and Ladies of the Watchtowers the new Wiccans and Initiates. With each of our Wardens we have specially designed Capes to acknowledge who they are within the Magick Circle.

- **Our Warden of the East**-wears a blue silk Cape that has been hand-painted with Wands, Sylphides, creatures of the Air, insects, birds, incense and the rising Sun.
- **Our Warden of the South**-wears a red silk cape that has been hand-painted with Swords, Salamanders, Dragons, Flaming Candles, flames, and the midday Sun.
- **Our Warden of the West**-wears a green silk cape that has been hand-painted with Chalices, Cauldrons, waterfalls, waves, Undines, feminine energy and the setting sun.
- **Our Warden of the North**- wears a brown cape that has been hand-painted with Pentacles, Pan, Satyrs, Gnomes, flowers and herbs, and Goats with large horns.

These capes belong to the Coven and are very special, they are usually only worn at festivals as a bit of elaboration. But represent something important within our Covens.

So, decorate to your hearts content and enjoy the beauty that they bring.

Heal a Tree

Trees like humans get sick, either through the absorption of pollution, unhealthy food (in their soils), too near passing traffic that chokes them, salt in soil content, cancer, root rot and a myriad of other problems. But we can help them.

All we to do is get your circle together, load up the car with supplies for a bit of a picnic, and essential tools for the healing; chalice for water, compost bags, nutrients, salt, and healing wands.

Write and make up a ritual that suits what you are doing, but remember when healing you are putting in so the energies are Deosil, when removing or destroying they are Widdershins energies. So maybe you have seen a place that has trees that are unwell and need your healing services. So, head to that place and make sure you are well prepared.

Take all your needs to the tree chosen or maybe trees are chosen, then it starts:

1. Introduce yourselves and let them know you are there for them and to heal and help them, also don't forget to ask their name and if it is ok for you to do Magick and heal them.
2. Then clear the base of the tree/trees and get everyone just to sit with their backs to the trunks, to absorb the trees energies, in this way the tree can share with you what is wrong.
3. When you are aware of the problem then start by walking widdershins around the tree and banishing the disease, removing it, see it being removed completely.
4. Then walk Deosil and give them your healing energies, if you have wands then now is the time to use them, heal the tree and surround it with love and light, knowing that it IS healed.
5. Open your bag of compost and place around the tree, as an offering and bury a healing crystal into the soil for the tree to absorb, knowing that the Goddess and Nature will now continue the healing Magick.
6. Thank the tree and send it your love and say your farewells.

Healing Blanket

A Medicine or Healing Blanket that we in my Circles always make and use. You can either buy a virgin unused clean blanket or quilt, or make one. If you buy one then wash it clean first with Hyssop and Lavender, then dry it carefully.

When you are ready make sure you have all your Coveners together to create this beautiful Medicine Blanket for Healing. Have fabric paints available, you can add crystals, feathers, shells, twine, dry leaves, but it is best to keep it strong and simple as to many heavy things can break or fall apart so think carefully first about what can be added.

It is good for all Medicine Blankets to have a border of connectedness, we got everyone together and placed our hands in paint of rainbow colours, and joined them together around the border of the blanket. Then we just let that dry whilst having a cuppa. Then comes the varied designs that we each place on the blanket with our own personal designs. I usually get 4 Wicces to each make a Medicine Bag (each one being of the Element etc) with healing items in it, and then in each corner of the Medicine Blanket stitch them securely.

Then we add symbols of power, healing and Magick. Circles, triangles, spirals, Pentagrams, astrological signs, moon signs, and any other Magickal symbol that comes to mind. These days at the markets you can purchase strings of crystal chips that have holes through them, they can be added to the blanket and stitched on there to add Crystal Magick.

Once your Medicine Blanket has been designed charged and completed then it is time to Consecrate it fully within the Magick Circle between a new Moon and up to the Full Moon. When the Medicine Blanket is done, fold it ceremonially and then roll it into a roll, and then it is time for it to do its work. Whoever needs the blanket borrows it for a said amount of time then returns it when finished with.

Mother Hertha House Blessing

Mother Hertha is the Goddess who lends her name to the Hearth within the home for family. As you can read in full my Mother Hertha Home Blessing Ritual in my second book of the series titled: "Complete Teachings of Wicca-Book Two-The Wicce". Where it gives an instructional chapter on the ritual for the Home Blessing.

We use the full coven to assist and bring something special for the house blessing. First step is a full Spring Cleaning, washing everything from walls to gutters. It also needs a small Magick Circle in the centre of your house (here you place your Altar and a large White Spirit Candle). Also have all your tools on your Altar specifically several more candles and incense sticks (one for each member).

You now perform the LBRP (again in full in Book Two). You then light your Spirit candle, incense, make sure your chalice has fresh clean water and your Pentacle has salt upon it. Have some nice relaxed music playing in the background, and now start moving Widdershins around your house each with their candles and incense to banish and clear the house of all negativity and dark energies, see with your mind's eye no dark places only places of light. Have each person use their element and tools to cleanse and purify the house.

You can use crystals, feathers, smudges, bells, drums, didgeridoos, oil, salted water, flowers etc. When the house has been completely done then continue to the outdoors and do the entire front and back yards including the sides of your property remember to go Widdershins, slowly working your way back to the centre of the house and your Magick Circle where you started.

Now it is time to be magnetic and start all over again but this going Deosil and being a magnet attracting all light, love and positivity moving again through the house and the yard, working your way back to where you started. Then take up your Hertha Box which is on your Altar that has photos in it, hair from your pet's ad each person living in the home, objects of power, crystals, etc. Bury this in the front garden for safety. End of the rite.

Holiday Slide-show

This is a great night just for show and tell, it is when you can share some of your adventures with each other. You may wish to show members photos or videos of your festivals for all to see, or maybe someone's great holiday to some sacred sites.

Not everyone is lucky enough to be able travel overseas, and the only experience they have is through television and maybe your slide show night.

Some libraries actually have DVDs and slide shows that are for lending, so this can be quite informative as they usually have professional speakers and commentaries.

I am lucky enough to have travelled quite extensively, but I am not good at photos, although I do have quite a few but should have mountain loads of them. I used to have dozens of Videos, but they were damaged and or stolen, so at least now I have my backup with my computer.

But whatever you do make it a night with popcorn, ice-cream and chips, and don't forget the drink.

Honouring the Earth

We do this all the time as Wiccans, but when scientists realise our truth, then it makes it easier to know more and speak to others about, it also confirms our beliefs. In the Nova television series is a show which explains the "Gaia Hypothesis". This is the scientific theory and belief through science that the entire planet the Earth and Her biosphere is one incredibly large independent organism.

How clever are they just these smart scientists?

Anyway, if you can get your hands on a copy, it is well worth viewing as a coven, with questions and maybe even a debate afterwards. Maybe you can copy it for educational reasons and as a teaching tool to new Seekers. If you are lucky enquire at your local libraries as they are usually able to get their hands on everything that is out there in this world. Even places like the ABC or television resource shops.

But do yourself a favour and do have a good look at this series is very warming and very beautiful to watch.

Honouring Each other

Honouring each other is a special night, where we go prepared. Prepared to be elevated emotionally by others speaking of you and all your positive and good traits. But also, you are speaking of all the positives and good traits of others.

You start by placing everyone's names into a small Cauldron, and then one at a time to withdraw a name. This then gives the chance for everyone to speak highly of and praise that Covener. We so often always confront the negatives and hear of bad things said about us, or maybe we attack ourselves due to lack of confidence. But as Wicces we must be confident in every way, and this does take a long process and a longer still time.

It is always hard to hear negative things about us, especially from those we care about, but it is usually harder still to hear of beautiful and positive things about ourselves from those close to us. It helps reiterate and reinforce the truths about our Coven, and brings us closer together. But please be honest, do not make up things just because others are saying nice things. It is very easy to find the negatives in ALL of us, but it is harder still to maintain our focus on the positive aspects that are real.

So, start the ball rolling, and do not stop until each member has had their dose of respect and love from everyone, no matter how small or intense it may be. We all possess the beauty and positivity of the Goddess within us, now is the time to accept that view and opinion form others.

Hot Tub Night

During the winter month and especially the Winter Solstice, at the end of the night we have for those who are brave to enter the Giant Steaming Cauldron (my spa or hot tub). There is no better way for close covens to get together in a beautiful bubbling spa, enjoying others company and the drinking and sharing of wine and laughter, and freedom of delicately nurtured senses.

It you do not have a spa, or know of someone with a spa, then know that you can actually rent one out for the weekend, and they are not too expensive if everyone puts in for it. It is also a great way to first experience nudity with others who may be a little shy. It is an easy way of revealing that you have nothing to hide, and that it is a natural show of harmony. We do not let these spa nights get sexual as that is not their sole purpose it is about freedom of expression and the release of removing our masks.

We have nothing to hide, and therefore it becomes a non-sexual event and people become safer and freer with those around them. If you wish to make it a sensual night then you can add massages etc later in the night, but this is if everyone is in favour and agreeance.

Human Sculpture

Unlike the Goddess Within Workshop, this is a very different way of seeing sculptures in your Circle. With this when all your Coveners have assembled in your circle, choose the first Artist, the Sculpturer who will use the rest of the members as a raw material. The artist then takes each member by the hand and places them in location and position, which best reflects their relationship to each of the other members.

When completed the human sculpture is a model of all the major relationships connection in the group as seen by one person. Then listen for a while whilst the Artist describes and explains their perceptions and reasoning.

Then disband the sculpture, stretch, and then let another person be the Artist and commence in their creation, it reveals how each person sees the Coven, and where each person fits in with the circle.

Hypnosis

Where relaxation comes from a quietening of the meta-identity (ego), hypnosis comes from an even deeper level of calmness. The meta-identity is relaxed, or quietened, to such a degree that your true self can come through to consciousness.

Your true self is the centre of your four basic drives; survival, sex/social, self-esteem and self-knowledge, it is only interested in fulfilling them, and your meta-identity is how society has told you to fulfil them. If you can reach your true self and suggest to it a more suitable way to fulfil its needs, then it will proceed to make appropriate changes in your meta-identity, or personality.

These suggestions many be anything you desire, e.g. more relaxed, happier, healthier, stop smoking or eating in excess. Either yourself or whoever is helping you into a hypnotic state can make these suggestions. The exercises for self-hypnosis use the same principles as the relaxation exercises, except that the theme is one of sinking deeper and deeper into your mind.

Lie down, and make yourself as comfortable and relaxed as possible. Now in your mind, state your intention or direction. *"I am now going to put myself into an hypnotic state, I will remain conscious during the whole experience."* This prevents you from falling asleep).

Take five slow deep breaths and say, *"Relax now"*. When you say this, you will be in a light hypnotic state. In your imagination feel yourself sinking slowly, this can be done in any way you choose. For example; you could be floating on a warm soft white cloud that is sinking gently to the ground-see the blue sky, feel the warm sun, smell the fresh air, feel the soft warm breeze, and hear the birds, feel yourself sinking very slowly into the ground, or you could be in an elevator, on the 10th floor of a building-press the ground floor button, and see and hear the doors close, feel and hear the elevator start to sink, watch the floor numbers lights as they change very slowly as you descend, 9-8-7 etc. until you reach the ground floor.

Or you could be solely walking down the stairs, or drifting down a tunnel of colours. These exercises are again, limited only by your imagination. Remember too, that when you visualise, use ALL your senses. Once you have done this exercise, it is a good idea to find out exactly what level of hypnosis you are in. there are five levels of hypnosis, the first three are the ones we are dealing with now. These are, simply called; light, medium and deep hypnosis states. A light – medium state is the best for things such as autosuggestion or any questions you may like to ask your subconscious.

Remember to decide exactly what suggestions you wish to make before you start the exercise. Write it into as simple a sentence as possible and when you are under hypnosis, repeat the sentence over and over, e.g. *"every day in every way I am becoming more and more healthy, happy, positive and stronger, etc."*

Deep hypnosis enables things such as pain control, etc. the easiest way to find out what level you are on, is to imagine a yard stick divided into three parts and ask your mind to indicate where on the yard stick you are. If you feel you are not deep enough, run through the exercise again so that you sink deeper, once you are happy that you are deep enough (keeping in mind that only a light state is needed for autosuggestion) then proceed with whatever you wish to use the exercise for, when you wish to come back, say to yourself; *"I am going to count to three and then be wide awake feeling refreshed and alert." "Count slowly 1- I am going to slowly wake up. 2-I am up gently waking up. 3-I am awake!"* remember that your imagination is your most powerful tool. Develop your visualisation and there is NO limit to what you can do.

For further reading on the subject, there is a great book by Leslie M. Le Cron; titled *"Self-Hypnotism"*. It is available in paperback and published by Signet Publishers.

Incense Making

I love making incense for my Circles, especially granulated incense, but also, I have found it quite easy to make stick incense these days. As you can purchase the basic incense sticks with no fragrance, just the pressed sawdust onto the bamboo sticks, all you have to do is add the fragrance or essential oils, then let them dry in the sun. This makes them sun dried incense sticks and the fragrance remains very strong.

But the art of making mixed blends in granule incense is far nicer and you can create some amazing Magickal blends, such as Goddess incense, Banishing, Love, Peace, Harmony, Dream, Courage, Happiness, etc.

You can make as many different types of blends that are needed in one's mortal and Magickal life. The art of making specific Magickal blends such as Kyphi from Egypt is very time consuming, but the result is absolutely magnificent, the aroma from Kyphi is my second most favourite blend. My favourite is an Australian Aboriginal blend called "Dreamtime Incense", I came across this quite by accident.

But since discovering it have realised how potent and powerful this incredible Magick blend is, and the aroma is the most elevating and incredible fragrance I have ever smelt.

If anyone wishes to try some let me know as we have plenty on hand, but a warning once you try it you will never try anything else.

Jack-O-Lanterns

This may sound simple, but in fact the art of pumpkin carving can be varied and amazing. There are so many artists out there with some incredible ideas of how to create the perfect Jack-O-Lantern.

You can make a competition out of it, but remember not to throw away the inside as it can be used to make the best pumpkin soups, scones, pies, baked pumpkin, and much more. So, have another competition of the best Pumpkin food delicacy.

For Halloween, yes, the tradition pumpkins are used, but for just everyday use, or even decorating your festivities and homes create some elegant and peaceful Jack-O-Lanterns. Carve some Goddess energy into them with beautiful natural designs of flowers, elementals faces, happy scenes to invoke a different scenario that Halloween ones.

You can carve symbols of power and healing into them such as spirals Pentagrams etc. Make them individual and try to get away from massed hysteria of evil ghoulish faced ones, to scare off the baddies.

When they are all carved and decorated then it is time to share in the feast of the heart of each pumpkin and feast in their produced culinary delights that are on offer.

Jam Session

This is a great time to get everyone to bring along their musical instruments, and if they don't have one then make one. Bring along drums, tambourines, guitars, mandolins, didgeridoos, cymbals, rattles, horns, clarinets, flutes, tapping sticks, etc.

And if you don't have one made, make a drum with a piece of hide over container, or a tin container and add a handle and make makeshift guitar. Even bring along a couple of short hardwood sticks that you have sanded and decorated to use as Aboriginal taps ticks. Even make a Sistrum with a long pole and collect dozens of bottle tops and punch holes in them, then add them to the pole.

You can even bring along some bells, or crystal bowls, even a Buddhist singing bowl. If not make your own with glasses partially full of water and then rub the rim with your finger to get the glasses singing.

Whatever instrument you have come together and make beautiful music (hopefully), if need do not forget to bring the ear plugs. This is the night to let go with your creativity and silliness, write your own music and sing your very own songs.

It is about just having fun and depending how good you are depending on how long the Muses will remain. But whatever you do, please tap and record your glorious Coven Orchestra.

Jesters Night

Every Coven has a clown, maybe two or three, so in having a Jester's night can bring out the Jester in everyone. We all have jokes that we have herd, some clean and some not so clean and some that should stay at home. The gift is not the joke but the ability to be Master of It and tell it correctly, so the punch line is not lost but cleverly Impacted on our sense of humour.

Even think of a clown's outfit or a Jesters outwit, to entertain your fellow fools. It is about making everyone love, a true comedian gets people to laugh at themselves, as they take them down the journey of silliness mixed with a little stupidity and creativity.

Maybe you can be the best Jester for the Coven Wiccelings, as they too deserve a good laugh, we always employ (without pay) the Coven Pixies at Yule to attempt in stealing the Wiccelings presents from La Bafana, this adds to a lot of humour and sometimes anger from the kids who may take them a bit too serious. Maybe the Wiccelings can learn a Banishing spell to be rid of the evil Pixies that want their gifts, and with enough Magick and power they can be banished in a big puff of smoke.

You could even hire a professional clown who is a magician to show the Wiccelings some real Magic (for sure). But the event is about laughter and having a fun time even if it is at our own expense.

Jewellery Making

Sometimes it is wonderful to know a jewellery designer and maker, and they can come and do a workshop on making jewellery. This is a great time to get everyone to bring along 2-3 crystals, or claws, feathers, shells, or rocks etc. that can be worn as necklaces. Purchase a couple of rolls of leather twine or even sinew if you wish

Then just thread or weave the leather through or around the objects which can make small woven cages to carry and hold your objects. With sinew you can wind it around your object or pierce it through after drilling a hole, but can be a lot tighter than wrapping an object unless you are aware just how to do this.

You may know someone who's a silver smith, and you can get them to make a mould of your Coven symbol (if you have one), my coven symbol or Church symbol is a sleeping crescent moon upon an interlaced Pentagram, my original symbol as my craft name which is Moondancer given to me by my Shaman Jungle Father Jubabe.

If you do not have a coven symbol then make one, you can use any design you wish even a spiral, a triangle, even a shell with a feather, a crystal with a Sigil.

It does not matter but maybe meditate on it for a while, even get your coven to do a ritual in creating the perfect Coven Symbol for your Coven. Get this beautiful symbol made up, and when people get Initiated into your Coven present them with this beautiful gift as a gift from the whole Coven Family.

Leylines

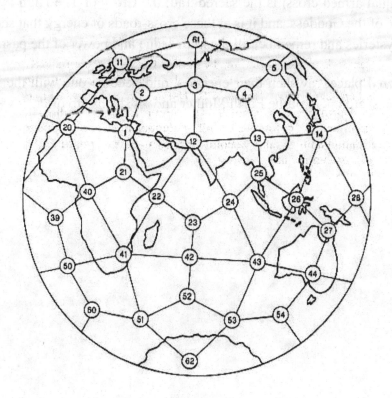

The whole Earth is covered with Power lines of energy, lines that are called Leylines. These Magickal energy lines were traced out by our ancient Priestesses who traced them out and walked them to find natural crossings of these Leylines, these crossed lines became the power centres where great shrines and structures of dedication were built in honour of the Earth Mother. They were the sacred places where the Samethoi, the Wicces of old built their shrines, temples and sacred stone Circles. These places were places of great stores of energy, of connecting with the ancestors, the Great Festivals, they are places where ancient wisdom is stored.

If you have sensitives in your Circle such as Aura readers, psychics etc. then get them to help your Coven find the perfect place in the countryside that can be a crossover of Ley energy, where you can create your Coven outdoor Temple. This would become the greatest treasure that your Coven would have. As it would offer up bountiful knowledge and power to be used as your Sacred Place.

The Cross, (equal armed cross) is the sacred Tau, the Cross of The High Priestess as the Representative of the Goddess, and it is at these cross-roads of energy that she can tap into the ancient Mysteries and remember all the knowledge and power of the past.

Find these sacred places, awaken their energies, and become one with the Breath of the Dragon and the sacred pore of the Earth Mother and all she has to offer.

Library Survey and Vigil

There are many ways to educate the community, but the best is through their education departments, especially their Libraries. Even if you do not frequent a library, you MUST become a member. This way you can keep an eye out for informational of Wicca, assist authors and get their writings out there for the public to read and to research. We must be vigilante in our surveillance of libraries, and they must have a decent selection, (correct selection) of books for the public, as they are the main front source of all information that is tried and true, they should have a good selection of books covering Paganism, Wicca, Wiccecraft, The Goddess, Earth Religions, Dianic Religion, Magick, Spellcraft, Ritual and Ceremony, The Horned God, and more.

It is necessary that they maintain up keep their selection of books, just by Pagans and Wiccans going to their local libraries and joining up, you can then have a word in their books by asking them to acquire certain books in their library. There are many Wiccans who may not be in a financial position to buy many books, so make this you're your mission to get the books in the public eye for your reading and for theirs. Make them a list of books you may wish to read. In all my books I usually have a list of recommended reading with a list of good factual books that are filled with sincere and honest information for the masses. It is important to fill our libraries with material that is the correct form of reading and information for the public and for fellow Seekers who are researching and wanting to know more about Wicca, and where and how they can get involved. So be vigilant with your Libraries and educate them into acquiring certain books for their library.

Life Masks

These are traditionally called "Death Masks", but "Life Mask" sound much nicer as they are of you whilst being alive and are also a wonderful gift for someone on your passing, someone who can place in a place of high esteem.

It is a beautiful way to remember the incredible and complex face of someone we love. They are easy to make even the menfolk can make one, if they are not bearded or have moustaches, or they may need a lot of Vaseline to cover them. It can become quite hard to remove plaster from your face if there is facial hair that is why we use Vaseline to prep the skin and face, so the plaster mould can be removed.

1. Mix up the plaster-of-Paris, that you can purchase from certain Craft shops, but ring around first as they may not stock, maybe use Google.
2. Get an assortment of cheesecloth to use and cut into strips or small squares, these then must be soaked in the plaster.
3. Now it is time for your model to wear their hair back with a head net, make sure that you also bring the Vaseline up over the front of the hair to not get caught in the plaster. Place three short straws into their nostrils and mouth so they can breathe and not panic, as they may remain in this position for up to an hour.
4. Now they are ready, sparingly cover their face with Vaseline, removing any excess as you do not need very much at all. Do not forget to do their ears and neck as well.
5. Now one by one put the gauze or cheesecloth piece into the plaster, scraping off any excess as well, as you do not need too much plaster as you will be doing about 4-8 layers, this makes it thick enough and strong enough as to not break.
6. Press the plaster gauze onto the face and neck, then get a fan of a hair dryer and dry their mask, allow to dry until it is touch dry before removing it. When you have got to that stage, gently and slowly lift off the mask and place it down on a tray of plastic, place close to the window as the sun on the window pane creates a thermal of heat that will dry the mask quicker. If you do not wish to use plaster you can use clay or latex, latex is the easiest to use and dry's the quickest, but it is easy to lose

shape later, unless you make it very thick. It is a personal choice I prefer plaster, it is messier than the other ways but has better results.

7. After about a week when you know that it has completely dried and hardened, then it is time for the next stage.

8. When all is done and ready now it is time to make your bust, your "Life Mask", here you place your plaster mould or latex into a tray of sand (this is the keep it from changing shaping or moving), you can buy beach sand at the local hardware). Make sure that whilst it is still a bit moist that you place into the back of it a "U" shape piece of wire, or a very thick rod of metal through its base to have it as a stand instead of on the wall.

9. When it is secure, then mix your plaster into another bowl or small bucket, making it quite dense, and then slowly pour it into your face mould. If you are good with fibreglass then you could also add a dye and glitter, which is how I made mine. My Life Mask is Azure Blue with gold flakes and gold glitter mixed throughout it.

10. When it has completely dried, you can either paint it (naturally), leave it alone except maybe a bit of sanding, or decorate it with whatever you feel you wish to adorn it. All I have done to mine is place a pair of diamond stud earrings in my ears, and then hand paint a crescent moon on my brow.

11. It is now complete and finished, keep it in a special place for all to adore.

Litha Fireworks

This little ceremony is about surprise and is not intended to awaken the earth but awaken ourselves, especially our Inner Selves or Higher Selves. This can be done by quick and sudden noises that shake and rattle us and wake us up.

Letting the fireworks awaken our Inner Wicce, and bring our souls back into the spiral staircase of light of the Goddess and the best way if to shell shock us so we become alert and aware of the Magick of the Universe starting with what is in the palms of our hands, microcosm and the macrocosm.

Fireworks are about excitement and the awe with every explosion. We love being surprised at every little display of colour and light in the heavens.

In fact, we should be like this every day of our lives, from our first opening of our eyes in the morning to when we fall asleep at night, Magick has ceased for many people because they have stopped believing in real Magick. Just open your eyes people and look all around you as the world of Magick in Natures changes every single day.

Lithomancy

Casting the Stones is called Lithomancy, it is the divination by the casting or throwing of stones onto a specific matt or divination cloth that is placed on the table top. This cloth is also used to wrap around the bag that you keep your Divination stones in.

There is a great system that many used that is explained in Doreen Valiente' book "Witchcraft for Tomorrow". However, I believe as I stated before that it is also best to make your own tools, so go for an Earth Walk to the local beach of running river and find yourself some flat-stones that can be used for your Lithomancy.

Remember that stones have an Earthly strength and when found with water like streams, rivers, oceans etc. they are also infused with that magnetic qualities of water. There are so many different systems that you can adopt in doing your Lithomancy, the oldest and strongest is the Runestones from the Nordic system, as they have ancient runes etched or painted on them giving them a story and each a Magickal energy.

You could even create your own Magickal Sigils and symbols for each stone, and write down what you believe that symbol to represent, this makes it a more in-depth and personal way of doing a reading for a querent and their many questions.

Magick Circle
Deosil v Widdershins, Southern Hemisphere
v Northern Hemisphere

I have always found this confusing, when I hear of people claiming that because we work in the Southern Hemisphere that we should place the Element of Fire in the North, and Earth in the South. Also, that energy moves differently in the Southern Hemisphere, so we should not move clockwise but anti-clockwise within the Magick Circle.

They say this is because the Sun moves across the sky from rising in the east to the setting in the west, so we should also move in the same direction (Widdershins). The truth is that the Earth is moving Clockwise, not the Sun, we are moving towards the Sun around the Circle. But that is not the only reason. The Magick Circle is the Epagomenes, the secrets of the 365 days of the Luna Calendar. Every 10 degrees has a meaning and sacred symbolism to the Wicce. There are 360 degrees' in a Circle, and when you add the Pentagram in the centre you get 365, representing the days of the year. Each month is approximately 28 days.

The Magick Circle is also following Nature, especially the Seasons, as the Circle is the Wicces year. North is Mid-winter. Solstice, the coldest and darkest time of the year. North-east is Imbolg, the warming and awakening of life, and East is Spring Equinox, fertility and a full bustling of wildlife and nature being born. South-east is Beltane, the lighting of fires to impregnate the earth and bring back the Sun. South is Mid-Summer Solstice, the sun at its peak, and the earth scorched and dry, the peak of the heat and masculine power times. South-west is Lughnasadh, the death of the Sun and the calling of the rains to fertilise the earth. West is Autumn Equinox, the letting go and release of the dryness and the welcoming of the rains. North-west is Samhain, the death of the old and the rebirth of the new. This is the Natural rhythm and flow of the Circle, the year and the Seasons. We cannot just flip the Seasons to suit our ways or views, Nature does not work like this.

I have also heard people say but water goes down the plug hole anti-clockwise and not clockwise as in the northern Hemisphere. This is also incorrect as I have travelled all over the world, and the water depending on its balance, even the turning of the inside of the taps can change the flow of water as well, but usually it goes both ways, mostly clockwise.

But this is a great topic to debate with your Coven, the pros and cons of Southern versus Northern and should the directional energies change. You decide for yourself, but make sure you are 100% in agreeance. Remember it is hard to work the mid-summer Solstice in the middle of winter, it makes absolutely no sense.

Magick Mirror

I love Magick Mirrors, I have had mine for decades, and have brought it out on very special occasions. These days you can buy mirrors everywhere, it is good to get a virgin mirror, one that has not been considered. Find one that is still in its box, something small enough but large enough to hold your full face.

With my Magick Mirror I actually made mine from a oval piece of glass that I bought from a glazier I wanted it to be nine inches wide by thirteen inches long, once I picked this up from the glaziers I automatically wrapped it in some cloth to take home. I then got my father who was French polisher/cabinet maker, to make me two ovals pieces, one for the back of the mirror, and then a front oval cover piece to protect it with a handle that was also thirteen inches long.

When he made these for me to my exact measurements, I then took them home and anointed them with my Magick Oil, this also protected the timber which was Oak.

I painted the back of the glass ovoid with matt black paint, and did three coats to make it solid and thick, so it was harder to mark. I then positioned my blackened glass shiny side facing up with glue to the back-oval board and centralised it, so it was positioned perfectly. When this was dry I then placed the oval circle frame and handle on the top of the glass, which was made with a cut in it, so the glass fit into it and timber frame surrounded it securely and fit like a glove. After about a week, it was time for the New Moon, so I consecrated it and then wrapped it in some black silk cloth that was padded to keep it safe, this then was placed inside my Magickal Tool Box.

Maidens Day-Ostara

On this special day we make it of importance to honour all Maidens, the first face of the Goddess, as they are the power of our future. This day is traditionally celebrated on the first day of Spring-Ostara, the 1st September in the SH, and the 1st of March in the NH. This is Maidens Day.

All young ladies between the ages of 13-25 are the Maidens, even older if they have not had children. We honour their capacity to be strong women and be great warriors who are ready to take the world head on. All Maidens should wear chaplets of flowers in their hair, this distinguishes them between the other ladies who are present.

We also have a special day for them by giving them facials, massages, weaving flowers through their hair prior to ritual. It is all about praising them, and honouring them in their prime, in readiness to bring forth the fruits of life ending their Maidenhood and becoming Mothers, the second stage of the Goddess, as the Crones are the third face of our Goddess. We do honour these stages at different times of the year.

This day they wear rainbow colours and are showered with flowers and grains of seed, which invokes love and laughter as nature dances with them in their strength, changes, and courage of their femaleness into the future as young Maidens of the Goddess. NONE GREATER THAN THE TRIPLE GODDESS!

Make Friends with the Night

Yes, I know we are all creatures of the night, and love the Moon and wolves and owls etc. but there are so many are creatures and beings that we do not communicate with. Make sure you are not easily spooked, when you are alone at night outdoors, especially in strange places.

Us as humans are day animals, but we need to open our senses to the night and the darkness. It is always good that as a Coven you visit the countryside away from humans, go as a group, but when you get there separate into different parts so as to be truly alone with the night creatures. Your Man in Black can make a fire somewhere close for all to see, so when you are done or get too nervous being alone you have a place of calm to head back towards. Do remember to ask everyone to bring with them a torch.

Sit and talk quietly in the darkness and the stillness of nature at night. Speak of your feelings, your fears and of your strengths. It is good to lean up against a tree and let yourself just open up to nature and drift freely into the silence and the Magickal sounds of the night. After about an hour if all have not returned to the fire then signal them all with a blow of the Conch, at this stage all convene and sit and huggle up and discuss their feelings and awareness of the night, did you make any friends, peak of your discussions and what you received from Nature. Whenever you are out in nature alone or not, remember to activate all your senses for safety.

Massage for All

Having a special day set aside for having professional massages is exactly what the body orders after a week of hard work and having the body tired and aching. We all know to a small degree the basics of massage, but if you are lucky to have a qualified masseuse in your Coven, or if you know of one, then that is even better.

You can make a group booking and get them to massage and explain in detail about massage. For this I would have at least several massage tables, so half can be massage at one time, then have a break and then the other half gets their massage.

If everyone has a table then that makes it easier and better for training, because as you are showing massage, you are learning and massaging your fellow Covener. Massage is an excellent art to learn, as it is the perfect healing agent and assist many in your circle. I believe that everyone should have the basic knowledge in massage for our partners, friends and family.

So, don't be lazy, strengthen those wrists with learning the skills of massage therapy and all that it offers, plus it feels so bloody goooood!

Maypole

Making a Maypole is traditionally made by the menfolk, as they find the perfect tree, ask for its sacrifice, and then cut it down with song and music. They then cut it to the exact height that they wish it to be, which should be either 11'or 15', as 2" will go into the ground or make it the exact height and secure it with steel fence posts. The width that is comfortable to carry so it is not too heavy (as it dries, it does get lighter, but make sure it is a good sapling with no cracks, or it will eventually split and be no good).

Get all the males to sand the pole down to make it smooth and clean, and then get a large tub of linseed oil (which is cheap at farm suppliers), as it is raw and used for horse's coats, whereas the city linseed oil is processed and is quite expensive. When it is completely oiled let it dry for a couple of hours, I recommend oiling it several times, as this makes the pole soak up the oils and makes it longevity better.

If you have metal workers make a secure wheel with a circular cap that fits tightly over the top of the pole, with spokes outstretched to a large circular wheel about 3 feet in diameter (this is where the ribbons are tired onto). This is to be like a wheel of a cart that is stationary and does not spin nor move.

Separately away from the men the womenfolk are making bowers of flowers (these are better to be plastic as they will last and not cost the earth, whereas buying flowers every time is very costly). The women make three long rows of flowers that can be wrapped around the top wheel with small lengths hanging down.

Then you would purchase rolls of the 9 rainbow colours of twine or ribbon of white, purple, dark blue, light blue, green, yellow, orange, red, and black. The white and black are to represent the positive and the negative of Magick in the Maypole.

The ribbons are measured at double the length of the pole, folded in half and then tied to the wheel at the top of the Maypole. Have them tight and hanging down, but secured at the base with another tied to hold them all together so they do not get tangled.

When components are ready, attach them all and finish the Maypole, wrap it in a cloth to keep it protected until it is need on the day after Beltane (the fertility Festival). On the day set aside for the ritual have it secure and set in the middle of your Magick Circle, and ready for the bards.

This is a day for all Coveners, family and friends to enjoy our Pagan Picnic. Start with the Morris Dancers weaving their Magick and dancing for the Earth. Then get all the Wiccelings under the age of 13 to come forward and take the colour ribbon of their choosing, we then get the bards to sing and play the Elemental Maypole Song, as the Wiccelings dance and play with weaving the ribbons to create and Magickal rainbow of colour and laughter, bring fertility to the Earth and all within and upon her.

Mediaeval Festival

I have been to some amazing Mediaeval Festivals, and they are spectacular, with all the components of entering and being a part of these Magickal times. They are always so inviting and exciting as if you are stepping into history and the very past.

They have so many events, with all Covens and groups coming together to create a full village theme, with stores, bakeries, gift shops, jousting, sword fights, and even the occasional Witch trial and burning.

This can start small and within time and good organisational skills can become and major event for not only Wiccans, Pagans and Mediaeval clubs but for the public community as a whole, as it is interesting and exciting for everyone in attendance, especially if everyone comes in costume as it adds to the theme of actually being in mediaeval times, it becomes more effective if everyone plays their role as if in a huge theatrical play.

So create a wonderful show of display and have your very own Mediaeval Festival that everyone can join in and make it more and more exciting as the years pass, and the festival gets notoriety and many expressions of interest of wanting to be a part of your festivities.

Media Press

When sending out Media and Press Releases you need to be quite precise and exact in what you are saying, it should be done by a professional if possible, because if you say the wrong thing at the start, they usually will not waste their professional time on something that is either very amateur or does not get to the point directly. The media need to be alerted and understand exactly what you are saying, without or the bells and whistles, they come later when you have rooved yourself professional with the media, and this may take many years. So, start slow and gradually you will feel more comfortable and learn to become better at speaking with the media and most importantly, think quickly about the questions they have asked, and give exact, truthful and direct answers that are full of information and qualified knowledge.

Start with:

- Subject
- Your name and qualifications
- Be direct to the point of what your media release about.
- Add your qualifications and experience in this field.
- Cover what you can discuss or talk about with confidence.
- Mention your public speaking qualifications (if any), radio, TV etc.
- Add now your contact details
- Then in BOLD say the word END. And then finish off with something as a finale to your Media Release.

This will help with your Media Release, but start with just your local Media contacts which can be found almost anywhere, always send by email or fax first, as this is the best way for your introduction.

Medicine Pouches

If you are not aware of Medicine Pouches, then know that these are an item that no Pagan in ancient times was without as it was their Talisman, their item of safety and security. It was a small handmade bag, which was usually made of animal hide, something that you may have caught for food, and used the hide for anything that you can make with it.

It is traditionally cut into a large circle (or as large or as small as you want your pouch to be, then punch into the dried hide 8 holes in its perimeter, these are form you to thread leather twine through them to make a drawstring, and with extra twine to have it worn around your waste or neck.

Inside are certain Magickal items that you have or have found such as feathers, shells, crystals, oil, seeds and grain, teeth, claws, fur, something personal or even something that belong to someone who was special to you and is no longer of this world.

Place these items in your pouch and Consecrate it by using the Elements; consecrate it with Water and Salt, Air and Fire, and then have it charged by the Earth Mother, Pachamama and the Horned God, Great Spirit.

This is now your sacred medicine pouch used and worn as a Talisman to keep you safe, strong, bold, good health, safe from bad spirits, and to attract good spirits and energies into your life.

Meditation

Meditation is the key to every circle, as it is the Wicces duty to better themselves on all levels, physically, mentally, astrally, psychically and spiritually. If they cannot be able to do this on the lessor levels, then how can they possibly do this on the highest levels.

Meditation is not about sitting down with a group and leading them on journeys, it has so many different levels. Our Mind and our Body must be healthy and be able to be relaxed, and strong, or we will never master Magick, as Magick will master you if you pretend without heart and soul. Being a Wicce means that we need to sacrifice much in order to gain much, so start your list of sacrifices knowing that what you give up, will be given back to you in a bountiful and more ascended manner.

If you have a proficient teacher of Meditation, then always ask them to offer their services at every gathering, as meditation should always be the first step of every ritual or ceremony. It is like anything that we do continually, we eventually will become proficient at it, and it will help us get to the level that we need to get to, to be a master of Wiccecraft and Magick. Talking about something does not make you qualified in it. It is about determination, hard work and much study and perseverance to take you to the highest levels of being a Wicce.

How can you be in touch with the World, and the Earth's creatures and the Goddess if you are not in touch with yourself in a healthy, focused aura. How can you love if you have no love for yourself? How can you heal if you are unwell? Loving yourself is about looking after yourself and knowing yourself.

Meet the Stars

"Let them that know the truth, look to the stars and homeward bound." A great way to experience the stars and the celestial bodies in our solar system are to get yourself a group booking at your local Conservatory.

The ability to have a small home telescope is great but in no comparison to the huge ones that they have at Conservatories. I have had many ventures with my Circles, as they are exciting and very knowledgeable and beautiful.

When you are aware that there is a special lunar or solar movement of change in the Universe, then if you are lucky you can book a tour on this night to see our massive heavens.

Using their massive telescopes are so incredible that you can never really believe what is out there until you sit the whirling masses with your own eyes, when you look through the lens of these gigantic telescopes you realise exactly how small we really are in comparison to the millions of solar systems that we do not even know about.

So, find a date in your Calendar that is special and book the Coven into a visit at the local Conservatory

Memory Exercises

This is an excellent way to keep Alzheimer's at bay. It also sharpens our memory. There are so many of us that have memory problems, whether it is short-term memory or long-term memory.

It helps to keep our mind sharp, and the longer you do this you better and sharper your memory will become. With the Memory Game it is best to start small.

Start by having 10 items on a tray that is covered with a tea towel, then when everyone is sitting around the table with pen and paper in hand, remove the tea towel and give everyone

5 seconds to view all the items, after 5 seconds place the tea towel back over the items and get everyone to write down what items they saw.

But that is not all folks, now get everyone to draw the diagram of where these items were positioned on the tray, then ask for their colours etc. When this has been done, get everyone to disclose their items, and check off how many they got right, and how many they got wrong.

Every time you do this change the items and maybe add a few more, gradually building up to 20 items, keep a Coven record and see if it is helping Coveners with their memories.

Morris Dancing

Morris Dancing is traditionally done by the menfolk, and most cities or towns have Morris Dancers, and maybe some of your menfolk can belong to such a group, and learn how to dance for the Earth, the Sun, The Moon and the Stars.

If you haven't seen Morris Dancing live, then you need to view some sites that show Morris Dancing, as they are quite gifted at what they do, and it can be quite spectacular and professional depending on long the group of dancers have been together. As their uniforms are great as well. They have bells attached to their wrists and ankles, and they use handkerchiefs and sticks when they dance, and they either throw them about or take hold and dance with them, they also hit their sticks against each other in a designed pattern that is all about Magick and Mystery.

Morris Dancing is just one form of dancing, and with my Circles we do a lot of Circle Dancing with traditional pieces of music. This differentiates the difference between our Circles and others, and we incorporate music and song with dance into nearly everything, we even sing the Quarters by singing and calling the directions.

Mother's Day

Yes, we all celebrate Mother's Day then society has told us too, but we should honour Mother's and have our own special day that we as Wiccan Honour Mother's, and not just the Mother's that we know, but all Mother's.

June is the perfect month to celebrate Mothers and especially nearest the Full Moon. But anytime that you decide to make it a special day for the Mother's in your Circle, and hold a ritual to honour all Mother's at all times, especially the Mother of us all, the Great Earth Mother Goddess, Pachamama.

It should be a day of not so much gift giving but doing something for her or them, helping them with their housework, looking after the children, maybe arranging a special day for them to have facials, massages, and a coffee at the local café.

But it must be all about them, and not their families or friends. If they are a great Mother and their children are young then they will be quite exhausted, so together as a Coven take some of the weight off their shoulders and give them some downtime. If they are single mothers then their jobs are much harder, and they will need more than a helping hand, give them as much as you are able too.

Mosaic Creations

I love making mosaics, I use to just go around to tile stores and ask for their broken tiles, even going to junk shops or the markets and finding old plates that are decorated or coloured add to your adventurous design.

When you have plenty of tiles broken or not, then all you need is the tools to make your creation.

- Have a board or something as a support backing for your design, make sure you know what size you are making. I used large old tiles and just did the mosaic designs over them, I also did our upstairs breakfast patio which was 4 meters square, this took me months to finish and a very sore back.
- You must have a pincher to break the tiles, or to chip off small pieces for your design.
- You must have drawn out a pattern, mandala or design that you want, and make sure you have enough broken tiles to complete it.
- You must have enough tile cement and a tile cement scraper to place the cement on the base.
- And you must have grout of the colour that you think is fitting, also a sealer to sealer the tiles and grout.
- When everything is ready with chalk sketch out your design and write what colours inserts you want where, this will help with time. Separate all your different tiles colours and pieces so they are easy to select when needed.
- Now just design away and enjoy the creativity as it unfolds.
- When you have finished tiling, and everything is pressed flat, when it is dry, then grout the entire infill areas to make them all sealed, and then make sure you clean as you go all the excess cement and grout before it dries, as it is much harder to remove when dry.

Movie Night

Movie nights used to be complicated and sometimes boring if people picked out the wrong movies. But in these days, we have so many choices. Everyone has a DVD or VCR, and you just have to come to an agreement on the movie or movies that you wish to watch.

I f you do not have room enough for a lot of people, and you do not have a large flat screen, then maybe make a night out at the movies and go to the theatre, as a group.

When I was younger we as a coven were all invited to attend the premiere of 'The Exorcist", the media were expecting us all to rock up in robes and regalia but we all blended in quite nicely and they did not even know who were the Wicces and who were not. It was an exciting night viewing this special movie, and it was quite scary, but when I watched it again many years later I found it quite tame.

You can hire the movies "The Wicker Man" 1 and 2. There are so many movies out there to choose, you can even get a rehash and watch the old series "Bewitched".

Whatever you choose just to make sure that the popcorn is flowing and the drinks, and don't forget the chocolate bombs.

Mural Painting

If you are lucky enough to own your own home, and you have a great artist in your Coven, then maybe get together and create a wall mural in your indoor temple room, start with the North, the realm of the God and Goddess.

Design a beautiful scene of mountains in the background with flowing water falls, and forests with giant tree's. Have a field of fruit trees and grain, and fields of flowers surrounding the Goddess/God who are frolicking in the fields.

Add some symbol such as Pentacles, spirals, zodiac signs, planetary signs, earth signs. Add your Elementals such as Gnomes, goats, unicorns etc.

You can get the artist to show everyone what to do and they can go around afterwards if needed and touch everything up. But these can be quite a beautiful thing in your home, and when meditating can easily take you into the realm of the North and the place of the goddess and God.

Museum Visits

Museums have changed a lot these days, as nowadays the world comes to you. You can attend the museum when they have massive toured displays from other parts of the world, from Egypt, Greece, Rome, Scandinavia, England, Native American Indian, Aboriginal etc.

They bring their treasures to you. When you visit the museums in your own towns, you only get to see about 30 percent of their relics, as they usually do not have the space to display everything. It is like the "Buckland Museum of Witchcraft and Magick, they have so many precious things but due to finances do not have the space to display everything. So, if you are to visit any museum at least visit this one, and donate, as they maintain and keep for safekeeping all our relics and regalia from the Wicce Elders of the World. They have some amazing items of interest for not only the Wiccan world but the community.

But do visit your local museum and support them, especially as a Coven, as the more you do as a group the stronger the bonds will grow. Keep an eye out in the media for museum shows that will and could interest all your members.

Remember Museums hold the knowledge of our past, that can teach us so much about where we have been, where we are, and where we are going. Museums are changing just as mankind are changing, but knowledge is still the essence of what we all need, all the time.

Mystery Guest

Having a Mystery Guest adds a bit of intrigue and mystery to your Coven. But usually it adds a little excitement as well. It has always been great to have guest speakers, but mystery speakers add a bit more Magick.

They maybe a special friend or someone that has experience in certain fields, such as a Psychometrist, dowser, author, magician, native elder, trance, High Magick, Ceremonial Magick, Herbalist, Naturopath, parapsychologist, hypnotist, astrologer, astronomer, aromatherapist, crystal bowl healer, palm reader, iridologist, geologist, environmentalist, Sea Shepherd, etc.

Or they may have absolutely nothing to do with these subjects but maybe just someone from the outer community that has a skill or qualifications, such as artist, sculpture, pottery expert, vet, nutritionist, fitness instructor, gemmologist, arts and crafts, etc. Or maybe even from a different religious faith, Buddhist, Taoist, Hindu, Judaic, Hebrew, Islam, etc.

Whatever their skill, knowledge or talent, be sure to give them respect for their knowledge and beliefs even if they differ from yours. They are not there to convert you but to educate you in their field or interest and maybe show you their area of expertise. I had on several occasions a Tanner, who tanned hides professionally and they showed us the many stages of how to tan our own hides. I also have a Doomsday Prepper come and share their views on being a prepper and how to be prepared for the worst, but pray for the best.

Name Tag Mixer

Name tag mixer is a fun way to get to know one another at a deeper level. Get all Coveners to take a supplied post card size blank card that they can write their name on in any way they like. Also get them to answer certain selected questions such as:

- Who is your favourite Goddess?
- Who is your favourite author?
- What historical figure do you respect and admire the most?
- What is your favourite book?
- What is your favourite colour?
- What is your favourite song or artist?
- What is your favourite sport?
- What is your favourite crystal?
- What is your best feature?
- What is your worst feature?
- What is your favourite hobby?
- What are three things you dislike about yourself?
- What is your Power Animal?
- What is your favourite plant or flower?

Now get everyone to sit in a circle and for everyone to honestly share their responses but in more detail, just get each person to answer one question at a time and then go onto the next person, so everyone answers the same question and then onto the next.

This can be quite fun and very revealing in getting to know your sisters and brothers.

Nuclear Free Zones

Now this may sound strange in some countries that do not have Nuclear Power Plants, like here in Australia. But we still have Nuclear waste and toxic waste that is transported through our towns and suburbs. We can legally stop this and avoid a catastrophe from happening.

So declare your homes, and your Coveners homes as a Nuclear Free Zone. Do this by notifying your local councils, and federal governments by letter and email that you will NOT countenance the manufacture, the siting and transport of any nuclear waste, weapons or toxic waste in your area.

It also helps to go up the ladder and write to your Statesmen and to foreign governments with a nuclear capability. Contact your local peace and environmental groups, as they can sometimes supply much detailed information about these sort of organisations, by giving you all the information that you require to take your concern higher.

You can also lobby by getting the registered voters to actually have your town, city, and even the entire state as a declared nuke-free zone. Just make sure you have many signatures to strengthen your letter of persuasion. Don't wait until it is too late, do it before it starts, this then adds to the hop that it will be impossible to change the laws and make it a nuke-zone.

Nudity Versus Robed

Since being involved in the Craft I have discovered that each Coven seems to have their own way of doing things, even though their structure is similar there are always subtle changes and differences, like some Coven prefer nudity or skyclad (dressed by the stars), and others robed all the time even in Initiations, and ones like ours that were both, in some rituals we were skyclad, and in others robed.

There is nothing more confronting than being completely naked with a group of people, this is why we always start with having some spa nights it helps people get accustomed and not have a shock effect of being around nudity. But being skyclad also shows everyone that you are open and free to the world, with nothing to hide or conceal.

It is also about timing, some rituals you need to be robed especially in winter, and others of higher Magick need not to be hampered by clothing that will get in the way and cause danger by running and dancing around flames and tools, as robes can catch of anything. Also, clothing does inhibit the power that is released from the bodies when we do higher forms of Magick and Ritual. Nudity is NOT about sexuality, it is not about being perved on or checking the tits or size of their Wigley's, it is about acceptance and a tolerance of the many differences, shapes and sizes of our bodies. We are not all perfect, and therefore should not act as though we are.

If you are shy and nervous that is fine as we all are at first, but then realise that no-one cares about the size or shape of your body, as we are all sisters and brothers and nothing more.

Once Upon a Time Storytelling

Storytelling is a great gift, and is excellent when the Elders can tell their stories and share their years of experience. Storytelling is not just about telling life experiences it is about telling the stories of our faith, the Gods and Goddesses of old and their creation myths, their stories, before they too get lost in the spirals of time and space.

I have written a book of Goddess and God Oracles, which will be later turned into an Oracle, book and card boxset to help guide our footsteps by listening to the words of the Great Mother, through her many names and individual cultures and ways.

The telling of the Goddesses stories is invigorating, my qualification in the Craft has always been as an Oracle, as the Goddess has always spoken through me, especially at Full and

New Moons, but usually whenever she has something to tell me, that she wishes me to pass on to others.

Even listen to some of the creation myths and stories of natives from the land you live on whether it is Australian Aboriginal, Native American Indian, Maori, Eskimo, Scandinavian, Germanic, Celt, Samethoi, Druid, Egyptian etc.

Every culture and every place have deity, and they have their stories that need to be shared and told, they have no voice in the 21st Century except though the Priests and Priestesses of Wicca, who can act as Storytellers or oracles and get their messages told and hopefully listened and adhered to.

Open Forum

Once a month I use to make myself available by holding an open forum, where people can ask me any questions that they like, and I mean anything. If I could not answer then I would try to either find out the answer they seek, or try to point them in the right direction to get some satisfaction from their answer.

None of us hold all the answers, but we all hold the ability to find the answers, it just takes time and research, hard work and many challenging hours of trying to get the answers that will put your mind at rest.

I believe that answers are always there somewhere ready to find, it is the questions that are hard. This is the reason I formed my first Coven, it was because none of my previous covens that I belonged to would give me the answers to my many inquisitive questions. I believe that if you have the knowledge to answer the question, it means that you are ready for the answer, maybe not the whole answer but enough to keep the inquisitive mind happy until the rest of answer is revealed to them when they are ready to receive the full answer.

So, if you have these open forum nights or days, then make sure you are prepared, but if not at least be honest. If you don't know, try to find the answer together. If you only partially know the answer, then let them also know this. But if you are smart and know the question and have the answer then reveal as much as you can or know, this is how our knowledge has lasted, by sharing with verbal talks and allowing all those that ask to be gifted with that knowledge, so they too can eventually pass on that knowledge to another. So, may it always be!

Outer Court Lectures

The Outer Court Lectures are the very first basic training that is required in every Coven, without these you are not ready for the path ahead. The term Outer Court implies exactly what it states, that it is the OUTER of the Circle (not yet Initiated).

In my first Book "Complete Teachings of Wicca-Book One-The Seeker", gives you a full training module of all the Outer Court Lectures that I used throughout all my years where I trained hundreds of Seekers, and brought most of them into the Craft family.

So, if you wish to use my Outer Court lectures please feel free to do so, just forward me an email and let know, then I can also be of assistance if you have any questions about them. The Outer Court lectures should last between 6-12 months and include all the written lore about Wicca such as:

- Meditation
- Chakras
- Self-Blessing Rituals
- The Elements and their Elementals
- Wicca versus Wiccecraft
- The Mother Goddess
- The Horned God
- Natural Magick
- Various Magick
- Colour Magick
- Candle Magick
- The 8 Festivals
- The 13 Full Moons and New Moons
- Death and Rebirth
- Book of Shadows
- Wiccaning and Initiation

- The Magick Tools of a Wicce
- The Hand-fasting Ceremony
- The Astral Plane
- Herbalism
- Astrology
- Healing Techniques
- The Priesthood
- The Wicces Calendar
- The Tenets and Laws
- Meeting the Coven Elders

All these and more are in my first book, so please have a good read of them, because once you know all these and still accept the ways of the Coven and Wicca, then you may be ready to take the next step and be Wiccaned in to the Coven and the Wiccan Community.

This means that if you wish to go further (but do not have to) to can study then and work towards being Initiated as a Wicce of the Old Religion, and then we say, "Blessed Be and Merry Meet".

Orchard or Garden Harvest

Around harvest time it is important to connect with the natural rhythm of what is happening in your neighbourhood. We must take notice of what harvest time is showing us, we need to be a part of this great time, and help in the harvesting.

If we have a member who has a coven herb garden, market garden or and orchard, then it is time to get the Coveners together to help a neighbour or friend "pick some fruit", many farmers actually allow you as payment to take home a fair amount of the produce to share and enjoy as a thank you.

If it is your orchard or a friend, then maybe discuss the idea of going organic and getting rid of poisonous pesticides and chemical sprays that are harmful to the plants and then us. When you get everyone together at an early time appointed meet and pick like crazy, but don't forget to hydrate and stop for mini breaks especially a nice picnic lunch, under the shade of your trees. This is the perfect time to get everyone together and make preserves, that everyone can take home and store for a special day when that fruit is out of season and you are just craving for that Mango or Orange fruit.

Whilst picking the fruit get everyone to sing merrily so as to make it more enjoyable and fun. Give thanks to the Earth Mother and the spirits of the Orchard for all their bounty, and give thanks and honour the Sun as the giver of life to this fruit through its warmth and sunlight.

Also, be aware that you do not need sugar, but if you do use sugar use brown sugar or better still as I do use Blessed Bee Honey.

Pagan Sled or Sleigh Rides

We don't have snow where I live in the tropics, but we do have sand-dunes, and these are great for sledding just as snow is great for sledding. Have you ever built your own sleds and tried in sliding down huge sand-dunes or snow fields, it is so much fun, and I mean for the whole family?

Get every Coven members family together and have a competition of family against family, and see who are the bravest and toughest. You can all put in a set amount and buy a trophy for the winner and for the loser.

Trophies do not have to extravagant, but they can be quirky and funny. You can also add some silly events like being blindfolded, or wear witch's hats and see who can fly the best, decorate your sleds to look like broomsticks etc.

The ideas are endless, unlike the sand-dunes and snowfields that do have an end, just make sure your breaks work or at least there is someone to stop you before entering the next universe.

Pagan Songfest

Well everyone has heard pagan chants, they have sung along with many Pagan and Wiccans songs, but how many have remembered them or written them down before they forget, so they can be added to their Coven Songbook.

We all love singing, even though some of us are not very gifted in the arts of musical notes and holding the right key, but it is not about the professional singer, it is about raises our voices and singing with love and happiness. I had created a Choir for the Church of Wicca, and they were all just members who loved to sing, and after a while they were so good, especially a couple of the singers, as they had beautiful voices, but then there were a couple that we kept in the back ground.

Bring out the old songbooks and get together around your campfire and sing to your hearts content. Bring out the old favourites and mix them with some new ones as this adds a little excitement. Maybe even have a little singing competition to see who the real stars are. Dust off the cobwebs from the musical instruments and give them a bash as well, this sort of this adds to the Coven and makes it more enjoyable and memorable.

Past Life Regression

Past Life Regression is something that we should all experience, I have several times been regressed, some were successful and others not at all. In my Coven I had a beautiful young lady whose grandfather was the creator of the Glaskins Technique of regression, whereas the other method is the Christos Experiment. Both are widely used but I actually prefer the Glaskins Technique, it is simpler and yet takes you deeper.

We also at one of the Spring Festival Camps has a wonderful pagan gentleman with us all the way from Ireland, and he did a full regression workshop on one of the attendee's, and he was absolutely brilliant, and very good at what he did. Even I was completely impressed, and it takes a lot to impress me.

The one thing about Regression is that it is all about trust, and being completely comfortable, so if you are to learn about regressions get an experienced person to guide you firstly, as it is quite involved and does take the patient in a very sometimes vulnerable position of facing their past fears and phobias.

Like everything never play Wicca, always be the Wicca and know before you commence, never going into something half-hearted and with only a small amount of knowledge. Especially when you have someone totally relying on you and your assistance in such a personal field, as there are many things that are private and can bring back past demons which can cause more problems than just a bad memory.

Pentacle Making

Every Altar and every Coven must have a Pentacle, as this is the principle Tool of the Magick Circle and the Wicce. It is a sacred key to the Portals and the Mysteries of the Goddess, it teaches the secrets of the Pentagram and the Magick Circle. It is more powerful than any other tool within Wicca and the Magick Circle.

We have several as my first Pentacle was shown to me by my first Traditional High Priest who showed me how to use and make a copper disc and acid etch in the top of it, leaving all the sacred Sigils that are needed. I still have this since my first Initiation in 1975.

I then discovered an ancient method of making wax moulds of the Pentacle, and so created a plaster mould and then poured latex over it to create and Pentacle mould, of which I then poured resin and bees wax onto it to make my Magickal Altar pentacle. This was made from Eucalypt resin, Dreamtime resin and beeswax, and within were placed some herbs and crystals to charge the Pentacle.

But due to me going to Bali several times a year, I ended up taking my design to some friends of mine in Indonesia and having them hand carve and make my new Pentacles out of wood. I still have many of them if anyone would like to purchase one from me just drop me an email on my website https://tamaravonforslun.com and I can send you the details.

Whichever way you decide to have your Pentacle, just make sure you have one, and that it is properly Consecrated before using it, and it is also needed for Consecrating all your other items and Tools on within the Magick Circle.

Photo Exhibition and Expedition

I love having the video camera at our Festivals and Full Moons, not within the Circle but outside so as to not be a distraction. But having video cameras as a teaching aid helps see things when you are to be focussed on the ritual and do not see everything. Also having some small cameras to take memorable snapshots for your scrapbook is well worth the memories.

It is always great to have a little exhibition and display your festivities, as it shows everyone in their happy modes and surrounded with Magickal Folk.

You can even go on a trip to identify plants, trees and herbs that are wild crafted. Taking pictures of the wild, is amazing as you may never witness the same Magick exactly the same again. Even when going on Earth Walks be sure to take some snapshots, as nature also loves being shot (with a camera that is).

With every Festival, event, or activity take photo as they are something you can display several times throughout the year and have an art gallery of all the Coven works. But remember to ask people first if they mind having their photos taken, as It may offend some people who are shy, or not yet fully out of the Broom Closet.

Photographing nature such as flowers, insects, spider webs, morning dew, leaves, the environmental damage and rubbish are all forms of art. But use them for the right reasons. Have a competition with the Coven for the best photo, the best flower photo, the best pet photo, the best Wicceling etc.

Pilgrimage to Sacred Sites

Many of us no matter where we live are lucky enough to have sacred Native sights in our vicinity. In Australia as I have already said we are about 30 kilometres from a sacred Taboo sight, which the Aboriginals do not go there as they call it the "Devils Playground", this place is called Boulder Rock and our Covens have been working our Circles there for over 40 years.

It was also put in our care by C.A.L.M. which were the land keepers of the place, but they did not do a good job at all. Whenever we go to this beautiful sacred place we ask everyone to bring some plastic rubbish bags, so we can do a clean-up as well before and after our Festival.

We honour this great place, where the Aboriginals legend states that the Shining Ones came from the stars and threw dice to see whether man deserved to stay alive on this planet or to be wiped out, due to their inability to take care of their paradise.

Well we are still here, so the dice (which were giant standing stones each weighing over 100 tons) landed in our favour, but it is up to us to take care of the bush and the very Nature that is our survival.

But there are many more sacred Places, just visit the local Native information sight, and ask where they are. It is well worth knowing what is in your immediate area that was termed Sacred, honestly the Natives see everything as sacred, so just look around you. Sometimes you can get permission from the local tribal council (or spirits of the ancient ones if there are no living guardians or caretakers). But any historical society or library will have relevant maps and books that can guide you to these sacred places.

Poetry Night

Everyone writes poetry even if they feel it is not very good. But all forms of poetry usually come from the heart and deep mind. Poetry seems to always stem from emotion which is the greatest platform for all types of creativity.

Have a Poetry night, and get all the masterpieces and not so masterpieces of Poetry together to a big event reading. I would also invite other Covens and make it a joyous event for all, even the shy may have some wonderful odes to the Goddess or to loved ones. But whatever the Poem, bring it with flare, don't just read it, make it sing with its own rhythm.

If you are not good at public speaking, then hopefully someone in the Coven if a great speaker. Get them to read the Poetry and read them with gusto, giving each a life of their own with feeling and energy.

When commencing the Poetry entertainment, do it alphabetically and make sure you have a couple of breaks, also add some nice snack and toilet breaks as well. Maybe give every Poem a rating, like a star rating from 1-10, and at the end of the evening let everyone see the scores for each of the Poems.

Have set categories under the Poetry reading such as; Poem, writing skills, public speaking, confidence, humour, seriousness, elegance, and maybe even Empowerment.

You may also give out small awards certificates or trophies, for most eloquent, best Poetry, worst poetry, weirdest poetry, funniest poetry, etc. But more than anything enjoys the evening especially giving confidence to those who are a bit reserved in the sharing of their poetry gifts.

Pollution v Global Warming

This is a great gathering especially for the Wiccelings, as the children seem to be more aware of the environment as they are educated at school. Maybe you could get the Wiccelings to do some talks or sharing on their aspects of the Environment and Pollution, and what can they teach the adults.

There is so much to learn and know, and our children have the best skills and knowledge in this area. An interesting surprise would be to have a guest speaker from an Environmental Protection Organisation. Find out all the things that are going on in your own neighbourhood, and ask what you can do to help or at least be a part of it. If we start to look after the Pollution and help the Environment in our own back yards, then like a stone thrown into a pond the ripple effect can spread outward, and gradually change the world.

Even think of doing Environmental Spells or Rituals as these can be more focused and do more than many a do-gooder who says one thing, and then does another. There are so many people that feel that they are too busy and do not have the time to do these extra activities, but if we start from just our kitchen rubbish and recycling, making sure that everything we recycle is properly prepared and cleaned, then it will not go into the waste. We all have our recycling rubbish binds, but if we do not do our jobs and remove labels, clean all the plastic and bottles, remove caps and lids, then they will all just get thrown into our rubbish tips to be buried. Ask your local council what information they have that can help getting out to people the right way and the wrong way to recycle. Mother Nature is watching, so honour her by our efforts.

Potluck Dinner

Potluck dinners are an exciting way to come together with different dishes. These are better during the winter months when everyone can bring their favourite hot dish. So everyone brings a casserole dish or saucepan/pot of a hot Potluck, and get the menfolk to bring the drinks.

You can have dishes from France, Spain, Mexico, China, Egypt, Greece, Italy, Polynesia etc. Having international Potlucks are the best, especially if you have a Maori member they can set up a Hongi, in your back yard, which is an exciting feasting. If you have not indulged in a Maori Hongi before then you are missing out.

But whatever the feast as a Potluck Dinner the theme is enough for all to taste and share, so make sure the plates are small, or what I use are small plastic cups, or small coffee cups, and make sure you get someone to make the bread loaves or roles. Here in Australia we love Damper, this is a fire made loaf of bread the way the Aboriginals make their Bush Tucker. You can add whatever your heart desires, heaps of butter and garlic in the middle, olives and herbs, cheeses etc. But they are a scrumptious way of filling the belly without eating all the Potluck Casseroles etc. and not having enough to go around.

Pagan Prepping

There is a lot of people out there who think that Preppers are fools, well I am a Prepper! The adage "Better to be prepared, than being sorry". Is true, if you think about everything we do, we are all Preppers to varying degrees. We all have extra food in the cupboards, freezers, etc. But Full Preppers prepare for anything that may or could happen, especially global problems; war, ice age, floods, cyclones, tornados, EMP attack, Nuclear Holocaust, invading thieves, and the like.

Being Prepared is the fundamental LAW of Wiccans, "PROPERLY PREPARED I MUST ALWAYS BE". This is the golden rule of knowing before you speak, it is about being prepared just in case, instead of later wondering why you did not be properly prepared.

If something did happen, how many of you can honestly say that you are Prepared. I know that being a Prepper we still are not 100 percent prepared. But when it comes to food storage, farm animals, vegetables, herbs for medicine, orchards of fruit, poultry, fish, gold and silver, firearms, etc. We are nearly there with all that we have, as we know that we must defend our property at all costs, because there is nothing worse than humans who are scared, hungry and angry.

We would only have enough for our close family and friends, and the rest we know we would have to reject, since for every extra that we take in, there is more of a chance of losing it all.

So the keys to remember in Prepping are: Preserved food, grains, rice, pasta, poultry, get a vegetable garden growing, even if you're in suburbia, and have some poultry. Money will be of no importance, but food and fresh water will be of great value. Also, medicines will best absolutely of urgency, as you may not be able to just run down to the local pharmacy or doctor, as they may not be there anymore. Just be smart and start small with important things, and get yourself a survival pack now this is a large list, so just make the list and then start the process from what you think are the most important to the least then cross them off when you get them, the list includes;

1. Disaster, Evacuation and bug-out Plan.
2. Survival Book
3. Multi-tool
4. Survival axe and spade
5. Led solar torch
6. Large first aid kit
7. Large full medical kit
8. Hunters knife
9. 550 Paracord 20-50 meters.
10. Spare set of clothes (winter and summer) including underwear and socks.
11. Rope 30 meters
12. Swag or tent
13. Sealed water proof bag with all legal docs, passports, d/license, birth certificate, deeds, will, bank accounts, tax numbers, etc.
14. Role of duct tape
15. Role of gorilla tape
16. Compass
17. Fishing rod, tackle and throw net.
18. Waterproof sealing bags
19. Some cash
20. Silver and gold coins and bars.
21. Role of snare wire
22. Water proof matches, lighters, flint, steel wool.
23. Camping utensils
24. Camping tools and equipment.
25. Hydrolyte tablets or sachets
26. Sewing kit
27. Suture kit
28. Spare batteries
29. Camouflage gear especially a jacket for the cold
30. Large bag of mixed nuts, seeds and fruit, for when you can find food.
31. Wellington or waterproof boots
32. Glowsticks
33. Sun hat
34. Survival bag/backpack
35. Water container

36. Whistle
37. Weapon of choice
38. Tea/coffee eyeglasses if needed.
39. Dust masks
40. Auto tools
41. Box rubber gloves
42. Well stored seeds of grain, vegs, herbs etc.
43. Camouflage surveillance system
44. Solar digital radio
45. Two-way walkie talkie
46. But out vehicle
47. Water storage and filtration unit.
48. LifeStraw water filters
49. Hermetically sealed jars and containers.
50. Canned food
51. Contact list details in writing
52. Thermometer
53. Ibuprofen
54. Codeine
55. Benadryl tabs and cream.
56. Allergy tabs
57. Ferro Gradumet (iron tabs)
58. Epi pen
59. Vitamin C, D, E, A, Iron, Calcium, Chloride, Selenium, Anti-oxidants.
60. Sulphur.
61. Mini and large pry bar
62. Pets survival kit as well
63. Children's survival kit.

Pregnancy Sculpture

This is one of the most beautiful things I have ever done for people, it is making a mould of the pregnant mother when she is in full bloom. I make sure that I get their thighs, tummy, breasts up to their neck.

This is such a beautiful thing to do for someone, as it is such a surprise to see the end result and then show your child down the track describing this was where they came from in mummies tummy. It is done the same way as the Goddess Within Workshop, with jar of Vaseline, plaster, cheesecloth in strips and a blow dryer.

- Get them to lay down skyclad but comfortable as they will be in this position for a while.
- Cover them with minimal amount of Vaseline.
- Then prepare the plaster in a bucket by adding water and not making it too wet, that way it will dry much quicker, remember she is pregnant and laying in the same position for a long time is painful and uncomfortable.
- Then just dip the cheesecloth into the plater and scrape of any excess and place over her body, you must do a few layers to make it strong, usually up to at least 10 layers, make sure it is all pressed down firm with no ripples or parts that stick out.
- Now get the blow dryers and dry as quick as you can.

When ready slowly and gently peel off and put it somewhere safe to full dry undisturbed. But when it is dry she can either decorate it or just keep it natural it is up to the mother.

Psychodrama and Role Reversal

If this is handled very sensitively, this can be quite hilarious and educational at the same time. It involves putting the names of Coveners in the small Cauldron and each in turn taking out a name, and then that is there partner.

So, two people pair off and switch roles (completely) and each will act in the character of the other, as they perceive it anyway. Just be sincere but not hurtful, select all their good and bad points and emphasize them with humour and even a learning curve.

Be careful as some people may feel embarrassed, misunderstood, even hurt by the way the other person mocks and presents them. Be sure that it is always respectful, if we cannot laugh at ourselves then we will never laugh sincerely at anything.

Make sure that you have a skilled facilitator on the ready, sometimes to start with it is best to mimic the positive traits of the person at least until you have judged their reaction to your display of theatre.

Psychometry

Psychometry nights are exciting, as they bring out the hidden talents of your Coveners. I usually do this with every new group of members, where I get them all to bring along a sealed envelope, with a personal object of their own inside. They are all placed inside the Cauldron, and then one by one I pick them out, and take them from the envelope.

I then begin to sense or feel about that person, and then hand them to the person that I feel it belongs to, I have been quite accurate with a count of about 90%, which surprises many people. I do not give readings on these people as I feel that is more personal and needs to be on a one to one basis.

Another method I use is by getting the Coveners to use their senses and feelings and get them to take up objects from the Cauldron and see what they can feel or sense from the object that they take up.

It is a great way to work with their own senses and it allows them to become more aware of their feelings at a deeper level, it takes them to a different space, and maybe a new career as a Psychometrist.

Rainbow Night

A rainbow night is all about experiencing the persons energies by what they are wearing, as colour Magick is of great importance in Wicca, as it creates a certain Magickal link and as every colour has specific meanings on different levels.

Colour Therapy is also a great way to get to know people, so what I do is ask everybody to come and wear their favourite or most powerful colour. They must be 100% in that colour, from underwear as well.

When they arrive, it is amazing to see what colours are present in the room, make sure no one wears white or black, as they are neutral colours. Everyone must wear the colours of the rainbow; red, orange, yellow, green, pink, light blue, dark blue, mauve and purple.

When everyone is ready get them to sit accordingly as the colours of the rainbow in sequence. Then get everyone to speak of their colour, and why they chose this very colour and what does it represent to them. After they have spoken get everyone to offer their opinion about what they feel the colour represents. This is an amazing way to also see other peoples' interpretations of what the colour represents to them.

Reflexology

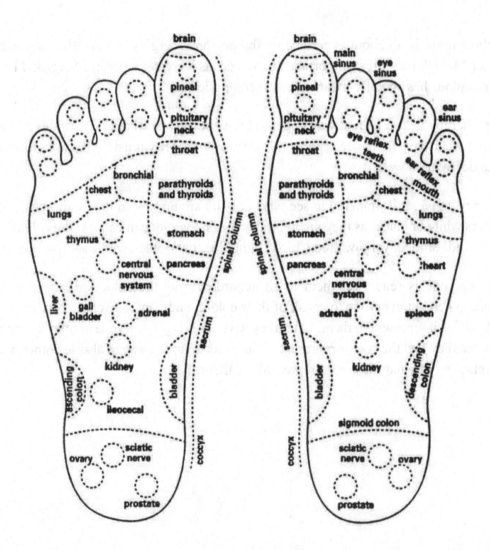

Reflexology is an art and a science which is thousands of years old, created by the Masters in ancient China as forms of healing and cleansing the body and soul. They work with the meridians and power points of the body of which there are thousands of special points that represent the organs of the body.

I do not know much about reflexology, but it is great and can be quite painful, as they really get into all your pressure points and find all the sore spots, actually they can create more sore spots, but at the end of the day they are professional and well qualified.

So do yourself and your Coven a favour and get a professional Reflexologist to come and give a bit of a talk to your group, as well as show you some reflexology. They do work all over your body but tend to focus on your hands and feet, which is great when they are gentle but not so when they are torturing you with pressure puncture.

But if you have not experienced Reflexology, then you should because many people prefer it to normal massage, but me I am a sook and my ore-tired body, does not do well with too much pressure or hard forms of massage, so give it a go and see what you think.

Religious Networking

How many of us really know much about other religions and their true ways? Not many I can imagine. It is always great to experience knowledge from another culture or spiritual path, especially in this world when there are so many paths, even though we know that they all lead to the same place.

But knowledge is power, and we must always understand other paths in a world where there are so many different paths such as;

- Christianity (hundreds of different forms and sects)
- Buddhism (again many varied sects)
- Hinduism
- Islam
- Judaism
- Hebrew

- Tao
- Shintoism
- Spiritualism
- Satanism
- And many more to research and learn about.

Rock Climbing

Rock climbing it a great way to face fears, especially fears of heights. I am not brave when it comes to heights, but rock climbing is about courage, focus, desire and being at one with the rock or hill, or mountain.

There are many rock climbing clubs out there these days, and many in-house rock climbing centres, which is also a lot safer, as they have professionals to watch you and guide you correctly, and if you fall you have ropes to hold you firm.

These I do recommend before hitting the outdoors away from safety and professionals. But do give it a try, the indoor centres are all about fun and courage. As a group booking it is fun to watch the ones with courage, and the ones who literally are panicking. With me I just think it is hilarious to see grown people swinging about trying to climb rock-walls without a clue in the world, but it is funny when they fall.

It is also great to see those who are gifted climbers. I also like races so with your Coveners get them to race to the top and then back down again, the fastest and most graceful is the winner. But no cheating it is not about the first person to fall to the ground it is about the first person to climb to the top and then make the plunge back down to the earth.

Rewards and Awards Night

All year you have Coveners that work hard within the Coven and without, you have members that are always early so that they can assist with the setting up of the Magick Circle, and those that are willing to go beyond.

These people are rare but if you have them in your Coven, then they should be praised and thanked openly in a small ceremony of Acknowledgement.

Just the acknowledgement is quite a lot for some people, but receiving a small certificate as an Award of their services and assistance throughout the year adds to a massive boost in morale for your Circle.

So, think of different categories that you can make these Awards for, even get other Covens together and make it a special Wicces Awards Night. Have such categories as:

- Best Mentor
- Best Service to the Community
- Best Tool Polisher
- Best Teacher
- Best Healer
- Best Chaplain of Service
- Most Important Wicce of Excellence and Achievement.
- Most Successful
- Best Sabbat Author and Conductor
- The Biggest Fool in the Community

Make up some categories and make a night of it, as it could be our own Globe Awards, or maybe Broomstick Awards.

Sabbat Contest

Sabbat Contests are a great way of getting everyone to write their very own ritual. In my Covens no-one can progress through to the Priesthood until they have written, performed and conducted a full Festival Full Moon, Ceremonial Magick and a Charge of the Goddess.

This then shows how much work they have done and how serious they are about their progression and ascension through to the levels of being an Ordained Priest or Priestess.

By having Coveners write their own Festivals it gives them the ability to be deeper in touch with the Goddess and God and what the Festival represents, teaching someone about Festivals is one thing, but having them research in-depth about the festival and write their own material makes them closer to the Magick of the night and the essence of what the Festival is all about. Always get them to use their own words and not the words of previous writers and authors, make sure they start with the Lesser Festivals first such as Spring and Autumn Equinoxes, Winter and Summer Solstices. As they are simpler and easier to write about. But as they advance get them to write a Major Festival such as Beltane and Samhain, Imbolg and Lughnasadh.

At the end of the year discuss which festival throughout the year that was their favourite and why, and discuss the different festivals, and together vote who did the best Festivals and why, maybe give them a reward such as a mini Broomstick trophy as best festival 2018.

Sand Painting Mandala

Sand painting Mandalas are so incredibly beautiful and Magickal as they invoke the powerful forces that are needed for what your Mandala is representing. If you do not know much about ancient Mandala's, then do some research even download some Mandala's that you can copy and do on a grander scale. Print them out and then sketch the design onto an art block, the size you are wanting to have as an art piece. You will need plenty of supplies, and the tools needed are:

1. A bag of sifted fine beach sand, white.
2. Some large syringes with large needles big enough to allow the fine sand grains to flow through them.
3. Seven different colours of food dyes; red, orange, yellow, green, pink, light and dark blue and purple, it is good to also get black, which can be used as border lines, if needed.
4. Large container of wood glue, that starts white and dries clear.
5. Some wooden skewers and flat orange sticks for moving the sand on your art board.
6. Can of heavy duty hairspray or a can of spray varnish or lacquer.

Make sure your art block is clean and dust free, sketch your design in pencil on the art block, and starting from the centre, work out what colours goes where. Then start your design onto the surface that has had the wood glue lightly pasted to where you are starting your design.

Your design if done properly and carefully can take many hours until complete, it is a good idea to have a tag team where you can rest, and others can take over. Make sure that all the dyed sand is gently pressed down onto the glued art block. Allow it to dry. When finished spray with lacquer or sealer.

Sand Witches Contest

Yes this is the fun part of creativity, design, infuse and then eat! This is where everyone can bring their own ingredients for their best Sand-Witches or Ham-burglars.

Some make massive burglars like leaning towers, and others fine and petite but delicious. You can award silly prizes or award Certificates in specialised categories: Tallest, most ingredients, heaviest, lightest, most Magickal, most natural, most beautiful, greenest, meatiest, spiciest, messiest, most unlikely to be eaten, most alien in appearance, most aggressive, ugliest, the most Godlike, the most Goddess like.

Even go with the Elements as the most Earthy, Airy, Fiery, Watery. Have them design an Elemental Sand-witch or Burglar. Choose which is the best overall Pagan temptation.

After selecting the winners and losers, carve them up and taste the spoils, because selecting the winners also comes in taste as well as design. Well for me it is in the taste.

Sea-sonal Ritual

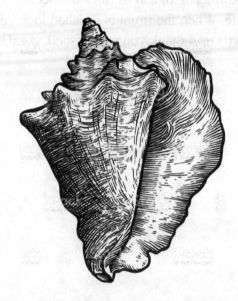

I am a bush baby, but I cannot be kept away from the Magick of the ocean and its dancing of ebb and flow. I try to make a Sea-sonal Ritual at least three times a year, this brings me closer to the beginning of where all life came from, and maybe in its Magick can teach me to where humanity is heading.

Try to gather all your Coveners at a designated place in a car park by the Sea, ask everyone to bring three offerings to be given to the Sea.

- A crystal of the Earth.
- A small bunch of herbs grain and flowers.
- Something that has been of fire, such as a small bag of ash or charcoal.

Also take along a bottle that you can place messages from every Wicce to what they are asking the Great Sea Mother, these messages get placed in the bottle and sealed, and then the strongest member will throw it as far as they can during the Ritual.

Get all to stand and meditate at the falling sun, as it leaves the land to darkness of night. Then concentrate on the waves as they come into your feet and then take away from your feet. As the waves crash on you feel the Blessings of the Sea, and as they withdraw feel them take away your worries, pain and negatives. When the time is right sing to the Sea Mother, and thank her for all she has given. Take your crystal and give to her as a thankyou gift, and then toss the bouquet of flowers, herbs and grain into the ocean as healing Magick from your Coven. Then toss the bag of ash to filter the oceans and remove impurities and cleanse the waters for all life. When the ritual is finished look down at your feet and see if the Sea Mother has gifted you as a thank you with a shell, coral, star fish etc.

Self Defence

With the world being as dark as it is, we must always think of what we can do to make our life safer and more secure and positive. Being able to defend ourselves is an important factor, and if you are lucky to have someone in your Coven who knows self-defence, or knows of someone else, then maybe they can come and give a few pointers to your Coven in self-defence.

There are so many basics that we should all be aware of and know and learn, as we must become confident in defending ourselves, and our family and friends. If you do not have anyone then maybe a couple of you can do self-defence classes and then come back and teach others Being aware if the first lesson of self-defence, the second is being unafraid and confident. Always have a mobile alarm with you or a very loud whistle, or if it is legal in your country some pepper spray. There are recipes online that show you how to make your own pepper sprays that are just as good if not better than the expensive ones you can buy.

I believe we all should carry at least a knife, but sometimes if you are not strong, a knife can be taken from you and then used against you. So, it is better to learn the basics of self-defence and have some pepper spray, and then run like hell.

The key is to know the soft spots, such as toes, groin, throat, eyes, and knees. Then run, but if you have a mobile phone take their picture then run.

Sensory Alert Night

We all rely on our eyes as the first and most important sense that we have, but sometimes our eyes lie to us, as we only use that sense alone, and we need to be able to use all our senses to keep us keen and sharp. Also by using a combination of our senses will heighten our senses and take us higher on a psychic level.

Have everyone in the Magick Circle, and choose just one or two at a time to be blindfolded, but do keep an eye on them as some people can lose their balance when blindfolded.

Let their visual abilities rest and shut down whilst you focus on auditory and kinaesthetic experiences, on sounds such as breathing and nature, use your smelling senses, and touch and taste. Also notice the feel of how your body moves when unsure and blind.

Once you are completely relaxed, you can learn a lot by opening up your senses, but try not to focus on your senses, but the Coveners and their voices that are with you, use your Higher Ears, touch their faces and know who they are, feel their energy and their love.

Take turns and try to do this exercise several times a year as it helps to add confidence, trust and can heighten the senses of the Coveners to make a higher and better working Coven. Having everyone use their senses that are heightened create the perfect Magickal Rituals and Ceremonies.

Sensuality Workshop

Sensuality workshops can be quite beautiful, but sometimes also uncomfortable when it is a mixed group of women and men. Just make sure that everyone knows the rules. Having this sort of Sensuality Workshop is great around the Festival of Beltane.

Have everyone change into their most sensuous outfits, but be serious and sensuous at the same time. It is not about sexuality, it is about sensuality. When everyone I suitably attired, then get everyone to join and come together a perform a Chakra toning and Attunement with chanting, breathing, singing, dancing etc.

Then when ready get everyone to sit and give each two pieces of paper and a pen, and get each person to write down their most sensual experiences that they would enjoy this very evening. You can include being fed grapes, hair brushing, foot massage, neck massage, scalp massage, aura-combing, etc.

Then divide the Coveners into separate groups of threes'. Each triune gather in a different part of the room where it is lit by candlelight and a fragrant incense or burning oil. Have available fragrant massage or healing oils. Select one person to be chosen as the receiver, and the other two are the givers, if their request was for hair brushing and foot massage, then each giver has their attention set differently.

Do this for a chosen amount of time say 30 minutes, and then exchange and change places, but have a little drink of something in between.

This is an enjoyable and very giving way of tending to our Wiccan Kin, where they may not be in a position in their private lives to have this sensuality, and we all need to feel alive and sensuous. After all, three have been indulged then all pack up and change and then have a light supper and a few drinks to discuss the evening.

Shrine creation

We should all have a Shrine of dedication to our Gods and Goddesses, and if you wish you may even have a Shrine to honour your Ancestors, those who have passed from the mortal toil and entered into the Summerland's. A Shrine is similar to an Altar but is set always for a specific purpose of honouring and devout faith, the reason being that we sometimes forget our spirituality unless reminded and as we continually walk past our Shrine we remember and think about our faith.

It can be decorated in any way you desire, but remember less is better, and try to always have offerings and fresh flowers or living plants on or near the Shrine as this helps keep with the theme of Nature.

Sigils and Symbols

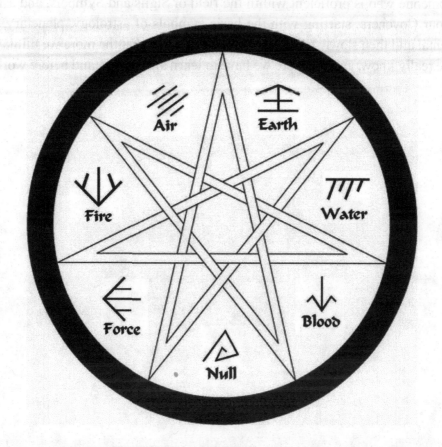

In Magick it is important that we all understand the symbolism behind everything that we do, as it affects everything on several planes of existence, such as physical, mental, astral, psychic and spiritual.

Everything we know omits an energy vibration, including colour, sound, symbols, etc. But Sigils or symbols are the key to each vibration, and without correct knowledge of them when using in an application of Magick can be dangerous. So please before using any Magickal symbols at all understand their full interpretation and sacred meanings.

It is like the Pentagram, it has hundreds of different meanings when working with it physically it represents totally different things to when using it mentally or spiritually. So at each level there is a different form of vibration that changes with each move up the ladder of the Gods and Goddesses. But some without correct knowledge take you on a ladder downwards, and deep into the dark recesses of one's ego, where things can go terribly wrong.

So find someone who is proficient within the field of Sigils and Symbols, and ask them to educate your Coveners, starting with the basic symbols of astrology, planetary, elements and elemental and then slowly work from there. Knowing that the more we think we know, the less we really know, and the more we have to learn and understand before working with them.

Silk Screening

Silk Screening is a beautiful art to learn, as you can make all specific Craft decorations for t-shirts, robes, capes, shawls etc. We had two people who were quite learned in this area and so we made shawls and t-shirts to sell at our festivals to raise funds for the Church of Wicca. They were very good at what they did, and everyone loved their shawls of a fertile and pregnant Goddess screened onto the back of the shawl.

Skill Share

Every Coven does courses and workshops on Craft related topics such as Tarot, Spells, etc. But many of your Coveners have skills that are invaluable in the outside world. What is their work skill knowledge, and can it be shared with fellow Coveners? They may be qualified in fields such as bookkeeping, nursing, chiropractic's, electrical, plumbing, painting, interior design, music, veterinarian, woodworking, horse riding, baking, security, yoga, sex education, mathematics, and a million other subjects that can be educational and interesting to learn.

Even some type of systematic sharing and discussion could possibly turn up an impressive assortment of skills and hidden qualifications amongst your Coveners.

Asking Coven members to share their skill set also adds to boosting self-confidence, and it also helps others with patience for those who are not good at public speaking. Be respectful of all skills even if you are not really interested, remember they are giving their time and knowledge to you, so be accepting of their skill and their method of teaching if they are inexperienced.

The essence of Wicca is to Listen, Learn, Laugh, Live and Love. Maybe then your spiritual family can all be more enlightened and closer to each other and to the Goddess and God.

Soup Cauldron Party

The main wonderful thing about Cauldron food, is that everyone brings a certain vegetable or meat that is to be thrown into the Cauldron and cooked within the Magick Circle whilst doing the ritual or ceremony.

Prior to the evening arrange for different people to bring certain items that go into the Cauldon Soup Pot; carrots, parsley, onions, shallots, mint, potatoes, celery, capsicum, chicken, fish or meat, herbs, parsnips, turnips etc. Make sure they are prepared before bringing them into the circle.

Then as each Coven member enters the Temple, they approach the Cauldron and place their offering into the Pot. If there are vegetarians, then maybe make it vegetarian at certain times.

It is also a great way to make some Damper (bread) baked in a small Cauldron and placed on the fire. Yu can add some butter and garlic or herbs into the bread mix, as this makes it perfect for the soup at the end of the night.

I prefer this method in the winter months as it saves bringing heaps of food for a feast at Full moons where it should be small, plus at Full Moons we always fast for a few hours prior to the ritual, so we are usually hungry afterwards.

Plus, you can enjoy it within the Magick Circle with good Magick Cauldron food, and warmth by the fire with songs and music.

Spell Swap

Having a Coven Swap Meet is a great way to make some extra funds for the Coven or for yourselves. So get each Coveners to go through their belongings and instead of throwing them out, box them up and bring them to the Covenstead.

There are always so many unwanted things that just sit in our cupboards for years without even thinking about or touching, it is best to get rid of it and make room for something else. You can do this amongst all the Coven and bring them together to create an event that occurs a few times a year.

Or if you have a large number of items such as clothing, old books, tarot cards, crystals, kitchenware, jewellery, knick-knacks, garden items, pot plants, herbal plants, incense, oils, etc. Then price them all up and get a few volunteers to help at the local markets and reveal your treasures to the public, you can be quite amazed at the amount of money you can make from you discarded items, that maybe trash to you but a treasure to someone else.

This can be an effective way of also meeting new people, and by having this event often, you can actually get the Coven to make items that can be for sale, such as your calendars and diaries etc.

Coveners can also throughout the year when they are spring cleaning just box items up and bring at their next meeting. But it can be a great way to make extra funds for the Coven and to meet other like-minded people who may not have been aware that there was a Wiccan group nearby.

Swap Meet

Getting all the members of your Coven together with all their throwaways and having either a Coven swap meet or even having a public Swap meet for all outsiders. Is a great idea. You can even join with other covens and get everyone together and hold this event every few months, it is also a great way to socialise and mix afterwards for a BBQ.

We all have so much unused or unwanted items in or around our home that can make you a few dollars at a Swap Meet.

Sweat Lodge

I love my Tepee weekends, as a friend of mine has several Tepee's, that range in sizes, one that fits 10, 25 and 60. So you can have whichever one it best for the size of your group. If you have the funds you could actually get one professionally made.

I like having this because we all bring food and drinks, all the womenfolk set up the Tepee, and all the menfolk set up the Nepee (sweat lodge). They also get the fire going as it has to start hours before use, so get loads of trees and branches make a base out of all the hard granite rocks or river rocks so they can absorb the heat from the fire.

Everyone needs to bring an old blanket each that will get very dirty, and also some firewood and large amounts of water. When you are at the place to build your sweat lodge, hunt and cut many lengths of green pliable wood branches that can be bent over to make your lodge. They can be tied with strips of rag, that has been dyed red, white, black or yellow. Before covering the lodge, dig a deep hole in the centre for the fire rocks.

Then when ready cover the entire lodge with thick plastic sheeting and seal it well, then place over the plastic all the old blankets that everyone brought. Make sure that you have an entrance or opening preferably in the west. Have a large tub or bucket of cold water just outside the opening with some large ladles or bowls to collect the water.

This s a sacred ceremony of purification, so make the experience meaningful. Each person that enters brings with them a water bottle, and you have a fire keeper who brings in the fire rocks, and one inside to place the water over the rocks, it does get extremely hot, some can only last 10 minutes some an hour. But enjoy the experience. You are back in the womb of the Mother about to be reborn!

Talisman Making

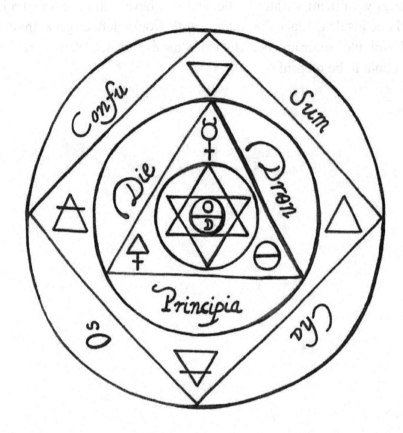

The making of Talismans is very in depth, and when you make them you need to be focused and have the area or Magick Circle charged with specific energies, because the energy for one talisman may not be right for another talisman. So be sure of what you are making.

I find the easiest way to make talisman is either with clay, or wood discs. High Magick requires certain Talisman be made of either tin, copper, steel, silver, gold, lead etc. But for this exercise just start the process with clay. Have at a hand all the tools you need especially some good and correct books on Talismans such as "Amulets, Charms and Talismans" by Lippmann and Colin, and my favourite "Amulets and Talismans" by Sir Wallis Budge.

Get everyone to work out what Talisman they wish to make, and research it and discuss it, and share it. Then make a sketch of it, and then start your craftsmanship, by making a small disc that can be worn around your neck, place a small holy through the top of it for hanging on a chain.

Now with a skewer start etching your design into the clay, and make it personal by focusing and charging your energies into it as you create it. It may be a great time to design a Coven Symbol and the make it out of clay and get the whole Coven to help make it and make quite a few for future uses, when you get new Initiates.

I started my Coven symbol this way and then found a great jeweller who hand made my Pentacles for me.

Tarot Cards Making Your Own

I have always loved Tarot Cards, and I have over the years seen many that are awful and many that are absolutely magnificent. But having a coven Tarot set, which is designed by your Coven is a great way of also making a few more dollars for the Coven Funds. But the most important thing is having something that is significant to only your group and no-one else.

I would get the most qualified to work together in designing the Major Arcana all 21 cards, and then split the men and women and have the menfolk design and create the fire (Swords) and air (Wands) cards, and the womenfolk design and create the earth (Pentacles) and the water (Chalices) cards. This will then have two entirely different energies in creating something rather spectacular. Do not worry about the prettiness of the cards but make sure that they have all the symbolism that is needed, and there are a lot, also colour is important as well.

Study as much as you can about the symbolism of each card, so it is truthful in its original representation, as the Tarot are used for many different rituals and ceremonies, and are used at different levels or planes as well.

But when you come together and see all the designs they can be quite spectacular, and have a great deal of meaning for the coven. Do not rush this deck, as it does not matter how long it takes as long as it is a workable Tarot Card set for the whole coven, get them photocopied so each member has their own special deck.

Tarot Games

It is amazing that the devil's cards as they use to be called only a few years ago, are now in nearly every home, and everyone reads Tarot Cards, some well and some not so well. But Tarot Games can be more fun and exciting. Again, take up the card deck and get everyone to sit in a circle, first person randomly selects a card and turns it down and passes the deck on so that everyone gets a random card. When everyone has a card the story starts.

The first person turns over their card and commences by telling a story of make believe using the card as its focus. After a few sentences, the next person continues the story by looking at their own card and imagery.

Each person does the same and story starts and continues with each person, so all the cards reveal and full epic tale of the tarot.

Or in a different way each person can take on the persona of the Tarot Card, so everyone has to guess who and what card they are. Combine them with politicians and have a debate between the King of Swords and the Fool, or maybe the Wheel of Fortune with Death.

Relax and enjoy and maybe you can think of new games to play with the Tarot Cards.

Tarot Meditation

Many people may not be aware, but the Tarot should be used for ritual and always within the Magick Circle, so lay your 21 Major Arcane cards around the circle in order, have them facing up. Then sit in the middle of your circle and meditate openly on the cards, do not focus on one, but let your mind flow with the energies of the circle.

Let the Tarot card call out to you during your meditation, when this happens acknowledge this by standing up and moving around your circle to where that specific card is situated. Then sit in front of it, take it up and look deep within its picture and symbology, allow the card to open up your mind by using the Tarot Card as a key to a different dimension of thinking.

Place the card back down in front of you and then envisage the card as a doorway and walk through into its portal and realm, and discover what message it has for you, you may also come across a Shining One who wishes to relay the message to you personally.

Enjoy the meditative journey into the realm of the Tarot Card, and when you are ready remember all that has been shown and spoken to you, and bring that memory back with you, thanking the Shining One of the Card, taking up the Tarot Card and kissing it and acknowledging all the knowledge that it shared, as soon as you can write down all that was given to you.

Tarot Visions

Cast your Magick Circle and when completely cast place all the lesser Arcane (Elemental Cards) around the perimeter in their specified directions, earth/Pentacles in the north, air/Wands in the east, fire/Swords in the south and water/Chalices in the west. When that is all down then in a smaller circle in the centre lay out all the Major Arcana cards (21 of them) in their correct order around the central circle. Also in this inner circle is the querent, the person all the others are reading for.

Then get all the Coveners to (without looking down) slowly walk around the Magick Circle and when they feel drawn to a specific section or card, they then sit and take up that card that they feel symbolises or represents that person who has been chosen. When everyone has made their selections, each Wicce then in turn will reveal their selected card, and explain to the querent why they feel this card best describes them, they then go on to speak of something important that they feel must be passed on to the querent. Each person does the same things as the querent listens carefully, when they have finished with their explanation the querent is given all the cards where they take a couple of minutes to study and take acknowledgement of them

Listen carefully and we all have something to learn, we then go again and move on to the next person doing the same, until everyone has experienced the same.

Tarot Readings

Having a day for all the Coven members where everyone can get together and either do Tarot Readings or receive Tarot Readings. It is also a good learning process in inviting other Covens to share on the Magickal Tarot Day, as members from different covens do not know you well enough, so their readings can be more rewarding and interesting.

Make it a BBQ day as well and in the middle of the day have a nice BBQ. Get everyone to bring along salads or meat for the BBQ, as a share meal.

Get everyone to bring along their favourite Tarot Decks, and share them with others. You may even have old Tarot Decks that you wish to sell to beginners, till they can find a deck that is suitable for them. I always recommend Waite and Rider decks for the beginner because of the original symbolism. For advanced Tarot and ritual use the Thoth Deck by Aleister Crowley.

My Oracle decks that I have created are from Aboriginal Artwork and the mystery behind them to the most ancient people on the Earth, it is titled "Dreamtime Oracles Deck and Book Boxset". I also have out the "Oracles of the Gods and Goddesses Boxset".

Tarot and Oracle are very different, so know which one is suited for you!

Thanksgiving

A Wiccan Thanksgiving is about thanking the Goddess and God for absolutely everything in our lives. As everything we have we should be thanking you for, but not only in thanking the deities but we need to thank each other for being in our lives, especially the ones who give the most, the provider, the hunter, the mother etc.

We need to thank the universe for all our bounty, the roof over our head, our jobs, our health, our family and friends, and our parents and children. We should each give daily thanks, for our food and the love and laughter that we share.

We must think of every step that the food that is on our tables and exactly how much was involved in getting to our table. Starting from someone tilling the sand, preparing the soil, planting the seed, the constant watering and taking care as in removing pests, the gradual process of growth and care, then the right time to pick and then clean and deliver, then it goes from farmer to shop, and then to you, and you bring it home and prepare it for your family. This is a long and incredible process that we never think of.

This is the livestock and how it came to be, the poultry, pigs, sheep, cattle, deer, fish, etc. Thank the spirit of that animal who gave his life for you and your family and friends. It is about honouring the many forms of sacrifice to make this happen and in keeping us alive, and we of humanity have lost the talent for growing and hunting and forget the painstaking endeavour that it takes to start this process and then the challenges all through the process and then the final removal and presenting for your livelihood.

So enjoy thinking about all the world and the process that everything takes to get to the end result, your dinner table!

Titles-Lords and Ladies

There has always been to common debate between covens having titles or not. Well most covens that are substantiated have been going for years, and they can have whatever their heart desires, and whatever works well for them. We should never judge another working Coven and their methods, if they work for them.

The Craft and Wicca have changed so much since the 80's. There was no mention of solitary Wicces, nor eclectic Wiccecraft, etc. Many terms that we use today are created to suit the changing tides of Wicca and Wiccecraft of the 21st century. Although I may not agree with all the terms, they do work for others, and that is what matters.

But in my time to be a Wiccan is a solitary choice, but to be a Wicce meant years of dedication in a fully training and workable traditional coven such as either Alexandrian, Gardnerian or Traditional. This was the only way to honestly earn the TITLE of Wicce (Sorry another title). Then to become a Priest or priestess meant also another few years of dedication and working within the Wiccan/Pagan community to gain this TITLE (oops there we go another title). Then to aspire in being a High Priestess or High Priest was another few years of training and dedication, and the desire to be a Lord or Lady of their own circle (another title).

This is where the term comes from being a Lady of the Circle is the representative of the Goddess, and being the Lord of the Circle was being the representative of God. It is a title of respect given to people who have spent at least 10 years of dedication and hard work as a student and helping the community, that they are now ready to be more responsible and become a teacher and Clan Mother or Father to their people. They do not call themselves Lord and Lady, but their community gift them this title as a badge of honour and respect.

The next and greatest honour is when a High Priest or High Priestess have trained several High Priests and High Priestesses that they have hived off to form their own covens, and when they have hive-offs of more than three covens, then they are given the title of Wicce

King and Queen. As this shows their dedication and loyalty to the community, in keeping not only the faith alive, but in helping it reach out to others and keeping the growth of the Craft moving forward and reaching all those that need to be reached.

But it is not title that you can just call yourself. To me the study of Wicca especially within my order, is one of similarity to a university degree, where you have honourably trained and succeeded in acquiring the badge of honour by others, not by you just reading a few books, stepping in running a coven without any formal training, and then giving yourself a title of High Priestess just for the ego of it. Would you go visit a doctor without any formal training or do you feel safe with his title as Doctor (another title).

I believe titles are a necessity, only when they are earned, and for all the many that I have Initiated, or Ordained to the higher levels I know for a fact that they have earnt that TITLE, as they have worked very hard under supervision by the elders of our community. So, a title with recognisable documentation of proof should be respected and honoured, but no documentation of proof, should be scoffed at.

I like the title of Lady and Lord within a Magick Circle, but feel it is not so important on the outer world of the mundane, unless it is of importance. So you make your own decisions or choices, but always be respectful of others, whether you like titles or not, that is your decision, you should abide by others and their personal reasons and choices to have or not to have TITLES.

Tool Making

Wicces Tools are a necessity if you wish to go through the stages and have all your Tools for your Altar and your Magick Circle. But remember there is no rush, it is a slow process, and if you rush you learn little, if you go slow, you learn much, for the mind maintains what it has seen and heard.

But not every member has the finances to afford expensive Tools that are needed. I believe that we should make as many of our Tools as we can, or make them simpler. My first Thurible was a $2 cake stand at a swap meet, and then a small brass bowl for the sand to go on top that was $1. This was beautiful when cleaned up, and it was my first. My first Chalice was a large Caracoles Shell, (Sea Snail Shell) that was perfect as the Chalice for my water.

In the second and third books "Complete Teachings of Wicca Book One-The Wicce" and "Tarot Mysteries of Thoth -Initiation and Inner Alchemy". They both have chapters relating to making or creating your own Magickal Tools. Everything from Altar Pentacles, Athames, Boline's, Wands, Chalices, Thuribles, Altar Clothes, Robes, Capes, etc.

But holding and having an item, a Magickal Tool that has been designed, created and brought to life through your own creativity and ingenuity, and then Consecrated with love and blessings of the Goddess and God, make it a relic that will be with you forever.

Tree Planting

Tree Planting is one of the most important Group activities, that is needed by all Covens and Coveners, even solitary Wicces, should be available for such an important aspect of giving back to Mother Nature.

As a parasite species upon this world, we have turned a paradise into a rubbish dumb, and have forgotten how to appreciate and resect everything that we take from Nature. Tens of thousands of acres of land worldwide are being destroyed at such an alarming rate we can never catch up to the demise and destruction that we are causing.

Make this event and annual event and spread the word amongst Wiccans, Pagans and Wicces worldwide. With every Initiation get them to acquire or purchase a sapling, that they need to take out and plant it somewhere.

Speak to CALM or your local council, or even Men of the Tree's and find out what areas need planting, maybe find an area such as an eroded hillside, create a new forest, start a wind break or even make a sacred grove for a Magick Circle. Just start small and gradually make it a yearly event at the same time each year and call it "Plant a Tree Week". Choose the right sort of trees that are to be planted, sometimes you can get them for free from men of the Trees, as they can share with you as to where to plant them.

Make it real and make it special, it is a great way to honour all life, especially in giving thanks to the Great Mother, the Earth.

Wicca-Ancient Religion or New Age Religion

Another debate about Wicca is that it is a new religion created in the late 40's but a group of patriarchal fathers of The Golden Dawn, Freemasonry and Druids to formulate a new pagan order.

But true Wicca maybe be a new creation, but it has its roots in the ancient Earth system of belief, with so many components that have been adopted from ancient teachings to form the Religion of the New Age. Every religion of the planet is relatively new, but they all take its teachings and knowledge from past ancient religious beliefs that had no names for their faith for the great Mother in the Earth or Father in the Sky.

So, when you argue that a religion is not ancient or old, be thoughtful as to its essence, as they are all of ancient (Pagan) belief systems that have through time changed to suit the ideals of the few that believe in its directions and its very Truth.

So, when I say that Wicca is an ancient religion, I mean that it has its roots in the ancient Dreaming Time of our first forefathers and foremothers.

This is a great discussion to have with your Coven, as we each need to find a compromise between us especially in this day when we have so many different groups with different titles and names that each feel theirs is the Truth, and everyone else is wrong (remind you of the Christians and of Islam). Should we be heading down this same path as judges and aggressive blind pagans who cannot see past their own noses.

Judge none, and then be judge by none, for only the Goddess and God can judge without bias.

Wicce Hats v Wizard Hats

Making Wicce Hats and Wizard Hats, and selling them just prior to Halloween, can also bring in some extra funds for your Coven, also sell them at a Samhain Festival for members. You can make them in all different sizes and shapes,

You can make them from as cheap as $2 right up to $100, depending on what material you use and how much creativity goes into them. They can be small for children, pets, or large for adults. My Wicca Hat (or Cone hat) is of velvet and large like with beautiful black lace and crystals on it.

What you need is:

- Wire to make frames.
- Fabric to cover frames.
- Wood glue for adding fabric signs and symbols, and super glue for crystals, stones etc.
- Iridescent fabric to cut into witchy designs like stars, moons, symbols, (have then glue hemmed before you start so they are dry).
- Thick card board for making cones and rims.

With the many sheets of cardboard, cut and create at least 6 different sizes and styles to suit all ages and styles. This also helps in measuring and cutting the exact same size fabric for the hats.

Wicce Stones

Witch Stones are my way of Divination with Crystals, it is an ancient way that Wicces used to divine. It is good to learn about the symbolism and meaning of crystals in your Witch Bag you will need 21 crystals that have been etched with certain symbols that empower and release the energy and Magick of the Stone. You will need:

- Velvet bag big enough for all your 21 etched crystal
- 21 tumbled crystals stones/
- Wicce Cloth for your divination.
- Book explaining symbolism.
- A small smudge stick and shell.

The stones are: 1. Jet-for the base chakra, 2. Jasper-solar plexus, 3. Agate-emotions, 4. Adamite-heart chakra, 5. Amethyst-third eye amplifier, 6. Indigo Aura Quartz-spiritual communication, 7. Aquamarine-channelling, 8. Azurite-higher self, 9. Feldspar-self-esteem, 10. Garnet-physical health, 11. Blue calcite-emotional release, 12. Amber-supports, 13. Gold Apatite-eliminates stagnant energy, 14. Kyanite-Dreaming, 15. Fluorite-healing, 16. Aventurine-Creativity, 17. Ammolite-transforms, 18. Rose Quartz-heart uplifting, 19. Bloodstone-grounding, 20. Jade-prosperity, 21. Hematite- balancing, 22. Witches Eye-Magick and Spellcraft.

Now place them in your Magickal Wicce Pouch and choose three stones one at a time, 1-for the question, 2-for the action, and 3. For the result. Make up your own small booklet to describe the meanings and Divine away.

Word Party

There are many people that enjoy such games as Scrabble, Dictionary games and Oxymoron's. But in this game, you get each member to find three unusual and hard words in the dictionary and to bring them with them, along with 3-4 answers and only one being correct. The more elaborate the answers the more confusing, and some are sure they all sound correct.

Rema digitation – 1. Someone who picks their nose in public. 2. Someone who has stumpy fingers. 3. Someone who enjoys sex with strangers all the time never sleeping with the same person twice. 4. Inter-tribal breeding between two different native cultures for a Magickal offspring. True answer number 4. But they all sound as if they could be the answer.

There are so many incredible words that we never hear or even know about unless looking them up in a dictionary, play the game with everyone and see who gets the best scores they then become the Wicce Professor of Knowledge, and am awarded something smart. Like a giant question mark shaped trophy.

This is an exciting game to play also "Forehead Celebrities", this is where you have a list of celebrity's names on a piece of card board with sticky tape on the back and that name tag is placed on their forehead, and whilst socialising throughout the night, they ask people questions to get closer to the answer, such as "Am I Female", if that is correct they move on to the next set of questions until they can guess who they are. It is a fun way to fill a night with people learning more about their celebrities.

Wine Tasting

This is a great way to check out the local vineyards and their wines, if you have some that do not drink Wine then maybe go to a beer house, or have fruit juice tasting. If you go to local wineries, you also have a guide who can explain and teach you about wines, you also get to sample much of the produce and get the chance to actually buy some bottles to bring home, or get your favourite Port for your Magick Circle as a Temple Wine.

Many wineries have experienced staff that take you through the spiel, but do not stress about the sales techniques that they use, as that is their main objective. Or else they could go out of business.

The best places to go are the ones that take you through the process and explain each stage carefully so you gain an insight into making wine at home or for your Coven. Each vineyard is different, and many focuses on specially selected wines, so it means you may have to visit a few to get a definite idea of all the wines, wink wink nudge nudge, (Probably a good idea to hire a small bus, or have a couple of non-drinkers to drive.

I had a friend who owned his own fruit winery and his tastings were amazing for a small little winery he had; raspberry wine, papaya, mango, blackberry, pear, kiwi fruit, pineapple and cranberry. They were delicious, he and I actually together made an ancient Pagan Malamel honey wine which we designed the labels and sold it at our Spring Camp. It did not last long!

There are also a lot of beer houses opening up and great place to test and try different beers from around the world, maybe have an excursion to an Oktoberfest.

Wine Making

For those who love wine drinking, and for that special breed of Pagans that love Mead, know that it is a great asset if you know a wine maker, or are able to make your own Coven or Temple wine. In our Circles we have actually made both wine and mead, and enjoy both.

Wine for the summer months is excellent and thirst quenching, and warm mead for the winter months is an addiction.

With wine making there are methods online of how to make wine, so take a good look and maybe if you have fruit trees instead of wasting the fruit make yourself a fruit wine, using all the excess fruit instead of throwing it away. Or you can jar it up for down the track.

But when it comes to mead, the method is exciting as you get all Coveners to bring an ingredient, someone to bring the good bag of white wine, someone to bring some apples, someone to bring some oranges, and then get different people to bring an assortment of herbs and spices such as cinnamon quills, star anise, loves etc. You can add different things and see what the taste ends up.

Allow it to cook in a small cooking Cauldron in the centre of the Circle whilst doing your ritual or ceremony. And when you have finished and ready for the blessing of the cakes and wine, maybe have the cakes as Damper cooking in another Cauldron near the fire, ready to share, and then partake of the warm Mead. It is a delectable taste.

Wishcraft

Wishcraft is something that we teach our Wiccelings. It teaches them to be cautious and careful about what they wish for, as it can have dire and bad consequences. But if their Wishcraft is true of heart and soul and unselfish, then it can be very rewarding.

Teaching your Children of Magick when they are young can also teach them of respect and the laws of Karma. When Wiccelings are aware of the word consequences, they are aware that they must think first, ask the Goddess second, and then if it will harm no-one then make their Wish.

Wishcraft is something we of our Circles teach all Wiccelings, as it gives them a small taste of Magick, and when it works for them in front of their eyes, then they hold their faith firmer and stronger, and believe more and more in the Goddess and their abilities as Wiccelings.

Always start teaching them with simple things like calling the clouds, calling the wind, using their mind to call to their pet without speaking, and also how to ask their parents for something without asking verbally to see if they can connect Magickly. Also get them to call to the Elementals such as the Faeries, Elves, Pixies, Gnomes, Unicorns, etc.

Yule Tree Decorations

Yule decorations are fun for the whole family let alone just your coven. You can make so many different styles such as tinsel, paper chains, or alfoil chains. Get some reflective Christmas wrapping paper and cut it into strips and then fold and glue into circles and make shiny paper chains for your Yule tree. There are so many things you can buy from craft shops to make elaborate decorations. For my front door, I go into my local bush and collect gum tree branches and leaves, ferns, honky nuts, pine cones, acorns, flowering gum, Banksia flowers and bottlebrush.

You can then make a circle with the small soft branches and gradually add the leaves, nuts and flowers to make as a front door Yule decoration, maybe even get some silver or gold glitter spray paint and spray it in patches for a more beautiful effect. You can even get the coven to make a Yule Log together, by using a small cut log about 13 inches long, drilling several small shallow holes into the top of the log to place candles. Then add natural bush decorations and maybe add some craft bought decorations to make it elaborate.

Wicces
Calendar

JANUARY:

World Peace Day	1 January
Sir James Fraser, author of "The Golden Bough".	
Fiesta of the Black Nazarene (the Philippines).	1-9 January
Nativity of The Goddess Inanna, Sumerian Goddess of Heaven and Earth	2 January
Advent of Isis from Phoenicia	
Earth is at Perihelion to the Sun, closest to the Sun than any other time of the year.	
Women's Fertility Festival, Pueblo Deer Dancers	3 January
Aquarian Tabernacle Church Australia by Lady Tamara von Forslun	4 January 1994
Day of the Goddess Isis and Hathor	
Doreen Valiente	4 January 1922 - 1 September 1999 *
Sir Isaac Newton	4 January 1643 - 31 March 1727
Eve of the Epiphany of Kore and Paeon.	5 January
Ritual to the Goddess Venus	
Feast of the God Poseidon	
Night of La Bafana who brings gifts to children, lump of coal if they have been bad	
Day of the Sacred Triune, Maiden, Mother and Crone	6 January
The Beatific Vision of the Goddess	6 January
Arrival of the magi to Christs Manger in Bethlehem	
Joan of Arc	7 January 1412 -
Decrees of the God Sokhit and the Goddess Sekhmet (Justice and Law)	
Magical Day of the Seven Herbs	
Magickal Day for healing with Herbs	
Old Druids New Year's Eve	8 January
Samuel Macgregor Mathers	8 January 1952 - 19 November 1918

Day of the Goddess Justicia, bringing justice
to the world

Day to Honour all Midwives

Day of Antu - Isis searches for Osiris   9 January

Day to gather Yarrow to dry for insect sachets
for dog's collars

Dirge to the Goddess Isis and Nephthys

Plough Day - until 1980 it was illegal to plough   10 January
the fields before this day

Securitas - Invoke when threatened

The Juturnalia   11 January

Day of the Goddess Carmenta - Goddess of
childbirth

Day of the African Mother Goddess Oddvdva   12 January

Basant Panchami Day - Day of Wisdom and Art

Day of the Goddess Sarasvati

Final Witchcraft Law Repealed in Austria in   13 January
1787

Festival of the God Faunus (St. Valentine's Day)

Day to bathe for purification in the Ganges River   13 January

Blessing of the Vines dedication to the Gods   14 January
of Wine

Official Confession of error, made in 1606 by   14 January
the Jurors of Salem Witch Trials

Hindu Festival - Makar Sankranti   14 January

World Religions Day   15 January

Day of the Goddess Vesta

Feast of the Ass

Day of the Goddess Concordia   16 January

Honour the Gods of the Eight Winds

Day of the Queen of the Universe in France   16 January

Day of Rest and Peace - dedicated to the   17 January
Goddess Felicitas

Women's Festival Honouring the Goddess Hera   18 January

Dorothy Clutterbuck	19 January 1880 - 12 January 1951
Day of Honouring the Goddess Minerva	19 January
Blessing of the Waters	
Dorothy Clutterbuck who Initiated Gerald Gardner	
Blessing of the Waters and all Water Goddesses	
Grandmothers Day	20 January
Festival of Peace and Harmony	
Feast of the Goddess Hecate	21 January
Day of St. Agnus	
Day of the Goddess Yngona (Denmark)	
Day of Visions	
Sir Francis Bacon - Philosopher	
Rasputin's Birth	
The Herb Mullein to be infused in olive oil for ear drops	22 January
Day dedicated to the Goddess Mawu	
Beginning of Aquarius	
Marija Gimbutas	23 January 1921 - 1994
Day to honour the Goddess Hathor by having a milk bath	23 January
Day of the Goddess Venus	
Sementivae Honour the Earth Goddess Terra	24 January
Blessing of the Candle of the Happy Women	
Tu Bi-Shivat - Hebrew holiday showing respect for trees and growing things 25 January	
The Shekinah - Sarah and Esther	25 January
Celebration of the Triple Moon	26 January
Day of the Goddess Cerridwen and Copper Women	
Day of the God Alacita, god of Abundance	
Dedicated to the Goddesses of the Grain and Harvest	
Gamelion Noumenia honouring all Deity	28 January

Up Kelly Aa (Scotland) Norse derived fire
Festival to sacrifice to the Sun
Peace Festival   29 January
Day of the Goddess Hecate
Feast of the Goddess Charites   30 January
Dedication of the Altar of peace and Harmony
Purification ceremony dedicated to the
Goddess Yemaya
Zsusanna Budapest Witch and author   30 January 1940 - 14 March 2008
Dr Frian - Alleged HP of North Berwick   31 January
Witches, executed in Scotland in 1591
Feast of the Goddess Aphrodite   31 January
Candlemas Festival
Festival of the Goddess Brigid
Day of the Goddess Hecate

FEBRUARY:
Festival of Lughnasadh Southern Hemisphere   1 February
Festival of Imbolg Northern Hemisphere
Festival of the God Dionysus
Festival of the Goddess Februa
Ethnic Equality Month   2 February
Original Ground Hog Day
Day of the Goddess Ceres and Proserpine
Day Dedicated to the Horned Gods
Lesser Eleusian Mysteries   3 February
Day dedicated to the Goddess Demeter and
Persephone
Halfway point of Summer in the Southern
Hemisphere
Lantern Lighting Ceremony Festival   4 February
Day of the Goddess Maat   5 February
Day to Honour Air Spirits
H. R. Giger   5 February 1940 - 13 May 2014

Feast of St. Agatha - Patroness of Fire Fighters
Day of the Goddess Maat - Goddess of
Wisdom and Truth
Festival of the Goddess Aphrodite   6 February
Day of the Goddess Artemis
Day of the Goddess Selene   7 February
Stuart Farrar passed into the Summerland's 2000
Death of Thomas Aquinas 1274 - whose
writings refuted the Canon Episcopi
Day to honour all Moon Goddesses
Chinese New Year   8 February
Eliphas Levi   8 February 1810 - 31 May 1875
Celebration of the Goddess Kwan Yin   9 February
Day of the Goddess Athena   10 February
Festival of Toutates
Feast of Our lady of Lourdes - visitation of the   11 February
Goddess
Day of the Goddess Persephone
Day of St. Gobnat
Day of the Goddess Diana   12 February
Day dedicated to the Ancestors   13 February
Day of the Goddess Vesta
Betrothal Day (later adopted by Christians and   14 February
changed to St. Valentine's Day)
Women's plea to the Goddess Diana for
children are granted this day
Heinrich Cornelius Agrippa   14 February 1486 - 18 February 1535
Day of the Goddess Rhiannon   15 February
Pope Leo X issued the Bull Toensure - that
secular courts would carry out executions of
Witches condemned by the Inquisition in 1521.
Day dedicated to the Goddess Juno Februata
Day of Lupa - The She-wolf
Day of Honouring Light   16 February

Christ accepted as the God Quetzalcoatl in South America	17 February
Festival of Women - dedicated to the Goddess Spandermat	18 February
Birthday of Ramakrishna - Hindu Mystic	
Day of the Wicces Sacred Tree - The Ash	
Day of the Goddess Minerus	19 February
Birthday of Copernicus - Astronomer	
Day of the Silent Goddess Tacita - averter of harmful gossip	20 February
Healing Day of the Goddess Kwan Yin	21 February
The Sun enters Pisces	
Holiday of St. Lucia - Goddess of Light	22 February
Sybil Leek	22 February 1917 - 26 October 1982
Day of Blessing Land Boundaries	23 February
The Regigugium -	24 February
Flight of Kings, when the Year King is sacrificed, and successor crowned by the Goddess	
Day of the Goddess Nut	26 February
Shrove Tuesday - the first day of Lent	
Day of the Goddess the Morrigan	27 February
Time of the Old Woman	
Anthesterion Noumenia honouring all Deity	
The Great Wicces Night	28 February
Sabbatu - cakes and wine offered to the Goddess for Prosperity and Luck	
Leap Year - when women rule the Earth and can ask men for marriage 29 February	
Day of the Goddess St. Brigid	

MARCH:

The Golden Dawn Founded	1 March 1888
The Covenant of the Goddess Wiccan Church was formed in 1975	
Day of the Goddess Hestia	
First Day of autumn	
Bale Fires are lit to bring back the Sun	
Festival of the Goddess Rhiannon	2 March
Day of the Goddess Spider Woman	
Women do not work on this day or the Goddess will send storms to destroy	
Doll Festival for young girls	3 March
Founding of the Church of All Worlds First	4 March 1968
Wiccan church to Incorporate in USA	
Festival of the Goddesses Artemis and Diana	
Feast of Flowers dedicated to the Goddess Flora and Hecate	
All Souls day – Greece	
Navigum Isidis of the Goddess Isis who opens the seas to navigation	5 March
Laurie Cabot Official Witch of Salem	6 March 1933 *
Junoalia —Celebration of matrons and young girls	
David J Conway author	6 March 1939
Day of the Goddess Ishtar	7 March
Ceremony of Peace	
Day of the Goddess Juno	
Birthday Celebration of Mother Earth	8 March
Day of the Goddess Ilmatar	
International Women's Day	
Mothering day - original Mother's Day	9 March
Feast of the Year Goddess - Anna Perenna	10 March
Day of Our lady of Lourdes - appearance of the Goddess Persephone	11 March
Festival of the God Marduk	12 March

Day of the Goddess Demeter

Discovery of the Planet Uranus - 1781   13 March

Bale Fires are lit to call in the Rain

Birthday of Ronald Hubbard - Creator of
Scientology

Jacques de Molay - Head of the Knights Templar   14 March

Festival of the Goddess Ostara   15 March

Pete Pathfinder becomes the first Wiccan Priest
elected as President of the Interfaith Council, 1995.

Day of the Goddess Levannah   16 March

Day of the Goddess Morrigan   17 March

Feast of Liberalia - Women's Festival of the God
Bacchus and the Maenads

Festival of the God the Greenman

Sheelah's Day - The Goddess Sheelah-na-gig of   18 March
Sexuality

Birthday of Edgar Cayce

Manley Palmer Hall   18 March 1901 - 29 September
                                                          1990 *

Marriage of the Goddess Kore to the God
Dionysus

Quinquatrus Festival of the Goddess Minerva`   19 March

Lesser Panathenacea - dedicated to the Goddess
Athena

Criminal Witchcraft Stature enacted under
Queen Elizabeth - 1563

Day of the God Aries   20 March

Day of the Goddess the Morrigan

World Forest Day   21 March

Day of the Goddess Athena

Day of the Autumnal Equinox Southern
Hemisphere

Mandate of Henry VIII against Witchcraft
enacted in 1542, repealed in 1547

Birthday of the Goddess Athena	22 March
Rev. Pete Pathfinder Founder of the Aquarian Tabernacle Church	22 March 1937 - 2 November 2014
Day of Fasting	23 March
Day of the Goddess Ishtar	
Day of the Goddess Bellona - Witches Power day	24 March
Lady Day - Feast Annunciation of Mary	25 March
Pope Innocent III Issues the Bull establishing the Inquisition in 1199	
Day of the Goddess Ceres (named for cereals)	26 March
Feast of Esus the Hunter	
Day of the Goddess Ceres, who lends her name to breakfast cereals	
Day of the Goddess Hecate	27 March
Birthday of Rudolph Steiner	
Elaphabolion Noumenia honouring all deity	28 March
Death of Scott Cunningham in 1993	
Birthday of Kwan Yin Goddess of Mercy - Healing Day	
The Delphinia - dedicated to the Goddess Artemis	29 March
Festival of the Goddess Athena	30 March
Anita Festival	
Festival of the Goddess Aphrodite and the God Hermes	31 March
Last Witch trial in Ireland in 1711	
Day of the Goddess Hilaria	
Day of the Goddess Rhaeda	

APRIL:

Veneralia Festival of Peace	1 April
Day of the Goddess Hathor	
April Fool's Day	
Feast of Ama - Goddess and Patroness of Fishermen	2 April

Birthday of Hans Christian Anderson

Descent of the Goddess Persephone into
Annwyn   3 April

Day of Ceralia - Seed Day

Day of the Goddess Ceres

Descent of the Goddess Persephone into
Annwyn

Honouring of Aesculapius, The Great   4 April
Healer

Day of Megalesia of the Goddess Cybele

Day of Fortune   5 April

Birthday of Kwan Yin

Birthday of Harry Houdini the Magician   6 April

Stanislas de Guaita Occultist and author   6 April 1861 - 19 December 1897

World Health Day   7 April

Church of All Worlds Founded in 1962 in
the USA

Day of Mooncakes   8 April

Day of the Goddess Ata Bey's

Empowering of Women day   9 April

Day of the Amazon Goddess of Women

Day of the Goddess Bau - Mother of Ea   10 April
(The Earth)

Day of Kista - Spiritual Knowing   11 April

Day of the Goddess Ceres

Day of the Goddess Anahit - Armenian
Goddess of Love and the Moon

Anton La Vey Founder of the Church of   11 April 1930 - 20 October 1997 *
Satan USA

Day of the Goddess Chy-Si-Niv Niv   12 April

Festival of Change

First Confession of Witchcraft by Isobel   13 April
Gowdie in 1662

Blessing of the Sea

Festival Honouring all Nordic Deity	14 April
Adoption of Principles of Wiccan belief at the 1974 Gnostica Witch Meet	
Day of the Goddess Venus	
Birthday of Elizabeth Montgomery (Bewitched)	15 April
Bernadette sees the Goddess at Lourdes	
Day of the Goddess Luna, Tellas and Venus	
Day of the Goddess Luna	16 April
Margot Adler Author and HPs of Wicca	16 April 1946 - 28 July 2014
Day of the Goddess Isis (Aset)	17 April
The Chariot Festival	
The Rain Festival	
Day of Honouring the Air Element	18 April
Day of Temple Offerings to the Goddess in Bali	19 April
Day of the Goddess Hathor, Isis and all Horned Goddesses	20 April
Astrological Beginning of Taurus	
Feast of the Goddess Pales	21 April
Roma Dea Roma	
Day of the pastoral Goddess the Perilya	
Earth Day	22 April
The Renteria	
The First day of winter	
Clothes Washing Day	
Festival of the God the Greenman	23 April
Pyre Festival of the Goddess Astarte, Tanith, Venus and Erycina	
Birthday of actress Shirley MacLaine	24 April
Children's Day	
First Seasonal Wine Festival of Venus and Jupiter	

Day of The Goddess Robigalia of Corn and harvest — 25 April

Passover originally dedicated to the God Baal

Day of the Goddess Yemaya — 26 April

Birthday of William Shakespeare

Mounikhion Noumenia Honouring of all Deity

Feast of St. George originally derived from the God Apollo, the twin of Diana 27 April

Festival of the Goddess Florala (Flora) — 28 April

The Ploughing Ceremony — 29 April

Women's Day in Nigeria

Walpurgis Nacht (The Wicces Night) — 30 April

Samhain (Halloween) Southern hemisphere

Beltane (Northern Hemisphere)

Remembrance Day

May:

May is dedicated to and named after the Goddess Maia. — 1 May

May Day and Samhain day dancing with the Maypole for fertility to the Earth

Day of the Goddess Maat The Goddess of Truth

Day of Moon Goddesses Asherah, Damia, Latona, Bona Dea and Dea Dia

Day of Ysahodhara the Wife of Buddha — 2 May

Festival of the Goddess Bona Dea for public welfare — 3 May

Chloris Tarentia

National Day of Prayer — 4 May

Festival of the Goddess Cerridwen

Veneration of the Sacred Thorn (Moon Tree)

The beginning of Hawthorn Moon

Rain Ceremony — 5 May

Day of the Goddess Maat of Truth
Birthday of Sigmund Freud   6 May
The Goddess visits Mut, Mother of Gods and Goddesses
Festival of the Earth Spirits   7 May
Hathor Visits Anukis the Goddess of the Nile
Festival of the God Apollo
Furry Day   8 May
Morris dancing for Maid Marion originally the Goddess Flora
Day of Honouring the Great White Mother   9 May
Joan of Arc canonised 1920
Day of Ascension
Day of Tin Hau the North Star   10 May
Celebration of the Goddess Anahit
World Nations Reduce Greenhouse Emissions
Day of Russali, the Triple Goddess - Ana, Badb and Macha   11 May
Shashti - The day of the sacred Forest   12 May
Founding of the Church of Wicca in Australia by Lady
Tamara von Forslun 13 May 1989
Procession of our lady of Fatima
The Goddess as a Young Maiden (Persephone, Athena,
Artemis and Diana)
Time of the Midnight Sun   14 May
The Panegyric of Isis - Her finding Osiris
Honouring the Great Stag   15 may
Honouring the Queen of Heaven   16 May
Festival of the Goddess Hathor   17 May
Goddess with Child
Festival of the Horned God   18 May
Feast of the Horned God Cernunnos
Day of Nurturance
Day dedicated to the Goddess Pallas Athena
Festival of the God Pan   19 May
The Goddess Hathor arrives at Edfu in Neb
Festival of Springs and Wells

Beginning of Gemini

Day dedicated to Night and Day being Equal   20 may

Birthday of the Bard Gwydion Penderwen   21 May

Biological Diversity Day   22 May

Adoption of the Earth religion Anti-Abuse Act 1988

Day of the Rose   23 May

Celebration of the Birthday of the Goddess Artemis   24 May

Festival of the Triple Goddess   25 May

Sacred Day of St. Sarah for Gypsies

Thargelion Noumenia honouring all deity   26 May

Day of the Warrior

Morning Glory Zell HPs and author of Wicca   27 May

Night Time Healing Ceremony

Scourge of Pythia - Seer at Delphi, the Delphic Oracle of the
Goddess 28 May

Feast of the Oak Apple   29 May

Family Day

Blessing of the Fields   30 May

Death of Joan of Arc 1431

Thargelia Honouring the Goddess Artemis and the God   31 May
Apollo

Honouring of Joan of Arc in Commemoration 1412 –1431
(19yrs of age)

Pucelle of the Goddess

JUNE:
June named after the Goddess Juno.   **1 June**

Festival of Opet in Egypt

Feast of the oak Nymph

Day of Epipi the Goddess of darkness and
Mysteries

Festival of the Goddess Ishtar   2 June

Birthday of Alessandro of Cagliostro Alchemist
and Heretic

Marion Zimmer Bradley author Mists of Avalon	3 June
Buddhist Blessing for young girls	
Free Women's Festival Skyclad (nudity)	5 June
Alex Sanders King of the Witches	6 June 1926 - 30 April 1988 *
Leave Cakes at Crossroads for the Goddess	
Artemis for luck	
Vestalia Festival of the Goddess Vesta	7 June
World Oceans Day	8 June
Day of the Goddess Rhea	
Mater Matuta Festival honouring all Mothers	9 June
Day of the Goddess Venus	10 June
Lady Luck Day	11 June
Dolores Ashcroft-Nowicki HPs and author	11 June 1929
Grain Festival to the Goddess Ashtoreth	12 June
Gerald B. Gardner Founder of Gardnerian	
Witchcraft 13 June 1884 - 12 February 1964	
William Butler Yeats author	13 June 1865 - 28 January 1939
Day of the Goddess Epona The Horse Goddess	
Day of the Muses	
Starhawk HPs and author	14 June 1951
Lesser Quinquatrus of the Goddess Minerva	
Day of Our lady of Mount Carmel	15 June
Feast of the Water of the Nile	16 June
Night of the Goddess Hathor	
Day of the Goddess Eurydice the Goddess of the	17 June
Underworld	
Day of the Goddess Danu	18 June
Birthday of King James 1st of England	19 June
Day of all Hera's Wisewomen dedicated to the	
Goddess within	
First day of Cancer	20 June
Midwinter Solstice (Southern Hemisphere)	21 June
Midsummer Solstice (northern hemisphere)	
Festival of the God Herne the Hunter	22 June

Final law Against Witchcraft Repealed in England
in 1951

Day of the Faerie Goddess Aine	23 June
Day of the Burning Lams at Sais for the Goddess Isis and Neith	24 June
Janet Farrar Alexandrian HPs and author	24 June *
Day of Praises to the Goddess Parvati	25 June
Skirophorion Noumenia honouring all Deity	26 June
Stuart Farrar Alexandrian HP and author	26 June 1916 - 7 February 2000 *
Day of honouring all Corn Mothers	27 June
Scott Cunningham HP and author	27 June 1956 - 28 March 1993
Birthday of the Goddess Hemera the Daughter of Ayx	28 June
Day of the Sun God Ra	29 June
Day of Aestas the Goddess of Corn	30 June

JULY:
Named after Julius Caesar.   **1 July**

International Save the Species protection day
Day to Honour all Grandmothers
Day of the Goddess Selene

The Coldest Day of the Year	2 July

Day of the Witch Gaeta

Day of the God and Dogstar Planet Sirius	3 July
Ceremony of the Mountain Spirits	4 July

Earth is at the Perphelion to the Sun-the
Furthest between the Earth and the Sun 5 July

Day of the Goddess Hera	6 July

Running of the Bulls in Spain
Day of the Goddess Hera

Day of the Goddess Hel Goddess of the Underworld	10 July
Let Fete de la Magdalene (Mary Magdalene) the Sacred harlot	11 July

Day of Justice	
Honouring of all Children	
Day of Forgiveness	
Dr. Margaret Murray HPs and author	13 July 1863 - 13 November 1963
All Souls day honouring the Spirits of	14 July
Ancestors	
Festival of the Sacred Rowan Tree	15 July
Day of the Goddess Carmen Healer and	16 July
Midwife	
Day of the Goddess Freya	17 July
Birthday of the Goddess Nephthys Goddess of	18 July
Death	
Lady Sheba HPs and author	18 July 1920 - 2 March 2002
The Opet Festival of Egypt the marriage of Isis	19 July
and Osiris	
Day of the Dragon	20 July
Pope Adrian VI issues the Bull	
Day for Binding the Wreaths for Lovers	
Mayan New Year	21 July
Feast of the Forest Spirits	
Beginning of Leo	22 July
Day of the Goddess Amaterasu	
Max Heindal Author and leader of the	23 July 1865 - 6 January 1919
Rosicrucians	
Day of Salacia The Goddess of Oceans	23 July
Hekatombaion Noumenia honouring all deities	
Day and the Games of the God Lugh	24 July
Day of the Serpent Goddess	25 July
Birthday of Omar Kha	
Death of Pope Innocent VIII	25 July
Feast of St. Anne	26 July
Sacred day to all Buffalo Gods and Goddesses	
Dr Carl Jung Occult psychiatrist	26 July 1875 - 6 June 1961

Day of the Goddess Hatshepsut Healer Queen and Architect	27 July
Procession of Witches in Belgium	
Day of the God Thor	28 July
Voudoun Sacred Day for Ceremonies	29 July
Day of the God Jupiter	30 July
Eve of Imbolg the Festival	31 July

AUGUST:
Named after the Emperor Augustus.

Imbolg Festival (southern hemisphere)	1 August
Lughnasadh Festival (northern hemisphere)	
Day of the Goddess Taitu	
Fiesta of Our Lady of Angels	2 August
Day of Saoka	
Day of the Dryads dedicated to Maiden Spirits of the Woods and Water 3 August	
Day of the Goddess Hathor	4 August
Day of the Lady of Snow	
Day of the Goddess Mara	5 August
Day of the Benediction of the Sea	
Day of the Cherokee Corn Dancers	6 August
Gaia Consciousness Day	7 August
Breaking of the Nile	
Day of the Goddess Nut	
Birthday of the Virgin Mary	8 August
Festival of the Goddess Venus	9 August
Festival of the Spirits	
Day to Honour the Star Goddesses	10 August
Holy day of St. Claire	11 August
Lychnapsia the Festival of Lights for the Goddess Isis	12 August
Helena Blavatsky occultists and author	12 August 1831 - 8 May 1947

Birthday of the Goddess Aradia Queen of the
Witches Born in Volterra in 1313 13 August
Celebration of the Goddess Diana and
Hecate of the Moon

Day dedicated to the Goddess Selene	14 August
Day of the Goddess Tiamat	15 August

Birthday of Charles Godfrey Leland
Celebration of the Goddess Dea Syria

Day of Giving	16 August
Feast of the Goddess Diana	17 August
Day of Healing the Past	18 August
Vinalia Thanksgiving	19 August

Day of Vinalia Rustica Venus of the Grape
Vine

Birthday of HP Lovecraft   20 August

Sacred Marriage of Heaven and Earth

Harvest festival	21 August
Metagetnion Noumenia Day to honour all Deities	22 August

Beginning of Virgo

Festival of the Furies   23 August

Festival of the Goddess of Fate Nemesis

W. E. Butler author and occultist   23 August 1898 - 1 August 1978

Festival of the Opening of the Mundas   24 August

Cereris the Womb of the Labyrinth to the
Underworld of Demeter

Opseconsia the Harvest Festival Ritual of   25 August
Thanksgiving

Feast day of the Goddess Ilmatar	26 August
Birthday of the Goddesses Isis and Nut	27 August
Opening the World Parliament of Religions	28 August

Birthday of the Goddess Athena

Birthday of the Goddess Hathor   29 August

Egyptian New Year's Day

Charistheria The Thanksgiving ceremony 30 August

Raymond Buckland HP and author 31st August 1934 – 27th September 2017

SEPTEMBER:

Awakening of the Women's Serpent 1 September
Power Life Force

Ostara - First day of spring (southern
hemisphere)

Festival of the Vine dedicated to the
Goddess Ariadne and the God Dionysus
2 September

Day of the Goddess Polias and the God
Zeus

Women's Healing Ceremony for the Four 3 September
Directions

Pilgrimage to test One's Soul 4 September

Day of the Goddess Cybele 5 September

Day of the Goddess Artemis 6 September

Day of the God Bacchus 7 September

Birthday of the Goddess Yemaya 8 September

Feast of the Shepherd

Birthday of the Goddess Yemaya

Day of Mercy

Te Veilat the Gathering of the Fruit 9 September

Reunion Festival 10 September

Marie Laveau Queen of the Voudoun 10 September 1801 - 16 June 1881

Day of Honouring all Queens of Egypt 11 September

Day of the God Bel 12 September

Day of the Goddess Nephthys 13 September

Ceremony for the Lighting of the Fire

Day of Honouring the Black Madonna 14 September

Day of the Goddess Kore 15 September

The gathering of Initiates

International Day of Democracy

Goddesses Ascent from Annwyn	16 September
Holade Mystai the Ritual bathing in the Sea	
Day of St. Sophia	17 September
Day of Faith, Hope and Charity	
Feast of St. Hildegarde	
Stephen Skinner author	17 September 1932 - 24 September 1997
Giving of Grain and Food to the Poor	18 September
Blessing of the Rain Goddesses	19 September
Boedromion Noumenia Day to Honour all Deities	20 September
Festival of Epopteia the day of Initiation	
Spring Equinox (southern hemisphere)	21 September
Autumn Equinox (northern hemisphere)	
Feast of Honouring the triple Aspect of Maiden, Mother and Crone	
Festival of Mabon the Wicces Thanksgiving	22 September
Day of the Goddess Demeter	
Beginning of Libra	23 September
Genesia Day to make offerings to the Dead	24 September
Day of Mercy	
Birthday of the Goddess Sedna	25 September
Day of Atonement	26 September
Birthday of the Goddess Athena of Knowledge	27 September
Day of Saleeb the Cresting of the Nile at its greatest height	28 September
Feast of Michaelmas (honouring archangel Michael)	29 September
Day of the Goddess Meditrinalia of Medicines and Healing	30 September

OCTOBER:

Day to Forgive Your Enemies	1 October
Neville Drury author	1 October 1947 - 15 October 2013
Isaac Bonawitz Druid and author	
Power Day for Arachnids	
Day of the Goddess Rhiannon	2 October
Feast of the Guardian Spirits	
Rosaleen Norton witch and author	2 October 1917 - 5 December 1979
Arthur Edward Waite witch and author	2 October 1857 - 19 May 1942
St. Dionysis Transformation of the Pagan God of Wine into Christianity 3 October	
Oddudua The Santeria Mother of the Gods and Goddesses	4 October
Fasting day for the Goddess Demeter	
Byzantine day of the Holy Spirit for the Goddess Sophia	5 October
Wine festival for the God Dionysis	
Day of the Goddess Artemis	6 October
Day of the God Bau	7 October
Francis Barrett occultist and author	7 October 1872 - 21 February 1941
Oschophoria the bearing of Green Branches to commemorate Theseus Return 8 October	
Day of the God Horus	9 October
The Eye of the God Festival	
Day of White Buffalo Calf Woman	10 October
Thesmophoria of the Goddess Demeter	11 October
Aleister Crowley occultist and author	12 October 1875 - 1 December 1947
Day of Women's Prayers	
Day of the God Eros	13 October
Victory day of Good over Evil	14 October
Day of Lady Godiva	15 October
Day of the Goddess Gaia and Nymphs day	16 October
Festival of Fortune	

Day of the Goddess Isis   17 October
Day of Clean Water   18 October
St. Luke's day The Great Horn Fair
Honouring Horned Gods Day
Day of Good Luck   19 October
Pyanepsion Noumenia Day to honour all   20 October
deities
Birthday of Selena Fox HPs and author
Day of the Virgin Mary
Kite Flying festival
Day of the Goddess Aphrodite   22 October
Sacred day of the Willow Tree
Timothy Leary   22 October 1920 - 31 May 1996
Day of the Goddess Aphrodite
Beginning of Scorpio   23 October
Day of the Goddess Lilith   24 October
Feast of the Spirits of Air
Day of the God Ge   25 October
Proerosia Festival Harvest
Festival of the Goddess Hathor   26 October
Honouring the Womb in all Female Life   27 October
Patricia Crowther HPs and author   27 October 1927 - 5 February 2009
Day of the Goddess Isis   28 October
Feast of the Dead   29 October
Day of the God Osiris   30 October
Day to Remember the Burning Times   31 October
Beltane Festival (southern hemisphere)
Samhain (northern hemisphere)
Wicces Remembrance Day

NOVEMBER:
Day of the Banshees   1 November
Rebirth of the God Osiris   3 November
World Communication Day

Stag Dances	4 November
Birthday of the Goddess Tiamat	6 November
Day of the Goddess Leto	7 November
Sacred day of Elphane	11 November
World Tolerance Day	16 November
Day of the Goddess Ereshkigal	
Israel Regardie author and witch	17 November 1907 - 10 March 1985
Maimakterion Noumenia Day to honour all Deities	18 November
Day of the Goddess Ishtar	21 November
Thanksgiving	23 November
Elders Day of Respect	
Lady Tamara von Forslun Elder HPs and author	23 November 1956*
Day of the Goddess Cerridwen	26 November
Day of the Goddess Sophia	27 November
Oberon Zell Witch and author	30 November *

DECEMBER:

Franz Bardon occultist and author	1 December 1909 - 10 July 1958
World Aids Day	1 December
Day of the Goddess Pallas Athena	
Day of the Goddess Arachne	2 December
Day of the Goddess Bona Dea	3 December
Day of the Goddess Bride	5 December
Dion Fortune author and occultist	6 December 1890 - 8 January 1946
Day of the Goddess Tara	9 December
Day of the Light Bringer	13 December
Day of the Goddess Sapientia	16 December
Festival of Saturnalia	17 December
Poseidon Poumenia	18 December
Day of Saturnalia	
Day of the Goddess Kwan Yin	
Day of Opalia	19 December

Day of the Goddess Selene and the God Janus	20 December
Festival of Evergreen Trees	21 December
Birthday of the God Mithras	22 December
Mid-Summer Solstice (southern hemisphere)	
Mid-Winter Solstice (northern hemisphere)	
Day of the Goddess Hathor	23 December
Festival of the Goddess Freyr and the God Freyja	25 December
Festival of the of Poseidon	25 December
Birthday of the God Horus	26 December
Birthday of Buddha	
Birthday of the Goddess Freya	27 December
Day of the Goddess Artemis	29 December
Festival of Father Time	31 December
Day of the Sun God Ra	

Epilogue

Well this is the end of my fourth book of my series "Complete Teachings of Wicca Book Four-Coven Tools and Activities". It is about other areas of Coven workings that many do not think about, but is needed in the connecting as a Spiritual Family, and that what a Coven must become. They must be a spiritual family that is all about the higher selves that are within.

This Book gives hundreds of different exciting ways that a Coven can learn and bond through fun activities, within the so-called classroom and outside the classroom. It is a book of activities that can take some considerable amount of time, and be an excellent way of sharing knowledge and the enjoyment of fun related activities. The building of a group of people is about shared experience some serious and focused non-serious and no focus at all.

My next book is a continuation from this book and it is titled "The Divine Feminine – Goddess of 10,000 names". It is a large book with over 400 pages filled with Goddesses from every culture, country, village and religion, even Judaic and their purposes and uses.

Throughout its pages I have hopefully given full accounts and details of each Goddess and their place of worship and there divine gifts to humanity and Nature.

Authors Books and Oracle Decks

Tamara Von Forslun
Witch of Oz

Complete Teachings of Wicca Book One – The Seeker
Complete Teachings of Wicca Book Two – The Witch
Tarot Mysteries of Thoth – Initiation and Inner Alchemy
The Witches Coven - Tools and Activities

Coming Soon

Oracles of the Divine Feminine – Goddesses of the World Book & Cards
Tarot Magick of Thoth – Journeys of the Arcana
The Shining Ones – Angels of Heaven and Earth
The Divine Feminine – Goddess of 10,000 Names
The Divine Masculine – God of 10,000 Names
Tarot Magick of Thoth Tehuti – Tarot Book and Card Boxset

Visit us on our websites www.witchofoz.com and https://tamaravonforslun.com
And on Facebook https://www.facebook.com/tamaravonforslun